The People and the Word

INDIGENOUS AMERICAS

Robert Warrior and Jace Weaver, Series Editors

Thomas King, *The Truth About Stories:
A Native Narrative*

Robert Warrior, *The People and the Word:
Reading Native Nonfiction*

Robert A. Williams, Jr., *Like a Loaded Weapon:
The Rehnquist Court, Indian Rights,
and the Legal History of Racism in America*

Daniel Heath Justice, *Our Fire Survives the Storm:
A Cherokee Literary History*

The People and the Word
Reading Native Nonfiction

Robert Warrior

INDIGENOUS AMERICAS SERIES

University of Minnesota Press
Minneapolis • London

An excerpt from "Philadelphia Flowers" by Roberta Hill Whiteman, from her collection *Philadelphia Flowers* (Duluth, Minn.: Holy Cow! Press, 1996), is reprinted by permission of Roberta Hill Whiteman.

Published by the University of Minnesota Press
111 Third Avenue South, Suite 290
Minneapolis, MN 55401-2520
http://www.upress.umn.edu

Library of Congress Cataloging-in-Publication Data

Warrior, Robert Allen.
　　The people and the word : reading native nonfiction / Robert Warrior.
　　　　p.　　cm. — (Indigenous Americas)
　　Includes bibliographical references (p. 　) and index.
　　ISBN 0-8166-4616-3 (acid-free paper) — ISBN 0-8166-4617-1 (pbk. : acid-free paper)
　　1. American prose literature—Indian authors—History and criticism.
　　2. Indians of North America—Intellectual life.　 3. Indians of North America—Historiography.　 4. Indians in literature.　 I. Title.　 II. Series.
　　　　PS153.I52.W37 2005
　　　　818'.08—dc22

2005013448

Printed in the United States of America on acid-free paper

The University of Minnesota is an equal-opportunity educator and employer.

12 11 10 09 08 07 06 05　　　　　　　10 9 8 7 6 5 4 3 2 1

For Margaret Kelley and Frances Hope Warrior

Contents

Acknowledgments

I want to thank the following institutions for the support they provided for this project during the years I was writing it, mainly through generous invitations faculty and students extended to me that allowed me to present my work to academic and professional audiences: the National United Methodist Native American Center, Claremont, California; Getty Center for the Arts, Santa Monica, California; Pepperdine University; Arizona State University; Duke University; University of Oregon; University of Lethbridge, Alberta, Canada; The Freedom Forum Pacific Center, San Francisco, California; Whitney Humanities Center and Beinecke Rare Book and Manuscript Library, Yale University; University of California, Davis; Instituto Cultural Oaxaca, Mexico; McMaster University, Toronto, Ontario, Canada; Ministry of Culture and Sports, Guatemala; Center for the Study of Race, Politics, and Culture, University of Chicago; Dartmouth College; Center for the Study of Sports in Society, University of Miami, Florida; American Studies Program and Department of Religious Studies, Yale University; National Conference on Race and Ethnicity in American Higher Education, Southwest Center for Human Relations Studies, University of Oklahoma; University of Missouri; Département d'Anglais, College de Lettres, Université de Limoges, France; Sequoyah Research Center, University of Arkansas at Little Rock; Radical History Workshop, University of Minnesota, Minneapolis; Osage Tribal Museum, Pawhuska, Osage Nation; St. Louis Artists Guild, St. Louis, Missouri; Département d'Anglais, Université Blaise Pascal, Clermont-Ferrand, France; First Nations House, University of Toronto; University of Wisconsin, Madison; Department of American Studies, University of New Mexico; Native American Religious Traditions Group, American Academy of Religion; University of North Carolina–Chapel Hill; Center for Race and Ethnicity, Brown University; Kenyon College; Harvard University; and Institute of Native American Studies, University of Georgia, Athens.

The following libraries and archives were great resources for this work, and I want to acknowledge them and the people who work in them: Barbara Landis and the Cumberland County Historical Society, Carlisle, Pennsylvania; Western History Collections, University of Oklahoma; the New York County Coroner's Office, Department of Records and Information Services, Municipal Archives of the City of New York; and Loretta Metoxen and the Oneida Nation Cultural Heritage Department, Oneida, Wisconsin.

The following individuals were generous in their willingness to read drafts of the manuscript, either in whole or in part: Jace Weaver, Vincent Lietch, Craig Womack, Simon Ortiz, Sharon Holland, Geary Hobson, Jean O'Brien, Lisa Brooks, Flora Quinata, Meredith Drent, and Charles Red Corn. Along with being wonderful readers, these are all people I value as friends and family members.

I thank my mother, Judy Warrior, for her continuing support of my work. My gratitude also goes to Michael Quinata; Archie and Ramona Mason and their children and grandchildren; Ted Moore and Terry Mason Moore and their children; Richard and Tammy Lux and their children and grandchildren; Talee Red Corn and his family; Russell Tallchief and his family; Veronica, Wilson, Rock, and Sharon Pipestem and their family; Jeri Red Corn; Moira Red Corn; Yancey and Miles Red Corn; Kathryn Red Corn; and all my Osage friends and relatives and their families. Lance Friis, Jane Mt. Pleasant, Joy Harjo, Homer Noley, Dan Cottom, Alan Velie, Catherine John, Elizabeth Parent, Sandra Drake, Mark Trahant, Paul DeMain, Janet McAdams, Steven Ray Smith, Paul Chaat Smith, and Jim Larimore have been great friends, wonderful colleagues, and tireless supporters. Richard White, Ramón Saldivar, and Arnold Rampersad deserve special thanks for their professional support during some challenging times. Doug Armato, Carrie Mullen, Laura Westlund, Jason Weidemann, Linda Lincoln, Kate Clements, Mike Stoffel, and everyone else at the University of Minnesota Press who has worked with me deserve special thanks.

During the year I was acting director of Native American studies at the University of Oklahoma I managed somehow to make tremendous progress on the final revisions to this book. When I was away from the office I always knew the program was in the able hands of Barbara Hobson, Jerry Bread Sr., and Edgar Heap of Birds. I am grateful to them for their friendship, good humor, and professionalism. I am also grateful to graduate students (especially my research assistant Phillip Morgan, and Veronica Pipestem, who helped prepare the index) in my seminars at OU, where I worked through many of the issues in this study.

Finally, Margaret Kelley has been an intellectual friend as well as a partner in life. Her dedication to her own scholarship and unflinching support of mine has provided endless inspiration and encouragement. She—along with Indigo, Hank, and Ice Cream—has helped me connect the life of the mind to the rest of what makes life sweet and good. Most of all, she has joined me in bringing our daughter, Frances Hope Warrior, into the world. Together they are the promise of new growth and hope for the next generation. My words and ideas are dedicated to them and the joy they have brought me.

Norman, Oklahoma
August 2005

Introduction

Reading Experience in Native Nonfiction

*T*hese four chapters—on the nineteenth-century Pequot writer William Apess, the Osage Nation's 1881 constitution, Native American educational narratives, and N. Scott Momaday's philosophy of language—are examinations, each in their own way, of two primary concerns. First, they focus on nonfiction texts by Native authors, texts that, taken together, narrate a North American history of Native American literature, with nonfiction at its center, from the seventeenth and eighteenth centuries into the 1970s.

Second, these chapters take up the issue of what it means for contemporary Native critical practice that this history exists. In these pages, I develop an idea I deployed in my book *Tribal Secrets*—that the history of Native writing constitutes an intellectual tradition, a tradition that can and should inform the contemporary work of Native intellectuals. Here, I am not reestablishing the existence of this intellectual tradition so much as I am further exploring some of the specific historical and theoretical ways that the Native nonfiction writing tradition challenges contemporary Native intellectuals.

Each chapter takes a different approach to these concerns. Apess, a Pequot minister who wrote in the 1820s and 1830s, becomes here a turning point in the history of Native writing. His work, essentially self-published without the benefits of institutional or programmatic support on the margins of the Native world, stands in my reading as a model for contemporary work. The Osage Constitution, which for over a century has been at the embattled center of my own tribal nation's political misfortunes, provides the unusual opportunity to consider a text that is communally authored and that directly connects to the political history of a tribal group. My own connections to its history and recent controversies allow for an exploration of the role of Native critics in confronting specific political situations.

Chapter 3, on Native educational narratives, deals with a major but underexamined theme in Native writing. These writings on education demonstrate the forward- and backward-looking ways that Natives have thought about their own futures in light of the institutions in which they have so often had to forge their futures' outlines. N. Scott Momaday's essay "The Man Made of Words" is a fitting topic for the last chapter. This essay, as presented at the 1970 First Convocation of American Indian Scholars, provides a vehicle for understanding work that has been regarded as conservative and quietist, rather than as speaking effectively to themes that had arisen in a broader social and historical context. Further, a reading of Momaday's work serves as an apt end for this work, given that I am seeking to highlight the long history of Native nonfiction in the midst of critical practice that so often has read Momaday as a starting point.

Taken together, these chapters allow me to create a historical context for Native writing and to demonstrate approaches to reading Native texts that highlight the existential and theoretical meaning those texts have in a contemporary context. Thus, the idea of reading is crucial here. Much of what has prompted the direction I have taken in my critical practice regarding Native texts is a conviction that the act of reading and what that act reveals are crucial to the enterprise of Native intellectual development. That enterprise and its implications for broader issues in Native America, I should say up front, are more central to the project I am attempting here than a concern for how this work contributes to the scholarship on Native American literature or the programmatic success of any particular field or academic institution. My overarching concern is working out how doing the work of the critic and intellectual can contribute to improving the intellectual health of Native America, its people, and its communities.

A fair question is, how can reading be part of such an improvement? Reading, as I use the term, moves beyond mining information from a text or merely extrapolating pertinent facts from the biography of an author. It is, in contrast, a process that highlights the production of meaning through the critical interaction that occurs between a text as a writer has written it and a text as readers read it.

Meaning is derived from the space between these two, and its production occurs in a context that includes everything that goes into producing the text and also what goes into making the writer and the reader who they are. Thus, language, history, genre, and form are central to the readings that follow. So also are the social location and circumstances of writers and critics. These readings, then, are self-consciously committed ones that take seriously the social and existential implications of intellectual work and proceed from the idea that what intellectuals do ought to matter and ought to make a difference in the real lives of real people living in real time.

The space between readers and texts is of special concern in each of the chapters that follows, and much of what I have tried to accomplish here depends on how well I garner the resources of imagination to tease out meaning from what would otherwise be ineffable. Momaday, as I detail in chapter 4, provides an important example of this sort of critical imagination in the way he has one of his characters, a female ancestor named Ko-Sahn, appear out of his language as he attempts to conclude his retelling of Kiowa stories through writing.[1] As I have imagined William Apess during his last, mostly undocumented days in New York City in the late 1830s, the writing of the Osage Constitution during the early reservation days of the 1880s, and the lives of boarding-school students as they can be read from one of the products of student labor in the print shop of the Santee Normal Training School in 1889, I have tried to do for my subjects something of what Momaday has done for Ko-Sahn.

I have also followed the lead of Rayna Green, whose insightful reading of a Frank Matsura photograph of two young Native women on a fainting couch from around 1910 provides an important example of how to read not only for what can be documented but for what the viewer/reader might see as possible in considering a Native subject.[2] Green conjectures that the young women on the couch in Matsura's photograph are kitchen help in the home of a rich white woman who found themselves somehow posing for the photographer. Matsura, she points out, made a habit of photographing Indian people in ways that showed them clearly inhabiting their contemporary world and its conditions. "In this world he shows us," Green writes, "Indians aren't weird, heartbroken exiles, or zoo animals for the expositions, endangered species preserved forever in photographic gelatin. Like those girls on the couch, they are changed, but in control" (52).

Green does not suppose however that the young women in the photograph simply dictated the terms of their own destiny. They were, after all, poor young women who lived in a world in which their people had been vanquished. The ways they reach through Matsura's lens to express their agency, however, demonstrate "that Indian survival was more complex and diverse than most pictures of it would have us imagine" (53).

Important to my agenda here, Green argues that complicating the world of Matsura's fainting-couch aesthetic complicates our own as well. She imagines how photographs of the present will be regarded in the future, saying, "How will I and my friends be shown—as mixed-bloods who've lost it, our briefcases clutched anxiously to our sides, our three-piece suits ill-fitting and never right?" (52). Green suggests that Matsura (and his subjects on the couch) caught truth in his photograph, though getting at it requires contemporary readers to work at least as hard to get "through the muck to see the possibilities" (52).

What I am addressing through these chapters, in the broadest strokes, is an agenda of Native intellectual work that considers practical as well as creative concerns. What guides my approach is the idea that intellectual agendas do not just set themselves but must be thought through, worked out, and implemented in specific ways. I am also concerned that, absent such specific discussion about the trajectories of Native intellectual work, what results is an inchoate body of knowledge that fails to speak to the aspirations and needs of people in the Native world—and this point is as true for policy and legal studies as it is for studies like this that concentrate on writing and literature. These readings, then, though focused on Native writing, take up issues of intellectual agenda-setting across a wide swath of fields in Native American studies.

The purpose of this Introduction is to elaborate on these two issues of the history of Native nonfiction and the way that reading that history informs the intellectual development of Native America. I will start with comments on the history of writing by Natives, then turn to some of the theoretical and existential dimensions that arise in considering that history. Specifically, I will discuss how the nonfiction tradition can be seen as giving rise to critical discourse and the theoretical usefulness of the concept of experience in developing Native criticism.

NONFICTION IN THE HISTORY OF NATIVE WRITING

Though contemporary fiction and poetry receive the lion's share of scholarly attention in studies of Native literature, the historical centrality of nonfiction in Native writing in English since the late eighteenth century is inarguable. Scholars of early Native American writing have differed on whether to focus on clear examples of published works or to include all shreds and fragments of Native literacy, but wide agreement exists that various kinds of nonfiction make up the vast bulk of early Native writing. Whether one is more interested in Samson Occom's widely disseminated "Sermon on the Death of Moses Paul," the Latin exercises of early Native students at Harvard, or the marginalia of Native converts of John Eliot's Massachusetts missionary activities, extant early writing by Natives is, except for some examples of hymnody, nonfiction.[3]

Until the 1820s, the Native writing that was published was almost exclusively produced by Native male Christians, with members of the clergy, like Occom, the most likely to become authors. By the time of the Removal crisis of the 1830s, the Cherokees and other southeastern Native groups had produced groups of literate male authors who were not clergy, some of whom engaged in writing and publishing as a way to respond to the political situations they found themselves embroiled in.

One of the most significant moments in this movement away from a male clergy-based literacy came in 1828, when Elias Boudinot published the first edition of the bilingual *Cherokee Phoenix*. Boudinot, who was executed for treason under Cherokee law for signing the 1835 Treaty of New Echota, which signed away Cherokee lands, has the distinction of being the progenitor of Native journalism in North America.[4] After the *Phoenix*, which in spite of some interruptions continues to be published today, hundreds of Native newspapers have provided news and information to tribal readers. Thousands of Native writers have plied their trade within the pages of these newspapers, writing tens of thousands of stories and many millions of words.[5] Against the grain of contemporary critical studies that assume the history of Native writing has been directed toward a non-Native audience, tribal newspapers have been usually addressed to literate people in Native communities.

Alongside this massive corpus of tribally based journalism, Native writers in the nineteenth century produced an array of books and made significant contributions to non-Native newspapers and magazines. The most common genre of Native writing in the period is autobiography, with texts by Apess, Peter Jones, and George Copway being important examples. But Native authors worked in other nonfiction genres as well, with Copway's histories, John Rollin Ridge's journalistic contributions (including the first English-language newspaper in California), and David

Cusick's writings demonstrating abundant proof that Native nonfiction is much more than autobiography.

The turn of the twentieth century saw a great flowering of Native nonfiction and was a time when significant numbers of Native women became part of the history of Native writing. Charles Alexander Eastman, Zitkala-Sa (Gertrude Bonnin), and others published dozens of books and articles while tribally based journalism continued.[6] This age of growth continued into the 1940s. Again, a good number of these works were autobiographical in nature, but many others, including Arthur Parker's *The Indian How Book,* John Milton Oskison's *Tecumseh and His Times,* Ruth Muskrat Bronson's *Indians Are People, Too,* and Ella Deloria's *Speaking of Indians* are not primarily concerned with their authors' life stories. Still other works, though often classified as autobiography, are more accurately hybrid works that combine various forms of nonfiction writing.[7]

As the nonfiction tradition grew, Native fiction was just beginning. With a few exceptions, including most notably Ridge's *The Life and Adventures of Joaquín Murieta, the Celebrated California Bandit,* Native fiction did not appear until late in the nineteenth century.[8] Native novels then began to appear in fits and starts, but not until the 1920s and 1930s would Native novels flow in an identifiable stream.[9] That stream slowed considerably in the 1950s and 1960s, though Native writing continued throughout the intervening two and a half decades.

Then, in certain ways without warning, the landscape of Native literature forever changed when N. Scott Momaday won the 1969 Pulitzer Prize for his novel *House Made of Dawn.* Many novelists found their way into print in the years following Momaday's breakthrough, and the decades since have witnessed dozens of Native novels and scores, even hundreds, of Native short stories.[10] Native poetry, as well, emerged at that time as critical to the development of Native literature.

The emergence of Native fiction and poetry coincided with the creation of Native American studies programs in North American universities. These programs, of course, were one aspect of larger political currents, including the worldwide movement against colonialism, the uprising of American youth against the United States' war in Southeast Asia, and political and cultural mobilizations for civil and gender rights. As Paul Chaat Smith and I have argued in chronicling that period, it was an era when American Indian people made significant strides into new forms of public life and political discourse. This confluence of literary achievement, social upheaval, and academic engagement helped pave the way for the academic legitimation of Native writing in the form of curricular offerings, recognition by the Modern Language Association, and the production of literary critical works.

Thus, this present critical work comes three and a half decades into the trajectory of developments from that period and, as such, is part of an ongoing attempt to recover the fullness of Native intellectual written work in the wake of the critical preoccupations that took root in the 1970s. Specifically, I want to ask why, with some notable recent exceptions, critical attention to Native literature has focused either on fiction, autobiography, and poetry, on the one side, or on oral traditional literatures on the other, when, in fact, nonfiction writing has been so vital for so long.[11]

The most obvious answer, of course, is that what has gone on in Native literary studies reflects what has occurred in the larger arena of modern literary studies in English over the past century. That is, in literary studies we have the full-scale ascendancy of the novel as the focus of modern scholarship, with poetry, drama, autobiography, and other genre literature taking up places behind. In the chapters that follow, I consider what happens critically when the force of the Native novel's ascendancy is blunted and nonfiction texts are given their due.

One result is the lengthening of the historical arc of Native writing. Leaving nonfiction out and treating the Native novel as the high-water mark or gold standard of literary achievement risks making Native literature a latecomer to the feast of modern literacy and literature. Native writers, in such a reading, are important insofar as they have produced novels of quality, meaning that Native writing lags behind until the flowering of the novel in the 1970s. The novel, indeed, is a remarkable genre in its modern form and it has been an enticing vehicle for Native literary expression. Yet, as Craig Womack argues, "[N]ot nearly enough . . . intellectual history has been brought to bear on a study of contemporary Native writings. Most approaches . . . have proceeded as if the Indian discovered the novel, the short story, and the poem only yesterday" (3). And if fiction and poetry have suffered from this sort of inattention, nonfiction has suffered even more.

Even during this most recent period, when fiction and poetry have become so prevalent in Native literature, Native authors have continued publishing at least as much, if not more, nonfiction. Natives have continued telling stories from their own lives, including Gerald Vizenor's highly literary *Interior Landscapes* and Victor Montejo's *Testimony: The Death of a Guatemalan Village,* a gripping account of the oppression of Mayan people in Guatemala under Efraín Rios Montt.[12] Other writers skirt the edges of fiction and autobiography, such as Jim Northrup in *Walking the Rez Road.*

Nonfiction writers have brought us impassioned pleas on behalf of Native peoples, accounts of crucial moments in Native history, profiles of people in contemporary Native communities, and explorations of dysfunctions, like substance abuse, in the Native world.[13] The Native nonfiction tradition, thus, is vibrant, complex, and worthy, in and of itself, of serious critical attention. This tradition of writing is the oldest and most robust type of modern writing that Native people in North America have produced as they have sought literate means through which to engage themselves and others in a discourse on the possibilities of a Native future. Scholarly attention to the novel, as I figure things here, has told us more about the preoccupations of literary studies than about the history of the critical contributions of Native writers.

One thing that emerges from reading across more than two centuries' worth of Native nonfiction is a remarkable overlap between writers who seemingly share little in the way of geographical, chronological, and circumstantial realities. I call these instances of disparate writers dovetailing and commenting on each other's work *synchronicity,* and I show at several turns how the opportunity to identify synchronicity is one of the main benefits of casting a wide historical and existential net in considering Native literature. Synchronicity, as much as any other contribution I attempt to make here, proves for me why these texts and the writers who produced them warrant careful attention.

SOME IMPLICATIONS OF HAVING A TRADITION

Having produced the foregoing paean to Native nonfiction, let me go on to say that my purpose here is not to proclaim the glories of Native nonfiction writing and place it on a pedestal. This is not ethnic cheerleading. Rather, I am interested in looking at the ways the Native tradition of nonfiction writing challenges and even critiques contemporary critical and intellectual work.

Nonfiction writing is particularly well suited to this purpose as it typically has allowed Native authors to speak more directly to the situations and conditions Native people face than fiction or poetry has. To give two contemporary examples, it is difficult to imagine how Lee Maracle's insights into gender issues or Taiaiake Alfred's call for a reformed political and philosophical approach to Native politics might fruitfully register in a fictional setting, in a poem, or even in a standard autobiography.[14] In this way, the nonfiction tradition has tended toward commentary and criticism. In two recent anthologies, to offer another example, the distance between the *writers* Simon Ortiz gathers to talk about writing and the *critics* Jeanette Armstrong brings together to talk about Native criticism is not far at all; both of their books take up the challenge of identifying the role that written discourse can play in addressing social problems.[15] Exploring the slight gap between Native nonfiction and Native criticism and developing critical approaches out of that gap is central to this project.

Examining Native writing with nonfiction writing at its center, then, not only promotes a view of Native writing as a literature with a long history but it allows for a critical conception of Native writing that relies more on its own terms than on the tastes and mandates of the contemporary conventions of modern literary studies. This conception of Native nonfiction writing defines it as developing alongside modernity, allowing for a much stronger sense of both how Native writers have engaged modernity and how Native criticism might most beneficially grow from Native literature.

This last point is a complex one and is part of the intellectual agenda that emerges in the chapters that follow. Suffice it to say here, though, centering on Native nonfiction is a way of seeing Native literacy as part and parcel of the growth of literacy in Britain, North America, and other British colonial holdings. Native writing participates in the same impulses that helped give rise to print culture and the public sphere in the seventeenth and eighteenth centuries. Criticism, arising as it does with the modern novel, draws those from the public sphere into its fold, demonstrating that literature is something to be not only consumed but considered. On the one hand this makes literature more available to more readers, and on the other it evinces the complex structures, sources, and histories of published texts. What this allows is a way both to recognize literature as a wonder of language and to affirm the fact that humans have wrought that wonder.

Thus, as writers, Native nonfiction authors have not only produced literary texts but have become a source for critical models for critics.[16] The doing of criticism, then, follows closely on the heels of writing nonfiction, thus providing links between what authors do in creating texts, what is happening in the daily lives of Native people, and the way critics go about constructing their work. Though my own view is perhaps a bit more nuanced, I am looking for the same thing Armand Garnet Ruffo seeks when he says, "[T]he literature itself tells what it is; theories of criticism, ways of approaching the literature, will necessarily come from the literature and not be foisted upon it" (667).

This position, of course, requires a specific conception of the work of the critic. As the late Edward Said, one of my teachers in graduate school and a scholar whose work has made deep impressions on how I think about critical and intellectual work, argues, "Criticism in short is always situated; it is skeptical, secular, reflectively open to its own failings" (*Culture*, 26). It is this sense of the critic being situated in a world of actual social realities in need of independent judgment that I hope these chapters evince. Further, I hope the work I have engaged in here helps establish the need for particular kinds of criticism in the indigenous world. "The inevitable trajectory of critical consciousness," Said goes on to say, "is to arrive at some acute sense of what political, social, and human values are entailed in the reading, production, and transmission of every text" (26).

Those familiar with the social realities of the Native world should be able to appreciate the need for this sort of critical consciousness. As Taiaiake Alfred says of the current situation of North American Native people, "Amid the seeming perpetual conflict that comes with defending our ideals, there is confusion, division, and sometimes despair. . . . Distracted from our goal, we wander a forest of frustration living inauthentic lives that make us easy prey for those who would enslave us. Such times constitute crises, and we are in the midst of one today" (xi).

Alfred argues that what is most needed in the midst of this crisis is leadership, and I would add that one of the leadership qualities that deep crises call for is the strength of judgment that derives from critical consciousness. That is, even in the midst of a crisis in which a siege mentality becomes tempting, a more fruitful choice is to develop the sorts of critical capacity that I will argue obtain in the finest moments of the nonfiction tradition. Each of the four chapters here speaks to the theme of leadership, and a premise of the book as a whole is that the sort of intellectual leadership so lacking in Native America needs to arise from the juncture of history, critical judgment, and experience.

EXPERIENCE IN NATIVE AMERICAN CRITICISM

While intellectual history is central to the chapters that follow, theoretical considerations play a constitutive role as well. Along with narrating what I hope is an instructive history of Native nonfiction and that history's potential in the development of Native criticism, an important part of this book's agenda is theoretically exploring the concept of experience and its relationship to the production of criticism.

Though I am interested in furthering a discussion of experience as it has emerged in recent work in Native American studies, I am also aware of the wide range of positions in contemporary scholarship on the topic of experience. From those who assert representations of their own experiences as a sure foundation of their scholarly position to those who are radically skeptical of our ability as humans to epistemologically access with surety our own, much less others', experiences, this is a topic that continues to generate a wide array of responses and reactions.[17]

Joan W. Scott explores both of these positions in her influential essay "The Evidence of Experience."[18] Scott finds fault with appeals to "experience as uncontestable evidence and as an originary point of explanation—as a foundation upon which analysis is based" (777). By taking experiences as "self-evident," we risk "naturaliz[ing] their difference" (777). Focusing on experience as something immediately available for interpretation, according to Scott, leads to ignoring how "subjects are constituted discursively" (793). Thus, linguistic discourses on race, class, and gender shape and mold the ways that subjects encounter the world, constraining their possibilities. "Social and political reality," as Scott argues, is made up of "complex, contradictory processes" (794).

Scott's perspective is an important one, especially for the way it cautions against the excesses of placing an a priori faith in articulations of human experiences of the world. In arguing against the idea of "a separation between 'experience' and language" and insisting instead "on the productive quality of discourse," she recognizes the limits of human understanding, even of our most sure knowledge of ourselves (793). "Given the ubiquity of the term," Scott writes reluctantly, "it seems more useful to work with it, to analyze its operations and to redefine its meaning. This entails focusing on processes of identity production, insisting on the discursive nature of 'experience' and on the politics of its construction. Experience is at once always already an interpretation *and* is in need of interpretation" (797).

Over the past three decades, a wide variety of scholars and writers from a broad range of backgrounds and fields have recognized, as Scott has, the danger of essentialism. As bell hooks has written, "[C]ritiques of essentialism have usefully deconstructed the idea of a monolithic homogenous identity and experience" (172). This is a concise statement on the problem of essentialist thinking. What marginalized group, after all, has its aspirations met if its personalities and characteristics are somehow reduced to a set of always-identifiable features? For whatever the formulation, such generalizations can be as easily turned against the group as they can be used to argue for the group's positive characteristics.

Yet, as hooks points out, marginalized groups have also found it "an active gesture of political resistance to name one's identity as part of a struggle to challenge domination" (172–73). Such gestures, whether in the classroom or in scholarship, have become occasions for accusations of the sort of uncritical deployment of experience that Scott bemoans. As hooks points out about classroom situations, and I would add critical discourse, what is almost always missing in such discussions is acknowledgment "that racism, sexism, and class elitism shape the structure of classrooms, creating a lived reality of insider/outsider that is predetermined, often in place before any class discussion begins" (176). Rather than ask participants in critical discourse to check their identity at the door to create an environment where everyone can supposedly feel included, hooks suggests a recognition that everyone brings experiential knowledge to the table.

Experiential discourse can become, according to hooks, not a place of competition for the most authoritative voice but a place in which "the concept of a privileged voice of authority is deconstructed by our collective critical practice" (177). Thus, even if experience is not self-evident, that does not mean it is not of vital importance. To shut down a discussion of experience runs the risk of using antiessentialist rhetoric to silence the voices of those who continue to face marginalization, while never interrogating the essentialist underpinnings of the discourse we all otherwise inhabit by default. This, Shari Stone-Mediatore argues, is crucial, as "experience-oriented writing brings into public discussion questions and concerns excluded in dominant ideologies, ideologies which sustain and are sustained by political and economic hierarchies" ("Chandra Mohanty," 126).

Like hooks and Stone-Mediatore, then, I believe that the positions Scott lays out are not mutually exclusive. This may be easy to miss for those who consider a position that privileges Native perspectives in the development of criticism to be antitheoretical. But I maintain that the choice between a theoretical sophistication that recognizes the impossibility of sure knowledge and an uncritical reliance on self-knowledge is a false one. Instead, as Stone-Mediatore argues, "[I]f we want to rethink self-hood in . . . pluralist, collective terms, we cannot simply assert fragmented identities; we need to reckon with the complexities of marginalized people's historically specific struggles" (127).

Craig Womack, in justifying his focus on his own Mvskoke tradition in his influential work *Red on Red* writes, "The critics of Native literary nationalism have faulted Native specialists with a fundamental naïveté, claiming we argue that Native perspectives are pure, authoritative, uncontaminated by European influences" (5). In response, Womack points out that Native perspectives do not have to be pure and uncontaminated to exist; determining that texts by Creek writers have enough in common to study them fruitfully alongside each other does not necessitate declaring that all Creek texts derive from a pristine well of Creekness. Revealing an essence underlying such perspectives, it makes more sense to argue, has been a particular obsession at various times in Western thought, not the Mvskoke tradition.

The assertion of Native perspectives is wrapped up in what hooks points to when she says, "[I]dentity politics emerges out of struggles of oppressed or exploited groups to have a standpoint on which to critique dominant structures, a position that gives purpose and meaning to struggle" (180). The resistance of those Womack argues against suggests a level of discomfort on the part of critics and writers who disagree with the goals and aspirations of such struggles, who fail to understand that such struggles are in fact going on, or who find no easy place for themselves within such struggles, even when they endorse them.

Such critics seemingly find solace in points of view that blur the specific realities of contemporary life. The late Louis Owens, for instance, in his reappropriation of the colonial idea of the frontier, misguidedly suggests that frontier

> stands . . . in neat opposition to the concept of "territory" as territory is imagined and given form by the colonial enterprise in America. Whereas frontier is always unstable, multidirectional, hybridized, characterized by heteroglossia, and indeterminate, territory is clearly mapped, fully imagined as a place of containment, invented to control and subdue the dangerous potentialities of imagined Indians. (*Mixedblood Messages*, 26)

Owens goes on to say that "Native Americans . . . continue to resist this ideology of containment and to insist upon the freedom to reimagine themselves within a fluid, always shifting frontier space" (27).

This statement, in replicating the broad outlines of postmodernism's worst tendencies to level all human identity to inchoate, unknowable haze, obscures the facts surrounding the many ongoing struggles for specific territorial homelands in Native communities across the Americas. Owens eschews the clear differentiation of political boundaries, while the history of Native struggle at nearly every turn seeks in some way to establish them. He endorses the use of a term, *frontier,* that has heralded unmitigated disaster in the history of Native America, revisiting it as if it is simply a convention to be employed, rather than an ideologically imbued term that has served as a primary weapon in the material oppression of Native people in the Americas. Owens points to important existential conditions for many Native people, conditions that critics and other scholars have too often ignored, but his assertion that Native people in general stand in defiance of the idea of discrete homelands ignores significant realities of contemporary Native life. Reflecting those realities does not require asserting a monolithic "Indianness" or denying the creativity of Native American people in finding new ways to respond to the experiential conditions under which they live.

Again, this is not to suggest that experience is an unproblematic category that is easy to pick up and use in explicating Native texts—far from it. In the case of African American women, hooks fears the way she and others "are treated as though we are a box of chocolates presented to individual white women for their eating pleasure, so that they can decide for themselves, and others, which pieces are most tasty" (174). Insisting on using a critical notion of experience in developing Native criticism, I am claiming the importance of working through the panoply of issues, some tasty, some not, that make up the complexity of Native texts. Experience, mediated in representations of it through language, is the material manifestation of the connection between Native texts and Native lives. But experience is not, as I have been arguing, the pure point of origin or the conclusion or be-all and end-all, but a crucial point for coming to an understanding, an interpretation, a reading of the world in which we live.[19] Reading experience in texts, as Stone-Mediatore argues, "is not an endpoint but a point of departure for readers to pursue further understanding of [our] history and . . . obligations" ("Chandra Mohanty," 129).

Scott's reluctance vis-à-vis experience, thus, may be well placed, but allowing that reluctance to lead to a dismissal of experience risks diminishing the power of experiential discourse. To offer just one example, Janice Gould's interpretation of contemporary Native lesbian poetry would not be nearly so powerful without the passion of her own experience embedded in it. As she writes, "I am aware, as I write, that this is an epistle from the borderlands, that liminal space of the Other, marked by the absence of legitimacy, security, and the known facts of the universe. Neither anthropologist nor tourist, I am a resident of this space. . . . I could name the place I occupy as a woman, a lesbian, an Indian, a mixedblood, or some other tag that belongs to me temporarily. But why is it important to hear from me?" (32).

Gould seems acutely aware of the limitations and finitude of her own experience even as she offers a powerful evocation of what it means to live on a particular set of margins. Perhaps most important, following hooks, Gould uses her own experience to expose the extent to which the normative experiences of others already operate within discourse. As she writes, "I am aware that in speaking about a lesbian American Indian erotics, and even more in speaking about lesbian love, I am being disloyal and disobedient to the patriarchal injunction that demands our silence and invisibility. If we would only stay politely and passively in the closet, and not flaunt our sexuality, we could be as gay and abnormal as we like" (32). In speaking from experience, Gould has not naturalized anything. Instead, she has unmasked the power of compulsory heterosexuality and created a space from which to articulate an alternative. Gould's comments demonstrate how Scott's position of reluctance is one that easily lends itself to contextualizing and problematizing at the expense of finally taking a stand and deciding that sometimes the witness of a literary voice demands action.

The need for attention to experience is true whether we speak of the issue of the relationship of Native texts to the social and political world their authors inhabit or to indigenous traditions of knowledge, including oral traditional literatures. Ruffo argues that Native writers confront "with an unblinking eye the realities of what it means to be a people under siege. For Native people, this is the history of the Americas and the legacy of colonialism" (663). Gloria Bird shares Ruffo's concern for the colonial context of Native literary production. "We are all products of colonization," she writes. "Five hundred years after the colonization of this continent, promoting the ideas of native peoples as Other . . . as we parrot Othering language when we speak of ourselves [is an] instance of the internalization of oppression—*is,* in fact, to speak the language of the oppressed" (6).

As Bird says, though, "In dealing with Native American literatures as a process of *self-evaluation,* at least in this country, there are no models that discuss the effects of colonization upon the literature in terms of internalization of stereotypes and oppression *as . . . subject[s]* of critical discourse" (2). Bird, in her concern for the colonial context of literary production, gives the lie to any idea that Native literature is always an extension of oral traditions. "As Native writers we are, after all," she writes, "walking the tightrope between the processes of colonization, and the simultaneous processes of our own decolonization" (3).

At the same time, Ruffo asserts the idea that Native literature draws strongly on Native oral and spiritual traditions. He manages to combine these, saying, "[M]y claim is that Native literature, while grounded in a traditional spirituality based on world-view, is no less a call for liberation, survival and beyond to affirmation" (664). This is an echo of Simon Ortiz, who was perhaps the first critic to work through the relationship between written literature, oral traditions, and the social and political conditions of Native writing. Ortiz recognizes the various ways oral traditions have informed Native writing, but argues that

> [i]t is not the oral tradition as transmitted from ages past alone which is the inspiration and source for contemporary Indian literature. It is also because of the acknowledgment by Indian writers of a responsibility to advocate for their people's self-government, sovereignty, and control of land and resources; and to look also at racism, political and economic oppression, sexism, supremacism, and the needless and wasteful exploitation of land and people, especially in the U.S., that Indian literature is developing a character of nationalism which indeed it should have. It is this character which will prove to be the heart and fiber and story of an America which has heretofore too often feared its deepest and most honest emotions of love and compassion. ("Towards a National Indian Literature," 12)

The ability of Native writers to imbue their work with a sense of what is at stake for the survival of their communities is no easy thing. Yet, as Jace Weaver has so convincingly argued, "[T]he single thing that most defines Indian literatures relates to this sense of community and commitment to it" (*That the People Might Live,* 43). Elaine Jahner speaks of this when she writes, "An important part of the excitement of Native American writing is the intimate bond between genuine need and the artistic response appropriate to the need. The appropriateness of the response also becomes the most important criterion of quality. Art and literature are true strategies of survival" (346).

While I concur with Ruffo, Ortiz, Weaver, and Jahner, an important point here is that literature and the reading of it are not self-contained political actions. I agree in this regard with Frederick Luis Aldama, who argues persuasively for a contemporary criticism that emphasizes the idea that "the most basic property of a literary text is that it performs within society (the consuming public, the reviewers, the critics, and so on) as a literary text" (7). The Native nonfiction tradition, in this way, is not a vein of experience to be mined. It is made up of texts, texts in need of interpretation. To treat them otherwise, as Aldama suggests, is to risk conflating "text-act and being" (5).

Thus, literary texts are, or it may be better to say, can be, part of larger processes of social and political engagement, and they are processes that Native people experience. Something similar is true of what has come to be known as the oral tradition. While even sophisticated scholars like Walter Mignolo recognize the gulf of difference between indigenous and European discourses in the Americas, few seem to understand that naming Native discourse *oral* privileges linguistic and graphic representation in a way that skews discussion toward Eurocentric norms.[20]

Embodied discourse that relies on memory does not always or even primarily rely on language and speech acts. Many actions in Native life are neither primarily oral nor even linguistic, such as ceremonially presenting someone with provisions, taking part in a ritual fast, being part of a societal dance, or cooking a communal meal. All of these actions can have complex levels of meaning within the confines of Native tradition, but those meanings are not necessarily best elucidated by textualizing them.

Calling into question some of the basic categories of criticism in light of Native experience affirms what David L. Moore calls "rough knowledge," which "is the pragmatic, incremental nature of dialogism. Radical understanding . . . is a humane, unremitting recognition of difference, of human fragmentation" (51). Jahner echoes this when she claims that Native writers have an "awareness of where meaning hides when threatened. Their awareness has been tempered by experience that one cannot touch by reading standard types of historical documentation. The inner history of a given tribe can be sensed only through the way each new generation uses the vital images that permit the transmission of all shared experience" (347). The use of experience as a critical category is an acknowledgment that Native texts exist in a real world—a real world that real people experience.

CONCLUSION

The four chapters here cover Native writing across generations and attempt to make sense of the situatedness of Native texts in various ways. The work of William Apess, the Osage Constitution, Native educational narratives, and Momaday's nonfiction provide different ways to develop a stronger sense of Native intellectual history, show the need for better categories of Native criticism, and demonstrate the importance of considering experience as a primary method for deriving meaning from Native texts. Experience and history, as I figure them here, are highly inflected by the social world in which they occur, especially in terms of familiar categories like race, class, and gender, but also by categories that impact Native lives in particular ways, like federal policy.

Apess's work speaks to this agenda in the way he uses his own experiences in Native New England as a primary vehicle for injecting himself into public discourse. The leaders who signed the Osage Constitution, on the other hand, embodied their cultural and historical experiences and their response to the exigencies of modernity in that document. Experiential discourse is crucial to Native educational discourse because of the way it points critical discussion toward those who are the subjects of that discourse, rather than to the policies that dictated conditions and those who implemented those policies. Momaday, in drawing intimate links between language, morality, and experience, propels the discussion from its historical roots into contemporary critical work. In a brief conclusion I will revisit all of these approaches, suggesting ways that experiential discourse can and should impact the development of Native intellectual history and critical studies.

I think of these writers and the texts they authored as figures along intellectual trade routes, a theme I elucidate in my conclusion. Trade routes, of course, are much older than modernity, and in the Americas they have been the loci of exchange for countless generations. Through them, tools, decorative materials, textiles, and foodstuffs have moved across mountains, plains, and rivers from tribe to tribe and community to community. Native intellectual history works for me in much the same way, as Native intellectuals participate in going out from and coming back to the places from which they came, learning along the way new ideas that inform the creation of new knowledge.

Linda Tuhiwai Smith argues that indigenous people seeking to recover and rebuild their communal lives are drawing on "considerable reserves of confidence and creativity [and] have generated a wide range of social, educational, health, and artistic initiatives. [They] have tapped into a set of cultural resources that have recentered the roles of indigenous women, of elders and of groups who have been marginalized through various colonial practices" (110–11). My hope is that these chapters articulate the importance of Native nonfiction as one of those resources and also demonstrate some of the ways that contemporary Native critics can and should embrace that tradition as their own.

Eulogy on William Apess:
His Writerly Life and His New York Death

"*A*nd while you ask yourselves, 'What do they, the Indians, want?' you have only to look at the unjust laws made for them and say, 'They want what I want.'"[1] These words, which I have chosen to open this examination of Native nonfiction, were spoken on two occasions in the Odeon Theatre in Boston in January 1836. They are among the last statements that history records the Pequot intellectual William Apess making in public. They come at the end of what is surely the pinnacle of Apess's intellectual career, his *Eulogy on King Philip*, a revision of American history in which Apess condemns the historical and contemporary practices by which Natives had lost and were continuing to lose their lands to invading Amer-Europeans. Apess delivered the eulogy on January 8, then again on January 26 (Apess, *On Our Own Ground,* 275).

The *Eulogy*, published in two editions after it was delivered, is the last of Apess's five books, all of which are nonfiction. He also published an autobiography, *A Son of the Forest,* in two editions (1829 and 1831); *The Increase of the Kingdom of Christ: A Sermon* (1831); *The Experiences of Five Christian Indians of the Pequot Tribe* (1833); and *Indian Nullification of the Unconstitutional Laws of Massachusetts Relative to the Marshpee Tribe; or, The Pretended Riot Explained* (1835).[2] Each of these books is remarkable in its own way, especially given the extremely modest background of the author. "Apess's work," says Jace Weaver, is "resistance literature, affirming Indian cultural and political identity over against the dominant culture" (*That the People,* 55).

Apess was born in 1798 in Colrain, Massachusetts, the first child, most probably, of William and Candace Apes.[3] His parents separated in 1801 and young William was sent to Colchester, Connecticut, to live with his mother's parents, in whose care he was physically abused. At age four, the city of Colchester bound him out to a local couple, who sent him to school until he was twelve. Apess's indenture was then sold to a judge in New London. Apess ran away from the judge's house several times before his indenture was sold once again.

During his time in New London, Apess began attending Methodist meetings and, on March 13, 1813, he had a conversion experience. His rebellion against his indenture, however, continued following this conversion and he ran away and joined the United States Army, serving on the Canadian front during the War of 1812. After mustering out of the army, Apess wandered around Quebec and Ontario before returning to Connecticut in 1817.

Returning to the Methodists, Apess was baptized by immersion in 1818 and began teaching classes and preaching. After marrying in 1821, Apess and his wife, Mary, had at least one and perhaps as many as three children. Apess worked in various places in southern New England and in 1827 was licensed by the Methodists to exhort. Following this, he began work as a missionary in the northeast. In the midst of a conflict with his sect of the Methodists over his ordination, Apess began what was an unprecedented publishing career for a Native writer.

Apess is one of several Native intellectuals from the eighteenth and nineteenth centuries to whom scholars have recently paid increasing attention, including Samson Occom, Joseph Johnson, Peter Jones, Elias Boudinot, and George Copway. Scholars have produced a range of work about these individuals, from extremely helpful and illuminating anthologies and articles built around recovered writings to full-length archival and textual studies of multiple and single authors.[4]

Rather than rehearsing and rehashing this often valuable critical and editorial work, my purpose in this chapter is to engage Apess at a critical nexus in which his realities, reflected in his ideas (as we can know them from his works and from history), inform a broader discussion about the tasks and responsibilities of intellectuals. Thus, my interest here is not so much in expositing Apess's texts as in arguing for a particular reading of Apess and his contribution to Native intellectual history. That is, through a consideration of his work and the emergent picture of the context in which he did that work, I hope not only to illuminate the life and career of this significant nineteenth-century Native voice, but to show how his life and work speak to a contemporary Native intellectual agenda. This connection is what is generally missing from the growing number of studies of Apess's work.

Further, I will argue that Apess's experientially based work provides a model for a more historically focused approach to Native life than one emphasizing static notions of culture or strict attention to texts absent the material realities, available through discourse on experience, that Native literature reflects. Crucial to this discussion is the way that Apess, rather than just relying on his own experiences writ larger and larger, uses those experiences to write more sophisticated nonfiction, culminating in the *Eulogy*. This example, then, establishes a major aspect of this study—that the nonfiction tradition in Native writing articulates a way of using experience to illuminate Native life in particular ways.

In taking this approach to Apess, I am interested in doing for his work something like what Alice Walker did for Zora Neale Hurston in her collection of essays, *In Search of Our Mothers' Gardens*.[5] That is, Walker argues that it is sometimes the responsibility of a critic to choose between divergent intellectual paths as represented in the writings of particular figures. In choosing Hurston as her primary intellectual progenitor, Walker not only evaluates and endorses Hurston's ideas, she takes up the mantle of those ideas and enunciates the truth that some ideas and approaches are better than others: they hold more promise for showing the way toward a more just future and provide a stronger basis for hope. Walker does not dismiss the work of those before Hurston, nor does she rely on a unitary intellectual consciousness for black women. Figures like Jesse Fauset were much more central to African American political life than the free-spirited Hurston, so Walker is not just extolling the virtues of an obvious intellectual progenitor. The challenge she places before herself is to make convincing arguments for her choice.

In a similar vein, and in a move not unlike the one Apess makes in his *Eulogy,* holding up King Philip as the greatest of all Americans, I will here make a case for Apess as the Native writer from before the twentieth century who most demands the attention of contemporary Native intellectuals. Read in this way, his work shines across the decades to provide an intellectual beacon. Much more than a stalwart to celebrate from the history of Native writing, Apess and his work stand, in this reading, in judgment of what has happened since. This is, as Scott Stevens has argued, different from what most scholars have done in their work on Apess, where attention to Apess's involvement in Christianity overwhelms other issues. I agree here with Stevens, who writes, "The complicated and painful history of Native America demands the careful study of such issues as acculturation, accommodation, and even assimilation without automatically denoting these as pejorative and then setting them aside" (68).

To make my case for Apess's centrality, I will discuss in detail the circumstances that brought Apess to his career as a public intellectual. Next I will look at some of the ways a reading of his life informs our understanding of his later writings. Following that I will look at the circumstances surrounding Apess's death in 1839, not in New England, but in New York City. Finally, I want to draw some parallels between the work of Apess and that of later Native intellectual figures as a way to flesh out what my reading means for a deeper appreciation of contemporary Native intellectual challenges. Along the way, I will point out how his nonfiction innovations continue to make him an exemplar of the best the Native tradition has to offer. Before turning to Apess's life, though, I want to briefly discuss what has come to be known of his death.

A NEW YORK MYSTERY

What happened to Apess after he departed the stage at the Odeon is shrouded in mystery; the contemporary realities of the 1830s and the attendant problem of Native invisibility in the northeast United States surround his story outside of his published work. A year after his orations at the Odeon, Apess published second editions of both *The Experiences of Five Christian Indians* and *Eulogy on King Philip*, but he has yet to show up in the historical record as having continued his life in the public eye. Indeed, the next places Apess shows up are in court in debt actions. Even in these records, an inventory of his household goods shows up, but he does not.

For years, that was all that seemed possible to know of Apess after 1836. One early critic speculated that his political activities had made him violent enemies and that he had been murdered, like his African American New England nationalist contemporary, David Walker. Others assumed he fell into dissipation and died anonymously (Apess, *On Our Own Ground*, xxxviii–xxxix).[6] Eventually, 1839 obituaries from New York City papers emerged in archival research, followed by transcripts of an inquest into Apess's death.[7] Until the New York obituaries were discovered,

Apess seemed every bit a product of New England and primarily a New England writer.[8] Then, somehow, Apess had moved from New England to New York City, where he died.

The inquest transcript, a handwritten document of just a few pages, offers no ironclad answers to the circumstances of Apess's death. In attendance were three witnesses: a fellow boarder, the daughter of the owner of the boarding house where Apess was living, and a wife named Elizabeth. Apparently, Apess sought medical attention due to pain in his right side and purging and vomiting that had lasted two days. A Doctor Viers prescribed something to help him purge more quickly. The next day, Apess felt better, brushing his teeth and eating some toast. The boarder who testified at the inquest reported that he spoke to Apess that day and reported that he seemed well. However, five minutes later, Apess was dead. The coroner concluded that apoplexy had caused his death, indicating that a sudden, strokelike event had ended his life. Barry O'Connell, who has traced out as much of Apess's history as any scholar, conjectures that bad medicine from Dr. Viers was really the cause, pointing to the woeful state of health care in those days ("'Once More Let Us Reconsider'").

The more likely possibility is that a long drinking career had caught up with Apess, which is consistent with the coroner's conclusion of apoplexy. All three who testified at the inquest reported that Apess was a heavy drinker, with the fellow boarder reporting that he was known to go on drinking binges that would last for some days, and then would not drink at all. His wife reported that "he has lately been somewhat intemperate" ("Inquisition"). O'Connell contends that none of this adds up to Apess being a victim of alcoholism, suggesting instead that perhaps Apess had drinking binges only occasionally. After all, over a hundred years later, the life expectancy for a Native male was still little more than the forty-one years he lived. However, the available evidence supports the conclusion that Apess's drinking career caught up with him in New York, a conclusion consistent with the combination of factors, including a history of heavy drinking, that Apess describes in his work.[9]

Why Apess would have moved from Massachusetts to New York City is also still unknown. Elizabeth testified at the inquest that she had been married to Apess for what appears to be either two or ten years (the handwriting is difficult to decipher), which is noteworthy since that could have her marriage to Apess overlapping with the publication of his wife Mary's story in *Experiences* (they married in 1821).[10] Furthermore, no record shows

Apess as being part of any larger community through which he might have gained an audience—a local Methodist church or society, for instance.

It is important to remember that nearly any of the evidence from the inquest could have been exaggerated, meaning that we might never be able to pinpoint the exact contours of Apess's last years. Perhaps Elizabeth Apess and the fellow boarder underplayed the extent of his drinking in his last days as a way of denying the unhealthiness of their own lifestyles. Certainly any interpretation of the inquest needs to take into account the dynamics of race, class, and gender that might have been at work as these men and women living on the margins of New York society answered questions about the personal habits of a racialized subject, questions being asked by men representing government power.

I want to speculate a little, after looking at some salient aspects of Apess's life and work, on the possible circumstances of his move to New York and his death. Using what history says about New York as a commercial, publishing, and intellectual capital in those years, I will suggest some reasons Apess might have made the move. Further, drawing a parallel to the 1960s figure Clyde Warrior, I want to suggest that he very well could have found himself in a state of intellectual despair that was exacerbated by excessive drinking.

I also want to relate Apess's experiences to other Natives who spent part of their careers in New York, including myself. By doing so, we can look for synchronicity between Apess and later Native writers, and thus learn more about what writers like Apess, who left so little in the way of detailed archives, might have done.

The idea of *synchronicity* is crucial. It helps build the case that a great many of the dynamics of Native intellectual production remain constant across the arc of history. Synchronicity, as an imaginative tool, helps in a consideration of the gaps of what documentary history doesn't reveal. To engage in speculation, as I will do in Apess's case, is not mere fancy, but a way of trying to grasp from the shreds and shards of evidence significant aspects of a Native intellectual patrimony. Imagining Apess, in spite of the limits inherent in the act, is to imagine his work on an arc with contemporary Native writing. Synchronicity is my way of making myself think of Apess beyond the abstract, seeing him as an intellectual living in real time. I want to suggest that this particular act of imagination, in and of itself, reveals its own kind of truth, however little we might be able to ascertain of the facts from the sparse historical record.

Whatever happened to Apess after the *Eulogy,* I will show that his re-markable life flowed quite naturally from his simultaneous act of going public while going Native. He placed himself in the public eye through his ministry and through his books. In so doing, he articulated a stream of experience that carried him along, defining him in certain ways as a Native, and making him part of the intellectual currents of his time in others. Apess's legacy continues to be the example that he set in learning to swim both in and against that stream.

BEING PEQUOT, BEING NATIVE

That we know so little of Apess outside of his own writings is testament to two particular sorts of American Indian marginalization in the Ameri-can northeast in the 1830s. First, by the 1830s Indians worthy of public consideration existed elsewhere for those who inhabited the region the Pilgrims had subdued two centuries before. During Apess's early life, the Ohio River valley was drawing the primary attention of the young re-public of the United States. Apess's public career (1829–36) paralleled the presidency of Andrew Jackson, whose Indian policy focused on remov-ing Natives from southern U.S. states to the other side of the Mississippi. The second sort of marginalization was that the last thing people in the northeast probably imagined when they pictured Indians was an articu-late Methodist minister writing books.

Focusing on this second sort of exceptionality has been the habit of most scholars who have written about Apess and his work—and for good reason. When encountering his work, compelling and even fascinating questions arise about how he came by enough education to produce his books, why he was drawn to Methodism in the midst of the Congregational history of southern New England, and where he developed the wherewithal to es-sentially self-publish five books in an era when next to no Native authors existed. The emergence of genius is, after all, no small thing, and charting the directions in which it takes someone like Apess is crucial.

But I will argue here that focusing on this second sort of marginality, Apess's exceptionality, has obscured the extent to which that first sort of marginality, Apess's experiences as a New England Native person, defines his life and is central to his work. In spite of his genius, his books, and his career as a minister, Apess is also not exceptional when considered in the context of Native history in New England. Yes, his books set him apart.

But as I will discuss through a review of Pequot history and an examination of the conditions of being Native in New England in the eighteenth and nineteenth centuries, his work emerged from his experiences of being Native in New England.

To understand the margins on which Apess lived requires first imagining what it meant for him to be Pequot two hundred years after the tribe was decimated in one of the worst genocidal wars in the history of North America. Two centuries before Apess's birth, the Pequots were one of the most powerful indigenous groups in what would become New England, numbering probably thirteen thousand people (Starna, 46). Though regular contact with Europeans would not begin until 1632, the first important genocidal moment in the encounter between the Pequots and the Europeans was a "plague" that significantly reduced Pequot population between 1616 and 1619 (Starna, 45; Hauptman, 71).

Periodic epidemics of various European diseases persisted among the Pequots and other New England Natives and what was almost surely a universal outbreak of smallpox occurred among the Pequots in 1633 (Starna, 46). The population of the Pequots subsequently dropped to approximately three thousand, a mortality rate of 77 percent since the beginning of the century. As William Cronin has shown,

> [t]o Puritans, the epidemics were manifestly a sign of God's providence,
> "in sweeping away great multitudes of the natives . . . that he might make
> room for us there." John Winthrop saw this "making room" as a direct
> conveyance of property right. "God," he said, "hath hereby cleared our
> title to this place." (90)

In the midst of these severe demographic shifts, the Pequots and other New England tribal groups became increasingly enmeshed in the developing market economy that the new European arrivals from England and Holland were introducing to the region. This trade was far from a one-way proposition in which the Europeans held all the power. Native men, in fact, were generally much more proficient hunters, especially of beaver, and Natives invented and produced the wampum that became a crucial staple in northeastern trade (Cronin, 92, 95ff.).

The Pequots seemed to occupy a choice location from which to exploit competition between the Dutch in upstate New York, the English of the Massachusetts Bay Colony, and those vying for control of the Connecticut River valley. However, less than five years after making their first significant contact with the English, the Pequots found themselves at war with their new neighbors. Armed conflict broke out in the midst of a Pequot attempt to satisfy the murder of a Virginia trader by a nearby tribe that paid tribute to the Pequots. The more powerful Pequots negotiated peace with the English. As part of the negotiations, the English were to send a trader to the Pequots so they would have easier access to trade goods. On his way to the Pequots, John Oldham, the trader, was killed near the shores of Block Island, probably by Eastern Niantics, or possibly Narragansetts (Drinnon, 35ff.).

The English struck back against the Pequots in what seemed as much an attempt to increase the reach of their power into the Connecticut River valley as reprisal for Oldham's death. Englishman John Endicott organized a military expedition that struck Block Island and then sailed against the Pequots. Endicott burned two nonfortified Pequot villages and demanded satisfaction for Oldham's death (McBride, 101; Hauptman, 71ff.). The conflict with the English exacerbated internal conflict between the Pequot leader, Sassacus, and his rival, Uncas. Uncas and his followers, thereafter known as Mohegans, separated from the larger group and allied themselves with the English and the Narragansetts against the Pequots (Hauptman, 72).

In April 1637, the Pequots attacked one of the villages the English had established in their territory, killing nine and taking two young girls prisoner (Hauptman, 72). This created the pretext for Massachusetts and Connecticut to engage in a full-scale war of extermination against the Pequots. The first act of retribution in this escalated conflict was a pre-dawn attack on the Pequot fort on the Mystic River by Captain James Underhill and Captain John Mason on May 26, 1637. Leading colonists and their Mohegan, Narragansett, and Eastern Niantic allies against the fort, Underhill and Mason found between four hundred and seven hundred Pequots in the fort, nearly all of them women, children, and elderly, who were at the fort for protection while the main force of Pequot male warriors was preparing to engage the main force of the English (Jennings, 222ff.).

The fort was in the palisade style, meaning it consisted of two semi-circular walls built of thick, tall poles embedded in the ground. The two walls came together to create a circle, with the only two openings coming at the offset points at which the walls met and overlapped. Once the Pequot defenders of these openings were overwhelmed, the English began to enter the wooden lodges inside, attacking the inhabitants and setting fire to their dwellings. By their own accounts, Mason and Underhill had led the killing spree. Those attempting to escape the conflagration were killed by those surrounding the fort.

Seven Pequots survived the massacre at Mystic. Underhill, justifying the complete lack of compassion with which he and Mason had led the massacre, compared the Pequots to the Philistines killed by the biblical King David. "Sometimes the Scripture declareth," he wrote, "women and children must perish with their parents. Sometimes the case alters; but we will not dispute it now. We had sufficient light from the word of God for our proceedings" (quoted in Hauptman, 76).

From then until September 1638, the Pequots were systematically reduced through capture, death at the hands of their enemies, and execution. They were sent to the West Indies as slaves or given over to the tribes that had allied against them. Of the three to four thousand Pequots alive at the beginning of the war, perhaps two thousand remained at the end (McBride, 104). Of those, many were scattered among other tribal groups and the population of Pequots in their former strongholds dwindled. The Treaty of Hartford, which formally closed the conflict, declared the Pequots to be dissolved as a nation (Drinnon, 55).

Less than four decades after the Pequot War, New England Natives found themselves plunged into a military conflict that would be another historical watershed for the region. King Philip's War, so called after the name the English gave to the Wampanoag leader Metacomet, was an attempt by coastal New England Indians to resist English encroachment in 1675 and 1676.[11] Metacomet, whose wife and son were captured and probably sold into slavery in the West Indies, died at the hands of one of the Indian allies of the English in a Rhode Island swamp in August 1676. His head was cut off and his body quartered and hung in trees. Though the Abenakis and others would continue various sorts of military action against the colonists well into the eighteenth century, by 1677 the more populous regions of New England were in a similar position to the Pequot homelands—vanquished militarily and overwhelmed by the social and economic weight of the European colonists, who had arrived not much more than half century earlier (Calloway, 4ff.).

The tide of history was rising for the colonists and swallowing up Native New Englanders. Whereas seventy thousand indigenous people had lived in the region at the beginning of the century, twelve thousand remained to face the brave new world that dawned for Indian people at the end of

King Philip's War (Cronin, 89). What emerged for Native American New Englanders was very much a diasporic existence.

Looking ahead to Apess, the question arises of what happened, given the misfortunes of the Pequots, that he and others still called themselves Pequots two centuries later? Essentially, the Pequots began making a resurgence a decade and a half after their near annihilation. Though technically barred from living in their previous territory, groups of Pequots succeeded in regaining parcels of their former homelands in the 1650s and 1660s (McBride, 105).

Yet, while the Pequots managed to survive the genocidal designs of the New England Puritans, their existence for the next three hundred years would be marked by social deprivation and constant threats to the status of their lands. And their reservation-based population continued to decrease. The population of the reservation of the western Pequots at Mashuntucket was 322 in 1725, 66 males above the age of fourteen in 1732, 72 adults above age fourteen (31 males) in 1755, and twenty to thirty families in 1762. In 1856, only six dwellings housing perhaps thirty people remained at Mashuntucket (McBride, 107).[12]

Clearly, just the continuing existence of the Pequots in the face of all they experienced is testimony to the resilience of generations of political leadership that refused to give up on the idea of the Pequots as a people. That idea, of course, required a land base, and some Pequot people held on to that base with ferocious tenacity. In the process, those Pequots managed to carve out a place for themselves in which they managed to endure. Their descendants would be the ones who, much later, set the stage for the contemporary rebirth of the Pequots as a people.

But what about those who left? The experiences of those who managed to find a way to stay connected to the dwindling land bases of New England Native nations are the exceptions rather than the rule. Much more common are responses to English colonialism that require the migration of Native people away from their land bases, away from the enclaves in which a sense of Native polity and culture could survive the onslaught of modernity in New England.

A Stranger in His Own Land

One way of understanding the transitory nature of Native life in New England in the early nineteenth century is through migration, which took a number of different forms. Poverty was at the root of all of them. The employment available to uneducated Indian people often was of the most menial sort, ensuring no more than a hand-to-mouth existence in which there was never enough money to get ahead and people were put at constant risk for debt peonage. As poor people, New England Indians' choices were circumscribed by the prejudices of white New Englanders, who controlled the local and regional economies. Even those Natives who managed to migrate to a place where they could make a living might find themselves having to move back to the town where they had been born if their circumstances changed and they needed local assistance.[13] William Apess would become acquainted with nearly all of these forms of migration during his life, as he reveals in his autobiographical work, *A Son of the Forest*.

Apess wrote the book sometime in the midst of the process of becoming ordained as a Methodist minister in the late 1820s. *A Son of the Forest* covers the period from Apess's birth until he wrote the book. In the beginning, as Weaver argues, "Apess through clever rhetorical moves is able to accomplish a number of important things" (*That the People*, 55). First, he claims family ties (though surely erroneously) to the Wampanoag patriot Metacomet, or King Philip. Second, he glides over his mother's almost certain African American ancestry, thus avoiding controversy over black-white miscegenation. Finally, according to Weaver, "the use of the language of evangelical Christianity subverts his readers' expectations about how Indians should talk and violates romantic stereotypes that were prevalent even in Apess's time" (55).

I will add to these the way Apess tells us how he was born into a tradition of using avoidance as a form of resistance, a strategy that was less and less possible for Native people by the end of the eighteenth century. In *A Son of the Forest*, Apess tells of how his father, "not long after his marriage . . . removed to what was then called the back settlements . . . where he pitched his tent in the woods of a town called Colrain, near the Connecticut River, in the state of Massachusetts" (4). This, I would argue, is a self-conscious move on the part of Apess's father to follow one of the common strategies of indigenous people around the world—moving as far as possible out of the way of colonial settlement.

Oral history among the neighboring Naragansetts suggests that many Native men "were reluctant to be identified by officials; they adopted aliases and took to the woods, unwilling to risk servitude under European

Americans" (Herndon and Sekatau, 121). Apess's father seemingly joined in a tradition of doing exactly that. Those with no desire to live among white people could make their way to sparsely populated areas. In the previous century, of course, options were more numerous, and someone like Apess's father might have decided to join other, more intact Native groups that had more opportunity to resist settlement. Though written evidence for this type of migration is even more sparse than what is available for other aspects of New England Native life, such moves of resistance provide an important backdrop for the story of New England Native survival and resurgence.

Crucial to this experience of migration and dislocation is the way gender circumscribed various life options. While ascertaining the number of Native men who managed to live out their lives undisturbed in the backwoods of New England may never be possible, a clearer picture has emerged of the ways Native men and women experienced life in the direct path of colonization. The whaling industry and the military provided Native men with a means to escape, at least temporarily, the vicissitudes of life in New England. Yet, as Jean O'Brien argues, "As a result of their participation in these activities, Indian men were absent for extended periods of time, engaged in dangerous pursuits that seriously jeopardized their lives and well-being and compromised their ability to function effectively within the English-dominated society" ("'Divorced' from the Land," 153).[14] Indeed, each major North American conflict, like the Seven Years' War, created difficulties for New England's Native communities. The New England divine Ezra Stiles reported that in the Pequot community at Mashuntucket in the early 1760s, 29 percent of its households were headed by widows, while the percentage in one Massachusetts community was 52.[15]

Whaling enjoyed its heyday among Natives in the Nantucket fishery in the middle of the eighteenth century, but Indian whalers continued to work in fisheries well into the nineteenth century. As with military service, the whaling industry was often only a stopgap measure for Native men. Worse, it often placed the men who participated in a state of debt peonage to those for whom they risked their lives at sea (Vickers, 104–9).

While Herndon and Sekatau stress the ways that the absences that whaling and the military caused in Native communities are continuous with earlier patterns of men hunting and fishing while women remained to tend crops, O'Brien argues that the new realities under English domination were far different. In the older way, she argues,

these periods of separation were scheduled, part of the seasonal rhythm
of life, and as such they rendered neither women nor men helpless. Newer
patterns of male mobility . . . frequently left women alone to experience
harsher circumstances than before, when kin-based social welfare and
flexible marriages had provided them with the means to alleviate their
wants. (154)

The main pressure for continuity of family and community life, then,
fell on women. O'Brien traces this phenomenon back to the end of the
seventeenth century, when, "as they successfully dispossessed and displaced Indians, the heirs of English colonialism seized the power to define the rules governing the social order, and they constructed surviving
New England Natives as peculiar and marginal" (145). Part of that recon-
struction was to pressure Native men into attempting farming, something
Native New England women had been responsible for in earlier times.

Native men did not in general make a successful transition to this new
gendered order of relationship to the land. O'Brien suggests that this can
be seen as a staunch rejection of English colonialism, and that it also had
the effect of altering the role of women in Native society. For while Native
men had the option of withdrawing from their conditions by going to sea
or into the military, Native women often found themselves in the crucible
of discrimination and oppression as wage laborers in the homes of New
England whites. An alternative for some women was the manufacture of
Indian-style crafts. "In their artisanal production," O'Brien argues,

women continued to cultivate the specialized knowledge required to
gather materials for fashioning baskets and other crafts. Their craft-
work represented a revealing accommodation to dispossession: reaping
basket stuff did not require "possession" of the land. At the same time,
in marketing Indian goods, they earned an income and reinforced their
"Indianness" in the popular perception. (150)

Yet, however much the act of maintaining a presence on traditional
lands or using traditional craft skills to make a living can be construed
as ways of persisting as Natives, the continuing disruptions of colonialism remained. This was especially true, O'Brien argues, for "[m]arginal
individuals, that is, those with few relatives or friends, Indian or non-
Indian, and little in the way of economic resources." These individuals,
says O'Brien,

suffered the most. Prior to Indian enmeshment in the market, caretaking and nursing constituted central kinship obligations. During the eighteenth century, as kinship networks thinned, families became fractured, and involvement in the market made prosperity precarious at best. Individuals could no longer count on thick networks of relatives to care for them when they were in need of shelter, sustenance, or support. Nursing and caretaking became commodified and unreliable. Even when an intact family was in place, taking on caretaking obligations in this changed context could spell the economic ruin of a precariously established family. (151)

The childhood story Apess tells in *A Son of the Forest* follows these outlines closely. From out of this crucible, Apess became a major intellectual figure whose work continues to challenge and enlighten readers over two centuries after his birth. The crucible shaped him and molded him. He overcame many of its limitations, but they carried him every bit as much as his genius.

Childhood and Violence

When Apess was born in 1798, his parents apparently were attempting to carve out an alternative within the crucible by starting a family at a distance from their world of domestic work. The family's location in the back settlements near Colrain, Massachusetts, lends credence to O'Connell's theory that Apess was a son of William and Candace Apes, both of whom were listed as working as servants in a household in Colchester, Connecticut. Candace was very possibly an Afro-Native domestic worker, perhaps a slave, in the household, and it could be that the elder William, upon marrying her, decided to live away from the watchfulness of people in town, including other Pequots. In the latest part of the eighteenth century, though, the lessening availability of such places might be the reason that William and Candace Apes moved back to Colchester not long after the birth of William, their oldest son. There, according to Apess, "our little family lived for nearly three years in comparative comfort" (*A Son of the Forest,* 5).

Then, however, circumstances changed. Apess's parents "quarreled, parted, and went off to a great distance, leaving their helpless children to the care of their grandparents" (5). While this separation between Apess's parents could be just part of the ebb and flow of New England family life, it is much more likely that the Apes family was feeling the particular pressures on family life that historians are establishing as more and more common. The move from Colrain to Colchester indicates very possibly some sort of economic difficulty that exacerbated other family problems—the loss of a job, perhaps, or the need to take time off to care for relatives.

The elder Apes could, at that point, have decided to do what many Native men in New England did, which is go to sea or into the military. Whatever his intentions, he apparently responded to whatever was ailing his family by doing what significant numbers of other Native men did. As O'Brien argues, "[S]ome men . . . abandoned their families to escape their predicaments; evidence may be found in scattered narratives of Indian men 'absconding' as difficult circumstances evolved into insurmountable economic and legal problems" (154). Following the departure of his parents, the young William found himself living with his siblings at the home of his mother's parents.

The year that followed can only be described as horrific. From Apess's description in *A Son of the Forest,* his grandparents were violent alcoholics, who, "when under the influence of liquor . . . would not only quarrel and fight with each other but would at times turn upon their unoffending grandchildren and beat them in a most cruel manner" (5). Apess writes of his grandparents' behavior, "I attribute it in great measure to the whites, inasmuch as they introduced among my countrymen that bane of comfort and happiness, ardent spirits. . . . I do not make this statement in order to justify those who treated me so unkindly, but simply to show that, inasmuch as I was thus treated only when they were under the influence of spirituous liquor, that the whites were justly chargeable with at least some portion of my sufferings" (7).

Apess and his siblings were not alone in their suffering, he argues. Alcohol was ravaging significant parts of the local Native community, and "the consequence was that they were scattered abroad. Now many of them were seen reeling about intoxicated with liquor, neglecting to provide for themselves and families" (7). Though writing about the contemporary American Indian world, Eduardo Duran and Bonnie Duran provide insight into the psychology of the Native New England communities Apess experienced growing up:

> Once a group of people has been assaulted in a genocidal fashion, there
> are psychological ramifications. With the victim's complete loss of power
> comes despair, and the psyche reacts by internalizing what appears to be

genuine power—the power of the oppressor. The internalizing process begins when Native American people internalize the oppressor, which is merely a caricature of the power actually taken from Native American people. At this point, the self-worth of the individual and/or group has sunk to a level of despair tantamount to self-hatred. This self-hatred can be either internalized or externalized. (29)

In this reading, Apess experiences his tribe's history through the actions of the damaged psyches of his grandparents. Thus, while Apess attributes responsibility for the social situation of his family to the material realities brought to Native communities with white ideology, he also seems to have an acute awareness of the complexity of what brought him to his familial situation.

Regardless of fault, it must have been tremendously scarring to have some of one's earliest memories be of grandparents being violent at home. Apess also describes a situation of extreme neglect in which his grandparents provided meals of a single cold potato or forced the children to dance around in the cellar to try to stay warm. Even today, most Native writers would be reticent to paint such a negative portrait of their own families and some might suggest Apess does so out of self-hate. Yet, clearly, Apess does so as a way to discover the truth of his own experiences and the reasons why he and others found themselves in such conditions.

"Truly, we were in a most deplorable condition," Apess writes, "too young to obtain subsistence for ourselves, by the labor of our hands, and our wants almost totally disregarded by those who should have made every exertion to supply them" (5). This is a child's view of Native life in New England in the early nineteenth century. Apess, at the point he describes, was four years old.

The situation came to a head when, as Apess tells it, his grandmother came home drunk "and, without any provocation whatever on my part, began to belabor me most unmercifully with a club. . . . She continued beating me, by which means one of my arms was broken in three different places" (6). This is hardly the usual portrait of tender Native grandmothering. Again, Duran and Duran provide an instructive perspective on the past, even as they analyze the present. "When self-hatred is externalized," they write,

we encounter a level of violence within the community that is unparalleled in any other group in the country. . . . What is remarkable about

this violence is that for the most part, it is directed at other Native
Americans. . . . From decades of work in the Native American community, the authors can attest to the astronomical incidence of domestic
violence within the Native American nuclear family. (29)

To the extent Duran and Duran are right, Apess would seem to be countering the self-hatred of his grandmother, rather than exhibiting his own.
Apess's uncle, who lived in an adjacent dwelling, saved the four-year-old
from further violence and told a neighbor, Mr. Furman, who had occasionally provided milk for the children, what had happened. Furman alerted
local authorities, who decided to bind the children out to local families.
As with so much of his early life, Apess's indenture is yet another marker
not of his exceptionality, but of how much he was imbricated in the life of
Native New England.

From One Bind to Another

Being bound out, or indentured, was a primary means of dealing with
indigent people, especially children, in New England. As Herndon and
Sekatau explain, "[T]own 'fathers' acted in the stead of natural parents
and placed poor and/or orphaned children of all races in more prosperous
households under a contract that obligated the children to live with and
work for the master until adulthood" (121).

By Apess's time, the historical record is muddled as to the proportion
of Native children who were bound out, but anecdotal evidence suggests
that the experience of the Apes children was part of a pattern of New
England Native life between the seventeenth and nineteenth centuries
that was in disproportion to other children, especially whites. According
to one study, in Rhode Island in 1774, "35.5 percent of all Indians in the
colony were living with white families" (Sainsbury, 379). Town records
around New England and testimony like Apess's suggest that Indian
people were doubly vulnerable to indenture—in part because they were
poor, but also because their subordinate position as people of color put
them in a social position in which they could supply the cheap labor that
made bound labor, in many instances, "only slightly disguised slavery"
(Herndon and Sekatau, 122).

Apess's first experience of indenture was, by his own account, on the
more humane end of the spectrum. The Furmans, who had rescued him

from his grandparents, took care of him for a year while his wounds healed, then accepted him as a bound servant in spite of doubts about whether he could be much help to Mr. Furman, who was a cooper. The Furmans sent Apess to school and Mrs. Furman exposed the young man to Christianity through the Baptist Church.

Still, his experience of indenture can be seen as positive only within a certain frame. Apess was, after all, bound to servitude. And Mr. Furman was hardly an enlightened antiracist; Apess reports him calling his young servant an "Indian dog" after a conflict in which Apess was wrongly accused of having threatened a young white woman with a knife (12). And any illusions about indenture being, in cases such as Apess's, a form of foster parenting are undermined by the fact that, when the Furmans became frustrated at Apess's behavior when he was twelve, they transferred his indenture to an elderly judge for twenty dollars and scorned his attempts to return to their home.

Life with Judge Hillhouse was on the other, even more negative end of the indenture scale. Apess reports that he was unable to continue in the religious teaching he had learned to value with the Furmans and was not well taken care of. "He had in the first place treated me with the utmost kindness," Apess writes, "until he had made sure of me. Then the whole course of his conduct changed, and I believed he fulfilled only one item of the transferred indentures, and that was work. Of this there was no lack. To be sure I had enough to eat, such as it was, but he did not send me to school as he promised" (16).

Apess rebelled against the situation and ran away, visiting his father some twenty miles distant. After a week, he returned, and the judge decided to sell his indenture once again, this time to the household of General William Williams, a man of prominence in New London. As Apess reports of this experience, "I was greatly mortified to think that I was sold in this way. If my consent had been solicited as a matter of form, I should not have felt so bad. But to be sold and treated so unkindly by those who had got our fathers' lands for nothing was too much to bear" (16). In spite of these objections, Apess found the Williams family much more hospitable than Judge Hillhouse.

During the time Apess was with the Williams family, he had his first conversion experience, with Methodists. He had attended Baptist, Presbyterian, and other Christian meetings since his indenture, but the Methodists appealed to him in a way the others never had. Their arrival in Apess's part of

Connecticut was controversial, no doubt because, in its extreme forms in the eighteenth and nineteenth centuries, Methodism demanded the fraternity of others across class, racial, and gender lines. The acceptance of such fellowship among white elites was ambiguous and uncomfortable, but the sheer fact of a group of poor people and wealthy people, white people, black people, and Native people meeting together in feasts of love was a striking response to the various injustices of the colonization and settlement of North America. That message clearly impressed Apess. "I felt convinced," he writes, "that Christ died for all mankind—that age, sect, color, country, or situation made no difference" (19). Thus, among the "noisy Methodists" Apess found a place where he was a child of God, not a bound servant, a neglected son, or an Indian dog.

"I enjoyed great peace of mind," Apess proclaims of his conversion, "and that peace was like a river, full, deep, and wide, and flowing continually" (21). However, following the pattern of American conversion narratives, Apess describes this conversion as not lasting long. Treated unfairly in the Williams household, Apess "absconded" with another of the Williams's servants. After Apess wandered around the region for a while, General Williams posted a reward for the return of his servant. Rather than risk return to New London, the fifteen-year-old Apess enlisted in the United States Army, which was then embroiled in the War of 1812. Soon, Apess "had acquired many bad practices. . . . In a little time I became almost as bad as any of them, could drink rum, play cards, and act as wickedly as any" (25).

By joining the military, Apess found himself yet again in one of the places that New England Natives migrated to in the nineteenth century. Being a soldier made a lasting impression on Apess. While in training to be a drummer on Governor's Island, off the southern tip of Manhattan, for instance, Apess reports witnessing the executions of two men who had been convicted of mutiny or desertion (26). Once in the field on the Canadian front of the War of 1812, he was placed in the ranks, rather than in the position of drummer, as he had expected. He deserted, but was brought back to his company. As luck would have it, he was later placed in charge of a team of horses that carried a piece of large artillery. Being able to ride on horseback no doubt helped him survive an extreme winter of meager provisions and sleeping on straw (27ff.).

After leaving the service, Apess found himself hundreds of miles from home with an overwhelming desire to return there. He wandered from menial job to menial job, sometimes spending time in Native communities with those he had taken to calling his "brethren," sometimes falling into a hard-drinking crowd, and occasionally making contact with Methodists, who reminded him of his earlier religious experiences.[16] Four years after having left Connecticut, he finally made his way back.

You Can Go Home Again

Back home in Connecticut, Apess became committed to the Methodists. Attending camp meetings and participating in the revivalist spirit of the era, Apess completed the conversion experience he had begun years earlier. In December 1818, Apess was baptized by immersion and began working toward becoming a minister. A crucial moment of *A Son of the Forest* comes when Apess relates a story from not long after his baptism, a story remarkable for its layers of potential meaning.

In the afterglow of his conversion, Apess makes a trip to visit his father. On his way there, Apess decides to continue on a road as the sun sets. "Unfortunately," he writes, "I took the wrong road and was led into a swamp" (42). The swamp gets the better of Apess as he struggles to find his way out. He thinks he hears a team of horses passing nearby and "penetrated into the labyrinth of darkness with the hope of gaining the main road" (42). Eventually, Apess is mired in the dark, surrounded by the swamp. "This was the hour of peril," he writes, "I could not call for assistance on my fellow creatures; there was no mortal ear to listen to my cry. I was shut out from the world and did not know but that I should perish there, and my fate remain a mystery to my friends" (42). Apess prays and manages to find his way out.

For readers of Christian narratives, the episode might call forth images of Bunyan's Pilgrim in the Slough of Despond. As Ron Welburn argues, it is also clearly a deeply Methodist moment in which Apess's faith in his experience of conversion is tested. "Encountering the swamp," Welburn writes, "Apess meets as a Christian the darkness of his uncivilized past, a time and place of pagan difficulties" (96).

For New England Natives, Welburn argues, swamps are especially ripe with meaning. For them, as opposed to Osceola's Seminole tribe in Florida, swamps came to represent places where Natives met death. From the massacre at Mystic, which took place next to a swamp, to the swamp massacres of the Nipmucs and Narragansetts and the murder of King Philip in a swamp, "swamp discourse" was something that prompted terror for New England Natives (Welburn, 87). Thus, by making it through the swamp, Apess's conversion is complete.

Yet, for Welburn, this is the low point for Apess. How, he asks, can a self-described son of the forest get lost in his own homeland? His enthusiasm for Christianity is so complete that the allegorical levels of his own experience blind him to culturally specific lessons he might have learned instead. As Welburn points out, in looking for the main road, Apess loses sight "that such thickets . . . are useful to informed fugitives and skilled hunters. . . . The physical entanglements become props warning him to avoid traditional culture's lore in order to better experience this darkness and rely on this new faith" (87).

Welburn, whose ancestral Assateague history in Virginia and long experience as a scholar in New England inform his learned work, prefers to read this episode forward against the Apess whose enthusiasm would wane as he took up what Weaver calls the communitist challenge of defending Native communities. Apess, according to Weaver, "increasingly reaches for an Indian Christian nationalism that aims at separatism" (*That the People*, 59). Welburn traces this back to Apess's experience in the swamp, which he calls "a lesson in traditional Indian survival ways," ways that Apess would only come to recognize later (87). The swamp becomes for Apess a place of "vision quest":

> The initiation ritual Apess undergoes is not simply passage into a new and white religion, but into a state of mind preparing his commitment first to "saving" the souls of his "brethren" and, more importantly, to his learning to negotiate the images of Christianity in order to attack white hypocrisy. (88)

Welburn suggests that Apess moves in the swamp toward what Duran and Duran see as necessary to healing Native psyches. As they say, "[I]ndigenous forms of knowledge were and continue to be relevant as we face the task of overcoming the colonial mind-set that so many of us have internalized" (6).

In that vein, Welburn speculates on "a way to project a detail into the Apess episode that would be perfectly rational and acceptable to southern New England Indian understanding today" (98). That is, "William Apess was tricked into the swamp by the Little People of the Pequots" (98). Welburn says that these beings, according to coastal New England Native traditions, use phosphorescence to lure people away from their paths. According to Welburn, they could have led Apess into the swamp only to make sure that he escaped safely. Methodism, in this reading, provides the stability Apess desires as he fights for the rights of Native people. "As a Pequot Indian," though, "he remains destabilized culturally—as are all Indians under colonialism—and spiritually displaced" (98). Apess, thus, is caught up in a spiritual contest that would unfold over the next several years.

Apess comes to recognize something of that spiritual displacement, but along the way he submerges himself in the pursuit of his new faith. In the process, he gains the pulpit and begins preaching. He was, he indicates, at least something of a novelty. As he says of one of his earliest sermons, "[M]y lips quivered, my voice trembled, my knees smote together, and in short I quaked as it were with fear. But the Lord blessed me. . . . Soon after this, I received an invitation to hold a meeting in the same place again. I accordingly went, and I found a great concourse of people who had come out to hear the Indian preach" (*Son of the Forest*, 44). This sense of novelty would continue, according to Apess, and he would have to deal with people in his audiences who were there to gawk. He seems to have made peace with his own novelty, differentiating between people in the "crowd[s who] flocked out, some to *hear* the truth and others to *see* the 'Indian'" (51).

Apess's ability to come to a critical relationship with the fact of his own novelty is one of the most remarkable aspects of his work. Later Native writers, including George Copway, Sarah Winnemucca, and Charles Eastman, would, in similar situations, "play Indian" for their audiences, to use Philip Deloria's influential figuration. Winnemucca constructed elaborate, bizarre costumes for her public lectures and Eastman often donned a feathered war bonnet as he lectured.[17] These are all important intellectuals who made crucial contributions to Native writing, but it is interesting that they all, to varying degrees, indulged their audiences with outward expressions of Indianness. They gravitate toward, as I have styled it, "the rhetoric of ancientness and novelty" ("William Apess," 200). The public discourse into which these figures emerge always seems to revel equally in the newness of the embrace of Indianness (no matter how simulated) and the ancientness of what is being embraced. Apess, on the other hand, resisted that same impulse. Elaine Jahner has called this sort of dynamic a "tyranny of expectations." Apess seems as aware as any Native intellectual of this tyranny and he seems to have worked actively against it.

His audiences most certainly didn't have a Methodist minister in a suit in mind when they decided to go listen to "the Indian," nor, as Weaver argues, did they expect him to use the language of evangelical Christianity. In short, he didn't strike a pose. Instead, his response to the tyranny of expectations and the rhetoric of ancientness and novelty was to offer an account of his experiences. And in the process he defined for himself the parameters of his own identity as a Pequot man in the nineteenth century. He didn't ask himself, as some recent readers have, whether he was Indian enough to qualify for his place as a public figure.[18] In spite of contemporary questioning of Apess's identity, he himself left little evidence that such doubts occurred to him, or, if they did, that they mattered.

Apess instead offers something more important. Throughout his work, the intellectual foundation he builds on is his own experience, as he recounts it in *A Son of the Forest*. Apess uses his own specific experiences as markers of what it meant to him to be Pequot. It is as though he is presenting a set of facts that readers need to take into account as he helps us figure out his contemporary reality. The church, for its part, provides a platform from which to tell his story. As Weaver notes, Apess "uses Christianity to break through his own alienation. He employs it to claim the full humanity of Indians and his own Indianness in particular" (*That the People*, 59).

What propels *A Son of the Forest* is the fact that Apess did his early preaching without the benefit of having a license to do so from the Methodists. For nearly the next decade, Apess tried to work within the structure of the denomination to gain standing as a minister. He worked as an exhorter (someone licensed to lead class, but not fully ordained to be a minister) and as a missionary to various Indian communities in New England. Along the way, he married a woman named Mary, with whom he started a family. Eventually, though, he found himself at loggerheads with the Methodists over the issue of ordination. It may have been during that period of conflict, in fact, that Apess first began to write of his own life, probably as a way of presenting the case for his own worthiness.

Eventually, Apess was turned down in his bid to be ordained in the Methodist Episcopal Church. This, as O'Connell points out, almost surely had something to do with the difficulty Apess had accepting the authority of the church, a constant anxiety of the Methodist Episcopals of the time (*On Our Own Ground*, 324). However, given the history of Christian churches and their reluctance to entrust the responsibilities of ordination

to Native people, Apess's complaint that ordination was denied to him because of white racism is difficult to ignore.[19]

After this rejection, Apess accepted ordination from the newly form-
ing Protestant Methodists, who followed a republican ideal. While the
Methodist Episcopals followed the lights of Francis Asbury and Thomas
Coke in focusing on moralism and piety, the republican wing of the church
sought to incorporate religious and political identity by trying to change
structures in American society that were unjust; this was a continuation
of the earlier egalitarian ideal in Methodism that Apess had found so appealing. But clearly, the Methodism in which Apess found acceptance and
that he found so appealing was falling further and further away from its
early ideals. The reason for the shift, most commentators contend, was
that the demand of living out egalitarian ideals severely limited the allure
of the Methodist message to the broadest base of whites.[20]

In other words, for the church to grow numerically it had to grow fi-
nancially, and thus the message had to appeal to people who owned slaves,
indentured servants, and tenements. Also, in the time during and after
the Second Great Awakening, which began at the turn of the nineteenth
century, evangelical Christians in the new republic were developing one
of the hallmarks of American evangelicalism: a highly individual, experiential polity in which political questions of the relationship of the church
to the nation were subsumed.[21] Apess's own use of experience stands in
contrast: his articulations of his experiences and those of others become
starting points for questioning the larger social and economic structures
that shape and constrain those experiences.

Apess and others who aspired to the older ideals of social egalitari-
anism in Methodism did remain firmly within the boundaries of John
Wesley's theology and the movement from which it sprang. As Russell
Richey argues, American Methodism has traditionally spoken in four languages: the popular or evangelical, in which the broad base of Methodists
expressed themselves through pietism and devotion; the Wesleyan, in
which Methodists questioned the necessity of a continuing relationship
with the mother church; the Episcopal, in which the church's leadership
tied itself to the Church of England; and the republican, in which the
church sought direct engagement with national politics. Richey argues
that all have a valid place within the Methodist tradition.

A Son of the Forest is in line with the popular, evangelical voice of Methodism, but the ways that Apess weaves his own experiences of discrimination

into his story point toward an engagement with the republican tradition. As with his African American Methodist contemporaries David Walker and Maria Stewart, the politically and socially engaged aspects of the Christian gospel were difficult to divorce from more personal aspects.[22] Apess, unlike Walker and Stewart, did not come out of a long tradition in which these voices were united in chorus. But when he broke with the Methodist Episcopals, he welcomed the opportunity to work within a structure more open to the ways that politics and spirituality intersect. The experientialism that emerges in his work, then, does not move exclusively inward, in a naïve attempt to seek out an essential self in the midst of the modern descent into meaninglessness, but it is rather a move that affirms the connection of individuals to larger groupings of people and the world in which they live. Putting his experiences into words helps him understand the racist structures in which he lives.

"I feel a great deal happier in the *new* than I did in the *old* church," he writes in the first edition of *A Son of the Forest*. Immediately after this he argues that those who opposed his ordination did so because of racism:

> [A]nd surely in this land where the tree of liberty has been nourished by the blood of thousands, we have good cause to contend for *mutual rights,* more especially as the Lord himself *died to make us free!* I rejoice sincerely in the spread of the principles of civil and religious liberty—may they ever be found "hand in hand" accomplishing the designs of God, in promoting the welfare of mankind. (323)

This was a much different public theology than that offered in the Congregational tradition of the Connecticut River valley or the increasingly secular tradition of Boston. The republican-evangelical Methodism of Apess, Walker, and Stewart was clearly devoid of the American Christian triumphalism of various expressions of Calvinism, as Richey outlines them. In general, the Calvinist approach to the politics of North America posited the complicity, indeed the authorship, of the Christian God in the history of the continent. Methodism offered an alternative in which something other than destiny and necessity had caused things to be the way they were. Methodism, in its most egalitarian forms, sought to address the oppression of those whose lives were laid waste by the march of American history.

Carolyn Haynes contends that Methodism's egalitarian ideals extended to the physical environment, undercutting New England ideas of the Christian God's gift of the region to invading settlers and their progeny.

"Given the Methodists' emphasis on the availability of grace to all believers regardless of race, sex, or class," Haynes argues, "and their stress on the continent's physical rather than political geography, their perspective on North America was necessarily not as exclusionary nor as oppressive as the dominant nationalist-expansionist view held by elite Protestants. No doubt the Methodists' view of the country as divided or bounded only by geography rather than by race was appealing to Apess and enabled him to construct a new vision or identity for the continent" (39).

Seemingly, Apess was attracted to the alternative, oppositional political rhetoric that Methodism provided. But it wasn't only the politics that attracted African Americans and American Indians to Methodism. The emphasis on the creation of community in the form of love feasts, conferences, and camp meetings must have also been appealing, along with the opportunity to use the body and the singing voice in worship. For groups of disenfranchised poor people, Methodism offered hope for a reconstituted present. Insofar as Apess was able to hear the good news in the Christian gospel, it is easy to imagine his ears welcoming the message. It had been a long time, after all, since his ears or other Pequot ears had heard much good news.

A Son of the Forest is, at its center, a telling of what that good news meant for Apess. As LaVonne Ruoff has pointed out, Apess follows the pattern both of American spiritual autobiographies, with their focus on the circumstances of individual redemption, and African American slave narratives, with their "emphasis on white injustice" ("American Indian Autobiographers," 253–54). If Apess had not written another book, he would have made an important contribution to Native literature. Perhaps most important, in *A Son of the Forest,* Apess provides the most extensive telling of an individual Native life in nineteenth-century New England.

But Apess did not stop with telling the story of his own life. And by going beyond his own story to the stories of others, participating in the liberation of others and developing a critical stance toward his own experience and history, Apess cements the place of nonfiction writing at the center of Native writing, a position it would hold for nearly a century and a half. He becomes the first great exemplar of a particular tradition within Native intellectual history. That tradition, as I will discuss in the rest of this chapter, has less to do with celebrating culture than it does with his creative engagement in the intellectual task of understanding the experiences and contemporary situation of Native people.

THE EXPERIENTIAL TURN

Apess returned to the theme of experience in his third book, *The Experiences of Five Christian Indians of the Pequot Tribe*. The book includes, as the title indicates, five autobiographical accounts of people in the Pequot community. Two of the accounts are of Apess and his wife, Mary, who does not identify herself as Pequot. The other three are of Anne Wampy, Sally George, and Hannah Caleb. These accounts were recorded and rhetorically shaped by Apess, and like *A Son of the Forest*, they provide both insight into nineteenth-century Pequot life, as well as subtle and not-so-subtle critiques of white Christian New Englanders. In highlighting the Christian experiences of other Indian people, Apess, whether he intended to or not, inoculated himself against a common misperception that Scott Stevens points out, the idea that "Indian converts . . . were lone figures." Stevens says that "[i]f Apess fails to be Indian enough" for some contemporary readers, "then so do his people, and contemporary scholars recapitulate the prejudice he experienced among whites—only this time in reverse" (73).

Hannah Caleb speaks of the experience of being bound out as a six-year-old girl due to the death of her mother. By nineteen she was married and soon had five children. Her husband died while serving in the French Army in Canada, and her children later died as well. She is included in the book, like the others, because of the exemplary Christian life she led, but Apess presents her as someone whose road to salvation had been made difficult because of the negative witness of white Christians. "I saw such a great inconsistency in their precepts and examples," she says, "that I could not believe them" (145). More than inconsistency, she points to the racism of white Christians against Indians as another obstacle to her conversion. "And not only so," she says, "the poor Indians, the poor Indians, the people to whom I was wedded by the common ties of nature, were set at naught by those noble professors of grace, merely because we were Indians" (145).

Importantly, Hannah Caleb represents her critique of Christianity as a very old one within the Pequot community. As in his own story, Apess presents Caleb as someone whose life had been spent experiencing the discriminatory actions of whites:

> But it is a fact that whites . . . would turn against their own kin, if the
> providence of God should have happened to change the shades of their
> complexion, although the same flesh and feelings. How must I feel, pos-

sessing the same powers of mind, with the same flesh and blood, and all we differed was merely in looks? Or how would you feel? Judge ye, though you never have been thrust out of society, and set at naught, and placed beyond the notice of all and hissed at as we have been—I pray God you never may be. These pictures of distress and shame were enough to make me cry out, Oh horrid inconsistency—who would be a Christian? But I remark here that I did not understand frail nature as I ought, to judge rightly. And I would remark here that these feelings were more peculiar 70 years ago than now—what their feelings would be now, if the Indians owned as much land as they did then, I cannot say. I leave the man of avarice to judge. (145)

Here, Caleb reveals several things. First, she understands herself as one deeply marked by race and poverty. Second, she sees herself as part of a community that has resisted in various ways its own dissolution and loss of land.

Why, then, does Hannah Caleb convert? The most obvious answer is that she found within Christianity comfort for her many afflictions. Indeed, she represents herself as being on the verge of suicide when "a voice seemed to say to me, 'Hannah, my mercy is as free for thee as this water, and boundless as the ocean'" (146). Not long after, she found salvation in solitude. But what seems most important to understand about Caleb and the other Christian Indians in *Experiences* is that they stand in judgment of the hypocrisy of white Christians, even as they find solace within Christianity. None of them testify that they are abandoning being Pequot in order to convert. Instead, they seem to lay claim to Christianity over and against white Christians.

As Caleb says near the end of her account, "I could say there was no more enmity in my heart, that I loved white people as well as my own. I wonder if all white Christians love poor Indians. If they did, they would never hurt them anymore. And certainly, if they felt as I did, they would not" (147). Clearly, Caleb's conversion was not a capitulation to white culture. It seems, rather, a challenge to white Christians, a statement that the degraded Native can better live out the demands of the gospel than the descendants of those who brought that gospel to New England.

The other two lives to which Apess gives voice do not have the completeness of his accounts of Caleb's and his wife's lives, but Sally George and Anne Wampy provide important glimpses into the experiential world of New England Natives. George describes herself as "a wanderer alone" in search of the peace that she would eventually find in the fold of the church. If, as O'Brien and others have suggested, the literal state of New England Natives was their lack of a place in a land that had once been theirs, perhaps we see yet another attraction of the Christian message—an end to landless wandering, even if only metaphorically and spiritually.

Wampy's is the briefest of the accounts, and is in the most halting English, but she is perhaps the most interesting of these converts. As she says of herself, "Me no like Christians, me hate 'em, hate everybody" (152). Yet her conversion, which apparently ended a drinking career that extended until she was almost seventy years old, seems to have been a genuine one.

Each of these conversion accounts includes elements of social critique. Reading between the lines one can detect Apess's interest in holding up the realities of New England Natives' experience to public scrutiny to bring the facts of Native poverty and marginalization to light. Yet these are also accounts brimming with a sense of piety and spiritual devotion. Apess ends Anne Wampy's account, the last one, by saying, "Should this happen to fall into the hands of any old transgressor, that has not become wise above what is written, I hope they will remember that they will want Master Jesus as well as Sister Anne Wampy. Lord help, Amen" (152). This is but one of many examples of Apess's true zeal for missionary Christianity.

In this way, these narratives are similar to *Poor Sarah, or Religion Exemplified in the Life and Death of an Indian Woman,* the religious tract that has been incorrectly attributed to Cherokee intellectual Elias Boudinot. The tract tells the story of a Cherokee woman who finds in the church solace from her impoverished life. Boudinot translated the story into Cherokee and published it in the syllabary that Sequoyah had invented. An English version followed and became a national best seller. As Weaver has noted of *Poor Sarah,* "Boudinot simply translated a preexisting pamphlet into Cherokee, though in an era when plagiarism rules were not as well defined as they are today, he claimed authorship" (*That the People,* 72).

Apess's accounts had a more political tone, even if much of the message was the same. "Apess," according to Weaver, "explicitly rejects the assimilationist message preached by the missionaries. . . . He makes clear that Whites have actually hindered conversion of Indians by sending among them preachers whose words and personal lifestyle are contrary to the gospel" (*That the People,* 58). And in publishing these autobiographical accounts Apess seems to have been making a transition to a voice with an even stronger edge.

At the end of the first edition of *Experiences,* Apess includes the essay "An Indian's Looking-Glass for the White Man." At the beginning of it, Apess asks "if degradation has not been heaped long enough upon the Indians?" (155). After having told his own story and those of the four women in *Experiences,* he makes one of the most vital turns in the history of Native writing. "Let me for a few minutes turn your attention to the reservations in the different states of New England," he says, "and, with few exceptions, we shall find them as follows: the most mean, abject, miserable race of beings in the world—a complete place of prodigality and prostitution" (155).

Apess paints a picture that historians are now increasingly reconstructing from town records and other scattered evidence. That is, to be Indian in New England was to live in an extreme poverty in which women were reduced to selling brooms and baskets or, worse, were forced into prostitution. Alcoholism was epidemic. Homes were most often headed by women. Appointed Indian overseers took advantage of their power by exploiting the lands of those they were supposed to protect. At the root of all of this, according to Apess, was the fact that "their land is in common stock, and they have nothing to make them enterprising" (155).

Apess then breaks away from the autobiographical and persuasive models he and others had followed and, at their best, had tested the limits of. He observes several things about skin color and, in doing so, abandons the strategy of keeping his anger masked between the lines of his prose. "If black or red skins or any other skin of color is disgraceful to God," Apess writes, "it appears that he has disgraced himself a great deal—for he has made fifteen colored people to one white and placed them here upon the earth" (157). He then writes what has become perhaps his most famous prose:

> Now let me ask you, white man, if it is a disgrace for to eat, drink, and
> sleep with the image of God, or sit, or walk and talk with them. Or have
> you the folly to think that the white man, being one in fifteen or sixteen,
> are the only beloved images of God? Assemble all the nations together
> in your imagination, and then let the whites be seated among them, and
> then let us look for the whites, and I doubt not it would be hard finding

them; for to the rest of the nations, they are still but a handful. Now suppose these skins were put together, and each skin had its national crimes written upon it—which skin do you think would have the greatest? I will ask one question more. Can you charge the Indians with robbing a nation almost of their whole continent, and murdering their women and children, and then depriving the remainder of their lawful rights, that nature and God require them to have? And to cap the climax, rob another nation to till their ground and welter out their days under the lash with hunger and fatigue under the scorching rays of a burning sun? I should look at all the skins, and I know that when I cast my eye upon that white skin, and if I saw those crimes written upon it, I should enter my protest against it immediately and cleave to that which is more honorable. (157)

Apess cuts to the heart of American racism and lays bare the roots of Native degradation. In holding up this looking glass to his white readers, he turns an intellectual corner in terms of his willingness to confront his public directly. In the 1837 edition of *Experiences,* Apess removed this essay and included a much shorter, much less confrontational paragraph (*On Our Own Ground,* 161). But by going public with this trenchant critique, he threw down the gauntlet in a way that few in the history of Native writing have equaled.

REVOLUTIONARY APESS

Apess's new militancy in "The Indian's Looking Glass" is wrapped up with his involvement with the Mashpee Revolt of 1833. He apparently spent at least part of his time in the early 1830s traveling to New England Native communities to preach and minister. Sometime in 1833, Apess visited the Mashpee Indians in Massachusetts. But at Mashpee, the largest Native community in Massachusetts, he became embroiled in a difficult political situation (Nielsen, 400). Arriving in a community where the local church was supposed to be ministering to the local Natives, who numbered over three hundred, Apess found a congregation made up of whites led by a Reverend Fish.

The Native community was nearby, gathered in a congregation under the care of a Baptist preacher named Blind Joe. Soon after visiting the Native congregation, Apess discovered their complaints against the Reverend Fish and their white neighbors (O'Connell, 171ff.). Fish was appointed to his position by the corporation of Harvard College, which administered the funds from which he was paid. The Mashpees contended, though, that he neglected his Native charges, using his position instead to minister to local whites. Also, the Mashpees were unable to protect their land and resources from local whites, who would take timber off Mashpee land without permission or compensation. Fish himself, along with his annual salary of $520, made several hundred more dollars per year selling wood from Pequot land that Harvard allotted to him (Nielsen, 403–4).

The Mashpees were a nineteenth-century version of the sort of contemporary community that Winona LaDuke describes so effectively in her book *All Our Relations: Native Struggles for Land and Life.* She writes of those like her who come from embattled communities that most people never notice: "We live off the beaten track, out of the mainstream in small villages, on a vast expanse of prairie, on dry desert lands, or in the forests. We often drive old cars, live in old houses and mobile homes. There are usually small children and relatives around, the kids careening underfoot. We seldom carry briefcases, and we rarely wear suits" (3). The Native people Apess met at Mashpee preceded LaDuke's present-day activists, about whom she says, "We have seen the great trees felled, the wolves taken for bounty, and the fish stacked rotting like cordwood. Those memories compel us. . . . We are the ones who stand up to the land eaters, the tree eaters, the destroyers and culture eaters" (3).

Apess encouraged the Mashpees to work through established channels to fight against these injustices. Adopting Apess as a member of their group, the Mashpees petitioned the commonwealth of Massachusetts and the Harvard Corporation for redress. "It was the spring of 1833," writes Mashpee historian Russell Peters, "and the Indian people of Mashpee felt that they had experienced enough oppression. Though fearful of the overseers and Reverend Fish, they decided to make a public protest." Their demands were as follows:

> Resolved, That we as a tribe will rule ourselves, and have the right to do so for all men are born free and Equal, says the constitution of the country.
>
> Resolved, That we will not permit any white man to come upon our plantation to cut or carry off wood or hay or any other article, without our permission after the first of July next.
>
> Resolved, That we will put said resolution in force after the date of

July next with the penalty of binding and throwing them from the plantation if they will not stay away without.

Yours most obediently as the voice of one man we approve the above as the voice of one man we pray you hear. (Peters, *The Wampanoags*, 32–33)

Nearly one hundred men and women signed the petition.[23] These demands made their way to state government officials and the Mashpees came to believe mistakenly that the Massachusetts governor supported them (Nielsen, 409). They elected their own leaders and decided to confront those who were taking wood from them. A small force guarded the road through the settlement and stopped a wagon filled with Mashpee wood. The Mashpees unloaded the stolen timber.

One thing worth saying at this point is that the Mashpee petition can be seen as a document that defies the rhetoric of ancientness and novelty. Rather than highlighting oral traditions and tribally specific ceremonies, it expresses what it meant to be Native, specifically Mashpee, in New England in the 1830s. Any disappointment the text and the people who produced it prompt, though, seems to have more to do with those who are disappointed than with the brave Native people who rose up and stood together as Native people against the injustice visited upon them specifically because they were Natives.

The act of blocking white people from stealing timber proved to be the breaking point for local authorities. Apess was arrested and charged with riot, assault, and trespass. He was tried and convicted, then sentenced to thirty days in prison. The case was a cause célèbre throughout the region. Apess, in the aftermath of Mashpee, found himself in the public eye and under intense scrutiny. For the community at Mashpee, the revolt was galvanizing. They attained "more control over their lives than since the English landed at Plymouth in 1620," and soon could boast of a town hall, school, and the Attaquin Hotel, which would stand until the 1950s (Peters, *The Wampanoags*, 35, 40ff.).

In 1835, Apess published *Indian Nullification,* his account of what happened at Mashpee along with reprints of regional press accounts and other relevant documents. But the book is a defense of Apess's character as much as it is about the revolt. "It appears," Apess writes, "that I, William Apess, have been much persecuted and abused, merely for desiring the welfare of myself and brethren, and because I would not suffer myself to be trodden underfoot by people no better than myself" (242).

The Mashpee Revolt succeeded at the level of gaining for the Mashpees rights to self-governance that predominantly white Massachusetts towns enjoyed. As important, it helped steel the Mashpee community against its enemies. More tangibly, the Mashpees reacquired their right to elect their own leaders in 1834. And Phineas Fish was eventually relieved of his post. Perhaps most importantly, the Mashpees sent a message to their neighbors—and to themselves—that they should control their own resources and destiny.

"The Mashpee revolt," according to Nielsen, "was a rare success story in a period of continual reversals for American Indians. . . . Such open defiance of authority occurred among no other tribes in nineteenth-century Massachusetts" (419). It was a remarkable event that demonstrates the potential for resistance that existed in Native communities scarred and beaten down in a long history of degradation.

That much of that message of resistance came in the form of writing is due, in the main, to William Apess. This event, in fact, seems an ideal example of what Scott Lyons calls "rhetorical sovereignty," in that the Mashpees stood in the face of a history of words that had been used against them and exercised, in Lyons's formulation, their "inherent right and ability . . . to determine their own communicative needs and desires in this pursuit, to decide for themselves the goals, modes, styles, and languages of public discourse" (449–50). For the Mashpee, the actions they took, both physical and rhetorical, were a great success.

For Apess, the revolt was something else. There are indications that his adoption into the Mashpees was eventually seen as detrimental, at least by some in the community. He would continue to be involved at Mashpee, but something clearly changed for him in the years following his most direct political action. *Indian Nullification* includes only shades of the evangelical language of the earlier work, and Apess himself became the center of attention, so much so that it seemed to distract from everything else he had done. As he writes at the end of *Indian Nullification,* "For troubling my readers with so much of my own affairs, I have this excuse. I have been assailed by the vilest calumnies, represented as an exciter of sedition, a hypocrite, and a gambler. These slanders, though disproved, still continue to circulate. Though an Indian, I am at least a man, with all the feelings proper to humanity, and my reputation is dear to me" (274).

For other Native writers, this kind of moment became an opportunity to become less concerned with specific issues and more concerned with the enterprise of their own celebrity. George Copway comes immediately to mind. Whatever else Copway's considerable contribution to Native intellectual history represents, he is unmistakably an odd man who named himself a chief and got caught up in the web of his own promotional schemes, so much so that practical solutions to Indian problems took a backseat to his creation of a persona.

Up to the Mashpee Revolt, Apess had worked differently, moving the focus away from himself to larger and larger frames. The progression of his work has him telling his own story, giving voice to the experiences of others, developing a critical stance toward those experiences and the sources of oppression revealed in them, and taking direct action to ameliorate the oppressive conditions imposed on Indian communities. The stage was set for what would be the final act of his public intellectual career, his *Eulogy on King Philip.*

King Philip's Revenge

Apess's *Eulogy* brings him full circle from the experientially based practice of his earlier work. In the *Eulogy,* he raises the question of history by arguing that Metacomet, or King Philip, was as great as Philip of Macedon, Alexander the Great, or George Washington. "As the immortal Washington lives endeared and engraven on the hearts of every white in America never to be forgotten in time," Apess writes in introducing his remarks, "even such is the immortal Philip honored, as held in memory by the degraded and yet grateful descendants who appreciate his character" (277). Further on, in fact, Apess calls Philip "the greatest man that ever lived upon the American shores" (290).

Throughout his *Eulogy,* Apess is interested in just this sort of historical analysis, which brings events from the past into relationship with contemporary experiences. As Anne Marie Dannenberg has argued, "Strategically choosing a pre-Enlightenment period (the late colonial era) as his focus and then repeatedly comparing that period with his own, Apess obliterates any notion that time has brought progress" (70).

Apess's last speech is a rhetorical treat as he takes up the history of Puritan New England. He describes the various moments of friendship and tension that led up to the war in which Metacomet and his allies struck out against the rapacity of the settlers in their midst. He tells the story of King Philip's War using the standard accounts available in his time, but frames his version with the ways that his contemporaries in New England had inherited the attitudes of their forebears. After telling how he himself had encountered racism on a daily basis in his travels, for instance, he says, "These things I mention to show that the doctrines of the Pilgrims [have] grown up with the people" (305).

In perhaps his most elegiac moment, Apess hearkens back to Philip's time and asks,

> How deep, then, was the thought of Philip, when he could look from
> Maine to Georgia, and from the ocean to the lakes, and view with one
> look all his brethren withering before the more enlightened to come; and
> how true his prophecy, that the white people would not only cut down
> their groves but would enslave them. Had the inspiration of Isaiah been
> there, he could not have been more correct. Our groves and hunting
> grounds are gone, our dead are dug up, our council fires are put out, and
> a foundation was laid in the first Legislature to enslave our people, by
> taking from them all rights, which has been adhered to ever since. Look
> at the disgraceful laws, disenfranchising us as citizens. Look at the trea-
> ties made by Congress, all broken. Look at the deep-rooted plans laid,
> when a territory becomes a state, that after so many years the laws shall
> be extended over the Indians that live within their boundaries. Yea, every
> charter that has been given with the view of driving the Indians out of
> the states, or dooming them to become chained under desperate laws,
> that would make them drag out a miserable life as one chained to the gal-
> ley; and this is the course that has been pursued for nearly two hundred
> years. A fire, a canker, created by the Pilgrims across the Atlantic, to burn
> and destroy my poor unfortunate brethren, and it cannot be denied. What,
> then, shall we do? (306)

To that question, Apess answered that whites and Indians must finally "bury the hatchet" and "become friends" (306). Yet, of course, the problem remained that whites held all the power and would have to be the ones to change their attitudes and practices to make real changes in the fortunes of New England Indians.

"What do they, the Indians want?" Apess's question, which opened this chapter and closes his *Eulogy*, resonates in various ways across the seventeen decades since he asked it. Reading William Apess is an invitation to think differently about how to answer that question, which has been asked in various ways over time. Each book is commendable for its own reasons, but the trajectory of the works as a whole is as important as any single piece. The author of *A Son of the Forest* made an important mark, but Apess's ability to move beyond the parameters of his early work is important as well. He does not merely articulate and celebrate his experiences—he uses experiential discourse to analyze Native conditions and add depth to his intellectual practice. Thus, in concluding this chapter, I would like to suggest that Apess's invitation is not only into the texts he left behind, but into an exercise of the imagination in which we seek to understand the ways he went about being an intellectual in his time, including the ways he recognized and defied the constraints he faced. The mystery surrounding his New York death provides the frame for explicating what I mean.

Apess in New York: Synchronicity and Speculation

In contrast to an insistence that he demonstrate his Indian authenticity, Apess offers chronicles of his experiences. As he represents it, his childhood was spent in the crucible of Native New England, where he was abused in various ways. He spent his adulthood giving voice to those who experienced the oppression of that world in silent invisibility. And when he became an appendage to the struggle at Mashpee, he left. Eventually, he departed New England for New York.

Why exactly Apess moved from Massachusetts to New York City is still not known and may never be. Though scholars may never be able to draw conclusions from boxes of correspondence, maybe we ought to suppose that Apess recognized that his own infamy was little more than an obstacle to those at Mashpee about whom he cared so deeply. And perhaps he had big plans for his days in New York, plans to make a bigger name for himself and a bigger impact on the world of Indian affairs than was possible from a New England pulpit or stage. Maybe he saw people like David Walker go out from Boston to Philadelphia, New York, and Washington and wanted to do the same.

New York in 1838 was in the grip of the economic aftershocks of the Panic of 1837, an economic collapse with national implications precipitated by runaway inflation and labor unrest (Burrows and Wallace, 603ff.). Following riots in February 1837, the city's infrastructure all but collapsed. Real estate prices plummeted, manufacturing was devastated, banks called in loans and mortgages, and bank patrons started pulling money from accounts. The ensuing depression lasted until 1843.

The time following the panic was not the most promising moment for Apess to make a move to New York City. But during the decade and a half leading up to the panic, the city had risen meteorically. The Erie Canal opened in 1825, connecting the city to western markets via the Great Lakes, the Mississippi, and New Orleans. New York, which had been an important place in the political development of the American colonies and then the United States, was poised to become a major metropolitan power. As Edward Burrows and Mike Wallace note suggestively for this discussion of Apess, "Not surprisingly . . . it was during these same years that Manhattan became the center of book publishing in the United States" (441). Access to readers in the West saw New York publishers like the Harper brothers flooding the market with cheap books. Further, they say, "[D]uring the 1830s New York was the fastest growing city in the United States, and at some point during the decade it surpassed Mexico City in population, becoming the largest city" in the western hemisphere (576).

Apess was no stranger to New York. He made his first recorded trip there when he ran away from William Williams and trained on Governor's Island (Apess, *On Our Own Ground*, 24ff.). As an adult in 1829, he deposited the copyright to the first edition of *A Son of the Forest* in New York City. In 1831, he published both *The Increase of the Kingdom of Christ* and a revised version of *A Son of the Forest* there (*On Our Own Ground*, xxxiv). Given these facts and the considerable gaps in knowledge of Apess's whereabouts for months and years at a time, one can surmise that Apess may have frequented New York City before moving there before his death.

Many aspects of New York might have beckoned to Apess, including the fact that in 1831 the state abolished prison terms for debtors except in cases of fraud (Burrows and Wallace, 522). Given his debt problems in Massachusetts, he very well could have made his way to Manhattan any time after the first of these actions in 1836, or perhaps he was going back and forth. If, in fact, his struggles with alcohol continued during these years, perhaps the relative anonymity of New York and the pervasiveness of its drinking culture drew him. Burrows and Wallace report that alcohol was a ubiquitous feature of Manhattan social life, especially among the lower classes. "Rampant overproduction," they say, "hammered the price down to twenty-five cents a gallon, less per drink than tea or coffee" (485).

Elizabeth Apess, the woman identified as William Apess's wife at his inquest, may be another part of the equation. She claims a marriage to him, depending on how one deciphers the handwritten inquest, of two or ten years. Regardless of length, this marriage is almost certainly different from his marriage to the former Mary Woods, with whom Apess had at least one and possibly as many as three children. The evidence indicates, then, that sometime after the first edition of *Experiences,* Apess left Mary and their children or, less likely given the logistics, maintained two marriages at once. Male abandonment of family, as previously noted, was rampant in Native communities in New England. Apess certainly had a model of that in his own father.

A slight possibility exists that Mary and Elizabeth are the same person going by different names, but if so, it is hard to reconcile Elizabeth's testimony of either a two- or ten-year marriage. Poor women in New York City were particularly vulnerable, especially when they were single. If anything, if Elizabeth and Mary are the same person, she would seemingly have wanted to make herself sound all the more respectable by claiming as many years of marriage as possible. "While a woman's wages might well be instrumental in keeping her household afloat," Burrows and Wallace write, "she could seldom earn enough to support herself on her own. This was particularly evident from the condition of wage-earning widows, who often lived closeted in tiny garrets or huddled in cellars or half-finished buildings, at the edge of destitution" (478). However she came to be with him, life without William Apess was most probably going to be grim for Elizabeth.

Thus, whether legally married or not, Elizabeth seems to be a woman with whom Apess was living as a married couple at the time of his death. New York, importantly, was a place where living together without being married was possible in a way it would not have been in Barnstable. And if they came across to most people as an interracial couple, sections of New York were much more tolerant on that score than most places.

Whatever the nature of his relationship to Elizabeth, Apess most probably left a wife and perhaps teenage children to face debt peonage in New England. Maureen Konkle, without citing any evidence, states that Mary Apess must have been dead by this time.[24] In this, though, she joins Barry O'Connell in marring an otherwise careful sifting of documentary evidence with a propensity to put only the most positive spin on it.

Positing Apess as having left a family behind in New England is the most obvious conclusion based on the evidence, as is his final illness being exacerbated by a history of drinking. Admitting that those obvious possibilities are the strongest does not necessarily demonize Apess. I would argue instead that Apess's failure to live up to his own moral code humanizes him and demonstrates the need to see him as a figure who lived his life within the frame of contemporary Native conditions. Doing so does not show that Apess had feet of clay, but that he just had plain old human feet.

Thus, this deeply gifted writer, who deserves the attention he has received in recent years, was also most probably someone with a drinking problem who very possibly abandoned his family to pursue his intellectual vision. Perhaps the children were, by the time he left for New York, already bound out to continue the cycle of servanthood so familiar to generations of New England's Native people and which Apess had opposed so effectively in his work. If so, he was certainly not the first or last intellectual to envision a moral world beyond his or her grasp.

In spite of all that, William Apess led an extraordinary life in a desolate time for Native people in New England. Born with no advantages, his early life was a descent into a hellish reality shared by many, if not most of, his Native contemporaries. Somehow, out of all of that, he managed to escape the worst of it, only to launch himself right back into the maelstrom of it all. Contemporary readers can rightly fault him for believing too much at times that white Christians and their churches could be prompted to make things better for Native people, but the history of Native writing is filled with people who did the same or who signed on to other dubious ideologies. To his great credit, though, Apess turned a corner, and by the time of the *Eulogy,* he envisioned his history and his experiences as illuminating a path toward a future outside the constraints of his life. However he got there, he broke out of his own provincialism and began to swim in the stream of the best aspects of Native intellectualism.

That, in the end, is what I hope drew Apess to New York before his untimely death—the palpable energy of intellect interfacing with the public in ways that were making the small press runs and the public lectures in New England a thing of the distant past. Observers in the mid-1830s reported people all over town voraciously reading papers like the *New York Sun* and Horace Greeley's *Herald* (Burrows and Wallace, 52–55). The *Sun* cost a penny and could be seen in the hands of common people. Also in that decade, William Hamilton and Peter Williams Jr. launched *Freedom's Journal,* the first African American paper in the United States. The press, according to Burrows and Wallace, "addressed something that had never quite existed before except in republican theory: a 'public' at large, a civic demos. In doing so, it offered New York's citizenry the technical and textual means to grasp their city's growing miscellaneity" (528). The Native politics of New England may have failed Apess, but he was on the front edge of a different dynamic in New York.

What an exciting time it must have been for a writer like Apess to witness the wholesale changes taking place in the intellectual currents of the United States. Beyond the popular press, the 1830s were the run-up to a significant intellectual age in the life of the United States. Whatever version of history you read, this period was a watershed, as New York was superseding New England. This was the era of Washington Irving, James Fenimore Cooper, Edgar Allan Poe, Walt Whitman, and Herman Melville. New England had its share of formidable intellects, including Ralph Waldo Emerson and Henry David Thoreau, but even a New Englander as luminous as Margaret Fuller was drawn to the new orbit of New York in 1844, when she took up reviewing for Greeley's *Herald*.[25]

To continue speculating about Apess, there is little doubt that whatever efforts he might have made to be part of this rising tide were thwarted. The literary clubs springing up around the city were for white men, most of them minor figures remembered for belonging to those clubs and not for the substance of their work. But I can imagine Apess picking up an issue of the *Knickerbocker* or the *Democratic Review* (two of the leading literary journals) and looking for an inroad into Manhattan's burgeoning life of the mind. I can picture him reading the literary gossip and being reminded of what it's like to be always on the outside looking in.

His Manhattan was no doubt one dominated by cramped quarters and short provisions in a crumbling tenement. "New York, it was widely agreed," say Burrows and Wallace, "was the filthiest urban center in the United States; Boston and Philadelphia gleamed by comparison" (588). Still, perhaps there were moments of magic that go unrecorded in the archives—a chance encounter with Cooper, a serious discussion with an editor willing to look at his work.

But an Indian in New York in the 1830s was pretty much what an Indian preacher was in New England—a novelty. Phineas Taylor Barnum provides a fitting illustration of just that. Barnum moved to New York in 1834 and opened his American Museum in 1841, two years after Apess died. According to Burrows and Wallace, Barnum

> stocked his [m]useum . . . with jugglers and ventriloquists, curiosities
> and freaks, automata and living statuary, gypsies and giants, dwarfs and
> dioramas, Punch and Judy shows, models of Niagara Falls, and real live

American Indians. (Barnum advertised the latter as brutal savages, fresh from slaughtering whites out west, though privately he groused that the "D__n Indians" were lazy and shiftless—"though they will *draw*.") (644)

That could easily have been the reaction of most New Yorkers who might have had the opportunity to help someone like Apess. If it was dressed up to appeal to the basest fantasies of contemporary America, maybe it would sell. Apess, never having had much truck with such commodification, may have passed on opportunities that have gone unrecorded.

All someone in his position could do was look at the intellectual stream that was flowing by and hope that the future would create new possibilities. I like to imagine, based not so much on evidence as the sense I get as a reader of his work, that in his brighter moments in those last few years, William Apess in his isolation peered into the future and imagined that he would not always be alone, that someday his books would be recognized for their genius and he would be celebrated for having provided a turning point.

Isolation continues to be a persistent feature of Native American intellectual life, a topic of conversation nearly every time and place that Native writers and scholars gather. All of us seem to know too well the realities of indifferent advisers, insensitive colleagues, insufficient resources, and a lack of intellectual camaraderie. Any graduate student or professional scholar can face these issues, but Native people in the academy are affected in particular ways. Many, if not most of us, know what it feels like to be the only Indian on campus, to be alone. Imagine, then, what it must have been like for Apess. He fought hard to make his way back home, then became by position and circumstances a leader more than a member of the Native communities to which he was connected. He ended up with no known intellectual associates, no one with whom to share the vicissitudes of his writerly life. Chances are good that he once shared a stage in Boston with Elias Boudinot (Konkle, 97–100), but he didn't really know a single other person like himself. So I hope he did allow himself a hopeful glimpse into the future, one that helped him believe that he would someday inhabit, if only as a historical figure, a world of his peers.

CONCLUSION

Comforting though it may be to imagine Apess caught up in such intellectual dreaming, a look at the end of the story is a reminder that such moments must have been fleeting, if they existed at all. It may seem odd to some readers that I make this comparison, but what makes me think of such moments as fleeting is a foreboding similarity between the end of Apess's life and that of Clyde Warrior, the influential Ponca intellectual whose career consumed a rather sizable chunk of my attention as I worked to undertand the contours of the Indian movement during the 1960s and 1970s.[26]

Apess and Warrior in many ways could not be more different—Apess a product of the absence of traditional Pequot culture, Warrior the product of the bosom of Ponca tradition. But they also seem so much the same, overcoming extreme poverty and reaching through empty rhetoric to confront Indian people and those in the society who dominate them with the question of why Indian people ought to settle for anything less than justice, anything less than the best. As intellectual figures, they both are immersed in Native experience and from that seek creative solutions to Native problems.

Yet, Warrior, in spite of his grand vision of a world in which tradition and modernity could exist side by side, was still overwhelmed by the depth of the problems facing the communities for whom he fought. He could imagine solutions, but the same brilliance of mind that gave him vision haunted his every moment. Having looked at his life from many angles over many years, I would argue that despair, in his case intellectual despair, came to define him. His drinking, much of it abetted by traveling in the circles of the official world of white people and Indian people who took part in Indian affairs in the 1960s, was legendary, and he succumbed to it before reaching the age of twenty-nine (Smith and Warrior, 56ff.). With so much work in front of him, he still managed in a relatively short time to become one of the most important Native intellectual and political voices of the twentieth century.

Did Apess face the same sort of intellectual despair? My guess is that he did, and, like Warrior, he seemingly abused alcohol as a result. The New York setting of his death, with its anonymity and separation from his family, adds to that argument. In coming to an understanding of Clyde Warrior, I found it impossible to comprehend the greatness of his contribution without also wrestling with the issues surrounding his tragic death. In almost two decades of reading Apess, teaching his work, tracking the scholarship about his work and life, and considering the limited archive that has emerged to illuminate the erstwhile dark corners of who he was in history, I have found the same need for grappling. Make no mistake, for my part I consider Clyde Warrior and William Apess to be giants in the intellectual history I have dedicated my scholarly career to interpreting. Part of what makes them giants, though, is the deep well of humanity—Indian humanity—from which they drew.

My interpretations of both figures, of course, are based on speculation, but engaging in speculation is a worthwhile enterprise insofar as it illuminates possible synchronicities, in this case between Apess and Clyde Warrior. Seeking such synchronicity is a way to imaginatively consider the gaps we inherit in studying the history of Native writing. Until recently that history has offered few direct connections between writers, few moments of one writer even making reference to another, much less encountering another face to face. Thinking in terms of synchronicity opens new vistas for viewing the history of Native writing as unified.

Apess's death in New York City makes him an intriguing figure to think of in terms of synchronicity. Before the facts of his death came to light, I sometimes found it difficult to place him as a figure, in spite of similarities between us. Like Apess, I found a home in Christianity after overcoming challenging circumstances, and like him I eventually sought to make an impact beyond its confines. But his move to New York makes me feel a stronger connection to him and has offered a new way for me to appreciate the breadth of his work.

Like Apess, I left New England for New York. I went as a graduate student in 1988 with hopes not only of earning a degree, but of being a writer. I wanted to leave some mark as a Native writer in a city whose intellectual winds blew around me in a way that stimulated me like no others. I looked for every opportunity to add my own energy to what was happening there, and I succeeded on my own terms. By the time I left, I had written for the *Village Voice, Christianity and Crisis, High Times, Lies of Our Times, The Guardian,* and lots of others. I was the New York correspondent for the *Lakota Times* (which later became *Indian Country Today*) and also wrote for *News from Indian Country* and helped found *Native Nations,* a short-lived national Native news magazine based in New York. Every time I published, new opportunities opened for me. I can only wonder what might have happened if Apess had had similar opportunities after he moved there.

New York in 1839 was not New York in 1990, but my experience leads me to ask what it must have been like for Apess to be a writer and feel like a writer and yet not find many avenues for his creativity beyond his self-published work. Maybe he was sitting on a pile of articles that not even minor publications were interested in. Or maybe by that time he was out of creative juice, unable to come up with the spark that led to the earlier work. That would still have been torturous in a city of endless energy with its promise of a national audience. I eventually found myself as a writer through my New York wanderings. Apess, who had already made a mark as a writer when he came to New York, perhaps found an audience that was unready for whatever he saw as the next step, an audience unprepared for the edges of his sharpness.

In this way, Apess catches the rising tide of New York at an intellectual crossroads. Something similar could be said of Ella Deloria, who went to graduate school at Columbia Teachers College while Franz Boas was institutionalizing American ethnography. Or D'Arcy McNickle, who by all accounts never fell head over heels for New York, but whose intellectual vision was shaped, at least in part, by its particular character. All passed through and left something of a mark that just waits to be noticed and pondered by those who come later. Some might prefer to treat it all like a random set of connections, but if Apess and those who came later to New York are understood as part of the same history, as moving in similar intellectual streams, the possibilities look different, if only because of the way the future can be figured through a consideration of history.

"What do they, the Indians, want?" That Apess went to New York and perhaps kept asking that question even if he didn't leave much more than a trace of his answer in the last chapter of his life adds something to his profile as a Native intellectual figure. As Dannenberg argues of Apess, "[T]he complexity of his political project has not yet been fully appreciated" (79). But what Apess did achieve was his way of doing the work of being a Native intellectual. By grounding himself within the lived lives of Native communities and allowing his social analysis to proceed out of that grounding, he points a way out of some of the quagmires of contemporary praxis. For Stevens, Apess's example is one for Native scholars that "shows the need for us to be the witnesses to our own history. To allow your history to be told by the group that vanquished you would be the ultimate defeat" (82). I would go one step further by adding that Apess's ad hoc method of cobbling together the parameters of his work, even as he addressed the needs and situations of Native people, establishes an important methodological precedent in Native letters.

Apess's precedent points present-day Native intellectuals in a concrete direction. In his seminal nonfiction, Apess raises questions about how an experientially aware intellectual praxis leads us to critical issues—not of how we might uncritically celebrate Native cultures, but of ethics, morality, history, imagination, spirituality, and intellectual development. Apess, in this reading, is central to a new agenda in Native American critical studies.

That new agenda is perhaps not so different from what Apess's contemporary, Ralph Waldo Emerson, the essayist who was then presiding over New England's intellectual rise, called for when he addressed the topic of "The American Scholar" in 1837. As he said, "Perhaps the time is already come when it ought to be, and will be, something else; when the sluggard intellect of this continent will look from under its iron lids and fill the postponed expectation of the world. . . . Our day of dependence, our long apprenticeship to the learning of other lands, draws to a close" (Whicher, 63–64).[27]

Scholars in Native studies have been anything but sluggards over the past three decades (though I suppose there are exceptions), but I believe those of us who are Native scholars have yet to ascend to the summit of our intellectual potential. Pondering that summit is all the more enriched when Apess's experiential wisdom suffuses a robust awareness of our own future. As Momaday put it much later, "The comprehension of the earth and air is surely a matter of morality, for it brings into account not only man's instinctive reaction to his environment but the full realization of his humanity as well, the achievement of his intellectual and spiritual development as an individual and as a race" ("First American," 35).

Apess offers not so much a specific, self-conscious program, but the most brilliant and challenging vision of being a Native American intellectual up to the middle of the nineteenth century. His turning point is my starting point for that reason. In the end, the important issue is not the one that has too often dominated critical discussion of Apess's work, about whether he is Indian enough to belong to the line of Native intellectuals. Rather, this last mysterious New York chapter of his story ought to lead those of us who make up this latest generation of Native writers and scholars to ask whether we have yet to live up to being a part of the same arc as his.

2

Democratic Vistas of the
Osage Constitutional Crisis

*H*alf a century after Apess ended his writing career, fifteen hundred miles to the west a group of Osage leaders facing drastically different circumstances penned the following words:

> The Great and Little Osages having united and become one body politic, under the style and title of the Osage Nation; therefore, We the people of the Osage Nation, in National Council assembled, in order to establish justice, insure tranquility, promote the common welfare, and to secure to ourselves and our posterity the blessing of freedom—acknowledging with humility and gratitude the goodness of the Sovereign Ruler of the universe in permitting us to do so, and imploring his aid and guidance in its accomplishment—do ordain and establish this Constitution for the government of the Osage Nation.[1]

Chances are, most of the leaders of my tribe who in 1881 signed the Osage Constitution, which included this preamble, had never read the U.S. Constitution, which provided a template for this preamble. They certainly didn't think about being part of the century-old tradition of Native American nonfiction writing.

Instead, the Osages borrowed this language and the rest of the language for their constitution from their neighbors, the Cherokees, who, in the midst of the Removal crisis, had modeled their 1827 and 1839 constitutions on that of the United States.[2] The Osage Constitution served as the basis for a working democracy in the last two decades of the nine-teenth century. A history of crisis, however, has attended this remarkable document since 1898, when the United States government declared that it would no longer recognize the Osage constitutional government as of April 1, 1900. More recently, the 1881 constitution has been part of legal and political struggles to restore constitutional democracy among the Osages.

This chapter focuses on the Osage Constitution and how a reading of it informs this critical history of Native nonfiction writing. Like the U.S. Constitution and the Declaration of Independence, the Osage Constitution of 1881 reveals something not just of the polity of the people its words seek to bind together, but the character and experiences of that people at the particular turning point at which Osage leaders felt compelled to draft and sign it. It is a political founding document, and as such it is a particu-lar type of nonfiction text, a text that can be considered from a number of different angles, including a literary theoretical one.

As a text, the constitution ranges from being transparently straight-forward to being highly layered in its levels of meaning. The preamble is followed by six articles: the first covering the boundaries of the Osage Nation; the second the separation of powers; the third, fourth, and fifth the responsibilities of the legislative, executive, and judicial branches of the government; and the final article all other issues, including a provision for making amendments. The text ends with a list of the sixteen signato-ries, the translator, and the constitutional convention's secretary.

My purpose here is to read this document against the background of its drafting and in the midst of the political situation in which it continues to play a significant role. As a partisan for it on one side of a significant divide in Osage politics, my reading advocates a particular view of this document, and, absent my own particular commitments to a standpoint I call here Osage constitutionalism, I cannot say what my reading of this document might be. This chapter, then, is a partisan document, a direct reflection of my politics and a clear argument for one side in a conflict that has defined Osage politics for a century. Though I do not speak for any other Osage, I do speak for my point of view, one shared at least in part by others.

At the same time, my long consideration of the Osage Constitution in the midst of the upheaval of the past century of Osage politics has al-lowed me to ponder the intriguing intellectual corners and shadows of this document in ways that can be beneficial to larger discussions of the history of Native writing and the importance of Native intellectual patrimony to contemporary Native studies. As an analysis of a situation that a generation of scholarship in Native American studies did next to nothing to ameliorate, I hope this reading of the Osage Constitution challenges scholars of Native writing and intellectual history to reconsider their ways of thinking about Native texts, textuality, and experience.

In reading the Osage Constitution, then, I do so as a political partisan and a scholar. Also, I perform this reading with the knowledge that Osages will be among my audience and will probably have the strongest responses. Osages, after all, care about these issues and have the largest stake in them. As a people, Osages occupy just about every subject position that can be imagined, from lawyer and doctor to cashier, clerk, and bureaucrat. My scholarly position is one more in that range.

The argument I make in this chapter is not just that Osages have gotten a raw deal—that much would be agreed to by a broad spectrum within Osage opinion. Instead, in the midst of my partisan reading I want to make the point that this document and others like it are examples of particular ways that Native people have used writing beyond fiction, poetry, and autobiography, which have commanded the lion's share of critical attention. In this way, the Osage Constitution is not only a record of history, but an expression of the modern intellectual aspirations of a people confronting the need to transform themselves on their own terms. The framers of the Osage Constitution provided a kind of intellectual leadership that, as was true for Apess, continues to resonate in the present. Though its words are copied, in large part, from other founding documents, this constitution remains an embodiment of Osage experiences. Before outlining and then delving into the critical issues that arise in this reading, I will provide some specifics on how the Osage Constitution came into existence and what its contemporary situation is.

On the Cusp of Modernity

Reading the Osage Constitution presents an entirely different set of challenges than reading the work of William Apess or the other authors in this study. Understanding Apess requires attention to a long history in which what it meant to be Pequot had lost much of the meaning it had for Apess's ancestors. When the Osages produced their constitution, on the other hand, they did so as a response to being on the harsh side of the cusp of a world of change that their ancestors could not have imagined when they first encountered Europeans two centuries before.

When they found themselves on that cusp, Osage leaders sent a small delegation to the Cherokees to study their constitution and they used what they brought back when they met in constitutional convention to come up with their own governing document (T. Wilson, *Underground*, 30). Seen synoptically, perhaps the most striking thing about these two constitutions is not just their identical structure, but that the Osages copied entire sections of the Cherokee version word for word. Exchange the word *Osage* for *Cherokee* and jimmy with the dates a little and much of the two documents is the same, especially prescribed oaths and qualifications for office.

After the preamble, the first article, which hews closely to the Cherokee model, marks the first significant difference between these two constitutions and the U.S. Constitution. Following the Cherokees, article 1, section 1 of the Osage Constitution sets out "the boundary of the Osage Nation." Section 2 declares the Osage government the only legal conduit for disposing of Osage lands or for making improvements on them. Reflecting the times, the Osage framers depart from the Cherokee text to make themselves the only legitimate body to approve allotment, an issue that was not germane in 1839, when their neighbors wrote their constitution.

The Osages made other significant alterations, indicating that the process for them was not merely one of switching some words to expediently and expeditiously create a document allowing them to argue for a modern political foundation in their ongoing efforts to secure their place in the world. The Osages, for instance, omitted Cherokee strictures against descendants of African slaves being citizens. The Osages also removed references to the right to a trial by jury, bail for noncapital offenses, and freedom of religion and conscience, as well as provisions against double jeopardy and unreasonable government seizures. Thus, in spite of their rejection of African slavery, the Osage framers did not embrace enumerated civil liberties in the ways their neighbors had in 1839.

I have not found written documents or many oral sources to illuminate the process by which this situation came to pass, but reasonable reasons for why the Osages struck these rights range from the fact that their traditional life had not yet exposed them to modern conditions that would prompt the need for such rights to their adherence to a priestly social organization that independent, unelected bodies like juries would undermine. By the time the Cherokees adopted their first constitution, they were surrounded by polities that used Western forms of government. The Osages had little of that kind of experience and still lived under at least the vestiges of a civil order and justice system that had structured Osage social life for centuries.

Osage leaders ratified their constitution at the end of 1881. For almost two decades, the principles articulated in that document, imperfect though they may be, provided the basis for Osage civil society in the transition from traditional to modern society. Albeit often rudimentary in form and sometimes only partially successful, the Osages made a remarkable transition to constitutional democracy.

Recently, Taiaiake Alfred has forcefully called for contemporary indigenous people to revitalize a sense of traditional indigenous values in governance. Far from being a primitivist return to an essentialized golden age, Alfred writes, "[C]ultural revival is not a matter of rejecting all Western influences, but of separating the good from the bad and of fashioning a coherent set of ideas out of the traditional culture to guide whatever forms of political and social development—including the good elements of Western forms—are appropriate to the contemporary reality" (28). This is clearly what Osage leaders were attempting to do when they adopted a constitution for their people. The Osage Nation was, for them, a vehicle for asserting not just political independence, but for retaining their sense of peoplehood and its distinctive features in the midst of a changing world.

In the years following the adoption of the 1881 constitution, Osage people became accustomed to casting votes for an elected National Council, which replaced the previous influence of the *Non-hon'-zhin-ga,* or Little Old Men, the village and tribal elders who had been invested with decision-making power in earlier generations.

At the first election in February 1882, the Osage cast their votes by selecting colored strips of paper representing the different candidates (T. Wilson, *Underground,* 33). They learned as the years passed to respect the power of district sheriffs and the judiciary that their constitution created. In spite of the fact that the framers had not endorsed enumerated civil liberties in the same way the Cherokee had, Osage civil rights were protected by guarantees that judges could not be involved in cases where family ties would interfere with their impartiality, as well as by guarantees of speedy trials, the right to face accusers and witnesses, and protection from self-incrimination. As Terry Wilson argues, "[T]he general tone of the constitution suggest[s] that the Osages were consciously attempting to create a pragmatic organ of governance in addition to making an assertion of sovereignty" (32).

The Osage Constitution of 1881 served the Osage people for nearly two decades at the end of the nineteenth century. Theirs was a fledgling democracy to be sure. In those years, the Osages made strides in the transition from being buffalo-hunting horticulturists to becoming ranchers and farmers. To varying degrees, Osages embraced their modern future in the form of the constitutional government they had chosen for themselves.

Undoubtedly because of the Osages' success in creating a constitutional government, in 1898 the United States unilaterally announced that it would no longer recognize the legitimacy of the Osage National Council, a move consistent with federal policy toward indigenous governments following the Curtis Act of 1898 (Prucha, 748). In 1906, in a move unique in its history with tribal nations, the United States Congress passed legislation that created a governing body, the Osage Tribal Council, to handle the economic, social, and political affairs of the tribe (Pierce, 1). The Osage Tribal Council, through the system created by this legislation, is elected through inherited shares of the tribal mineral estate; by the 1990s, fewer than two thousand out of seventeen thousand Osages held shares of the mineral estate and were enfranchised to vote (Pierce, 48ff.).

The dream of restoring Osage democracy has endured in every generation since 1906. The 1960s and 1970s was a particularly active, though finally disappointing era for Osage legal challenges to the situation. In 1990, a group of Osage constitutionalists filed a lawsuit in federal court seeking recognition of the Osage National Council. The suit came to be known as *Fletcher v. United States,* with the lead plaintiff being William Fletcher, a widely respected Osage man with deep roots in the Osage community (Pierce, 49).

In a move that surprised many, in 1992 U.S. District Court Judge James O. Ellison reached what can be seen legally as a decision in equity and mandated a process through which the citizen-members of the Osage Nation (most of whom were ineligible to vote under the tribal council system) voted, over the course of two years, in a referendum process to reinstate their National Council.[3] The new National Council took office in June 1994. In establishing the new government, Osages were living out what Russel Barsh points to when he writes, "The essential question of today is not whether Indians were victimized, but what role they will play in future society" (208). On June 10, 1997, however, the Tenth Circuit of the United States Court of Appeals in Denver, Colorado, reversed the district court's ruling, effectively ending the Osages' three-year national government restoration.

Understood within the confines of U.S. jurisprudence, the court of appeals decision made legal sense. The judges of the Tenth Circuit essentially decided that Judge Ellison, in seeking an equitable remedy for what he saw as the valid complaint of Osage constitutionalists, had violated the sovereign immunity of the Osage government, which the U.S. Congress had created in 1906 after it abrogated the Osage National Council. The court ruled not against the rightness of the constitutional position, but for the power of the United States–imposed government, never commenting on the prior sovereign immunity of the Osage National Council, which the United States had violated with its 1898 edict.

Thus, the logic of the decision vis-à-vis the legal system of the United States was not, especially in retrospect, surprising. It was, however, no less devastating. In June 1997 when the decision came down, supporters of the new Osage constitution fought for their reformed government. Calling the decision "a setback for the cause of Osage democracy and for the recognition of all Osages," Vice President Dudley Whitehorn said he wanted to "assure the Osage people, all Osages, that the Osage Nation will do everything possible to protect them against this attack upon their fundamental rights."[4]

In the midst of the crisis, some people went door to door and called around the country to raise money to send a secret delegation of elected Osage leaders to Washington, D.C. It was reminiscent of one of those moments in the nineteenth century when tribal leaders would decide they needed to see the Great Father face to face. For the Osages in 1997, though, it was summer in D.C. and the Great Father was away. The delegation came home with little to show for their efforts.

On October 1, 1997, those who had led the charge against the restoration, the Osage Tribal Council, were reinstated as the official governing authority of the Osage people. Acting Commissioner for Indian Affairs Ada Deer, famous for her efforts in restoring her tribe, the Menominee, after the United States terminated their right to indigenous nationhood in 1961, signed the order that terminated democracy among the Osages. Partisans of the National Council hid the records of their three-year-old government. The democratically elected Osage leaders stepped down, their constituency disempowered, disillusioned, and, of course, disenfranchised.

Recently, the reinstated tribal council has succeeded in addressing some of the major issues that led to *Fletcher.* I will discuss these developments in brief in concluding this chapter, but the most basic issues that arose during the restoration period remain unresolved.

READING THE CONSTITUTION

My purpose in writing about the Osage Constitution is twofold. First, as an Osage constitutionalist, I am interested in promulgating the history of this remarkable document as widely as possible. That is why, in the months following the Tenth Circuit's decision in June 1997, I started talking about this situation at every opportunity I could find. For the next several years, whenever someone invited me to speak on a program and asked what I wanted to talk about my immediate answer was the Osage Constitution.

I have now talked about the crisis of Osage democracy dozens of times on college campuses around the United States and in Guatemala, Mexico, Canada, and France. Usually, these talks have been opportunities to demonstrate to audiences one of the basic facts of Native America, that the struggles of indigenous Americans are ongoing and immediate, occurring all over the continent even though most people never hear about them. Sometimes, though, my talks have provided moments of remarkable intellectual synchronicity.

In 1999, for instance, I made a presentation at the first Congress of Indigenous Writers of the Americas in Guatemala. Young Mayans in the audience took great interest in the Osage Constitution, their leaders having so recently negotiated written peace accords themselves after decades of brutal repression and civil war. Seeing the way these young people connected to my Osage ancestors, who struggled to articulate a vision of their peoplehood in a moment not so different from the ones Mayan leaders were facing, was deeply moving and clarified for me the synchronicity between what I was doing as an Osage and what other indigenous communities were facing.[5]

Thus, being able to narrate the history of Osage democracy and detail the contours of the recent crisis were crucial for responding to this political emergency. Conferences, lectures, and other invitations became opportunities to develop intellectual discipline of a certain sort as I confronted the need to find ways to speak clearly and concisely, whether for five minutes or five hours. But I had a second purpose as well, that being my interest in coming to a deeper understanding of my responsibilities as an Osage intellectual in the midst of such a crisis. To what extent could this political emergency, which struck so close to my heart, help me comprehend better the possibilities and positionality of contemporary Native intellectuals? This second purpose, as I will discuss in the conclusion to this chapter, has helped me clarify, more than anything, the extent to which Native American studies has only started to face the challenge of being accountable in meeting the intellectual needs of Native communities.

The Osage Constitution of 1881, then, has become for me an intriguing test case against which to consider a set of questions that have arisen in my scholarly work. First, to what extent can we consider this document, copied in large part word-for-word from other sources and whose authorship is communal, a part of the tradition of nonfiction writing in Native written intellectual and literary history and what is the nature of the intellectual leadership the Osage framers practiced? Second, how do we properly contextualize a text like this given its peculiar history? Third, how does taking up a text like this speak to the development of tribally centered intellectual and literary histories? Finally, what challenges to current notions of the responsibilities of Native scholars does reading this text evince?

The intellectual issues that arise from this political emergency and the text that inspired it are myriad. After narrating some of the history of the Osages and the creation of the constitution, I will turn to some of the theoretical and conceptual issues that arise from that history. In addressing this set of intellectual challenges, I have relied primarily on work done by Osage writers and in Native American studies, but I have also turned in two directions outside the field in an attempt to gain a broader understanding of these issues. First, I have sought to gain insight into the hermeneutic conditions of Native materials through an engagement with Frantz Fanon. Second, I hope to bring the Osage constitutional crisis into focus by looking at an American text that is contemporary with the era of the roots of the Osage crisis.

That text is Walt Whitman's 1871 essay, "Democratic Vistas," which marks one of the few occasions on which the United States's first great modern poet engaged in nonfiction prose. Whitman wrote his essay out of the chaos of the Civil War. Having personally witnessed the carnage of the war in hospitals in Baltimore, he turned his attention after the war to the difficult question of what kind of future could be wrought on American soil, which was so thoroughly and deeply disfigured by a history of slavery and secession. Far from the exuberance of his "Song of Myself," "Democratic Vistas" joins in essay form the gut-wrenching postwar poems like "When Lilacs Last in the Dooryard Bloom'd" as a testament to a sharp, opposite edge of the American experiment in democracy.

Which is not to say that Whitman didn't see a way out of the terrible mess. As he writes in a typically long, single sentence:

> Our fundamental want to-day in the United States, with closest, amplest reference to present conditions, and to the future, is of a class, and the clear idea of a class, of native authors, literatures, far different, far higher in grade, than any yet known, sacerdotal, modern, fit to cope with our occasions, lands, permeating the whole mass of American mentality, taste, belief, breathing into it a new breath of life, giving it decision, affecting politics far more than the popular superficial suffrage, with results inside and underneath the elections of Presidents and Congresses—radiating, begetting appropriate teachers, schools, manners, and, as its grandest result, accomplishing . . . a religious and moral character beneath the political and productive and intellectual bases of the States. (506)

What interests me most about "Democratic Vistas" is the opportunity it provided Whitman to ruminate on the future while facing the postbellum crisis. Whitman confronts the depth of challenge the Civil War represented to his own vision of the best the United States had to offer to the world. This kind of forum is one the Osages have rarely had during the long century of our constitutional crisis.

In comparatively engaging Whitman's essay, my hope is not only to gain insight into the conditions of the Osage crisis, but to violate the rhetorical boundaries within which a Native American situation of crisis calls forth outrage, demands for reform, liberal guilt, or acrimonious charges of hysterics and politics—in short, everything but sincere analysis and creative attempts to find viable solutions to Native problems. It is just this sort of scholarly intervention, I would argue, that is a central need in the academic and intellectual consideration of Native Americans today. Just as Apess worked as a writer and leader in an era where much of the infrastructure for his work did not exist, so did the Osage framers. Whitman's text does not so much fill in the gaps as it helps identify where those gaps are.

Moreover, the essay helps identify the two major dynamics that have typified Osage encounters with the United States—at times a glimpse of a potential future in which the new realities of modernity and the integrity of Osage peoplehood might coexist, and at other, more crucial times, an arbitrary unilateralism in which the worst aspects of U.S. history block and disfigure Osage aspirations. Thus, however great the promise of an Osage future in relation to the United States, this other aspect has emerged concomitantly in history to betray that promise. This, I hope, will become more clear as I draw the outlines of the Osage constitutional crisis.

PAYS DES OSAGES

Given their history with Western ideas and institutions, especially American ones, the Osages of the latter half of the nineteenth century seem unlikely candidates to so enthusiastically endorse constitutional democracy. Until the beginning of the nineteenth century, the Osages had flourished in a homeland that provided for them prodigiously. For the greater part of each year, they lived in the fertile mountain region south of the Missouri River, an area now called the Ozarks. In the Ozarks, the Osages tended gardens and hunted small game. Then, in the summer and fall, the entire group left the lush hills for biannual buffalo hunts on the prairies of what is now Kansas, Oklahoma, and Colorado. When they returned from the summer hunt, their abundant gardens were ready to harvest.[6]

The Osages shared this region with a number of other tribal groups, including the Kaws, Wichitas, Missourias, Otoes, and Quapaws, but the Osages were the dominant group. On eighteenth-century French and Spanish maps of the region, for instance, the names of all of these groups appear, but the region as a whole is called *Pays des Osages* (Din and Nasatir, 40–41). As Willard Rollings notes, "Osage hegemony was based upon several factors: a large population, a strategic location, abundant resources, and an adaptable culture" (7).

To the south of this area were the Caddo people, who, for reasons that have been lost in the dim recesses of historical memory, were the mortal enemies of the Osages. The Omahas and Missourias lived along the Missouri north of the Osages. They helped create a buffer between the Osages and the Lakota, Nakota, and Dakota people, whom the Osages had been part of in an earlier age; the Osage language, in fact, is a Siouan language (T. Wilson, *Bibliography*; Rollings, 5).

This close linguistic relation is one indication that the Osages had once lived somewhere else, probably further to the east. The story of Osage

origins, though, says that the people who became the Osages had their beginnings in the stars. At the behest of their creator, *Wah'kon-tah* (the Great
Mystery), three groups of people descended to the earth, and these three
groups encountered a fourth group, the Isolated Earth People, living in
extreme chaos. The three groups from the stars invited the fourth group to
join them in finding a new way to live together and organize themselves.
This invitation to "move to a new country," as it is figured in the story, was
geographical, philosophical, and spiritual. And each time the Osages made
a major change in their social structure, this was the phrase that marked
the occasion (Mathews, *The Osages*, 7ff., 53ff.; Burns, *History*, 47).

The lifestyle that arose from the combination of horticulture and small-
and large-game hunting in the Ozarks and on the plains—along, no doubt
with favorable genetics—made the Osages inordinately tall; it was common for men to reach a height of six feet, six inches and seven-foot tall men
were not unheard of. Their formal name for themselves was *ni-u-ko'n-ska*,
or Children of the Middle Waters, but in general they called themselves,
in what was certainly an ironic gesture, the Little Ones (Mathews, *The
Osages*, 7). To top off their tall girth, these Little Ones shaved all but a
four-inch wide strip of their heads in a distinctive "roach" style that set
them apart from their neighbors (Rollings, 17).

The Osages first came to know Europeans in the seventeenth century,
when bands of explorers made their way into the tribal homeland. As tribal historian John Joseph Mathews writes of these early encounters,

> The people along with the chiefs would believe that the strangers could
> have no dignity, and must represent a tribe of little dignity, therefore of
> little importance. In the village they flashed their eyes everywhere and
> let them rest for long moments in the women and girls. There were grease
> swipes from their fingers on their buckskin leggings. They were like camp
> dogs who wag their tails and slaver when there is fresh meat to be trimmed,
> and the same cajoling expectancy was in their laughs. (*The Osages*, 101)

In 1673, the Catholic missionary Jacques Marquette and French trader
Louis Jolliet found their way to the Osages. It was Marquette, in fact, who
recorded the name of the tribe as "Wah-Sha-She," gallicized and later an-
glicized to "Osage" when he heard from Native people on the east side of
the Mississippi that that was the name of the people the missionary would
encounter after crossing the river (Mathews, *The Osages*, 107).

From that point in the seventeenth century, the Osages would experience successive waves of pressure on their domain. As the French and then the Spanish established trading relationships with the Osages, the lifestyle of the tribe changed little. Metal, or *mon'ce,* brought new tools, which in time prompted new names and ceremonies among the Little Ones, and various new invisible biological agents caused new illnesses, called *we-lush-ka,* or Little Mystery People, but the Osages' clan system and ceremonial structure remained strong (Mathews, *The Osages,* 16, 233). The Osages, in fact, often thwarted the plans and schemes of the European powers through their resistance to encroachment.

Over the course of the eighteenth century, the Osages became a formidable presence, ideally situated to take advantage of the colonial powers vying for dominance in North America. With their homelands bordering three important rivers (the Mississippi, Missouri, and Arkansas), Osages controlled access to a region that could connect Spanish holdings in the southwest, French holdings in Canada and Louisiana, and English territories to the east. The French, whom the other powers recognized as having rights to the Osage homelands, were easily the most desirable of the three powers to deal with. Not being in a position to seriously consider settling the trans-Mississippi west, the French concentrated on establishing commercial relationships with the Osages (Pierce, 7–8).

The French, furthermore, were more than happy to arm the Osages as a means of protecting their western territorial interests from British incursion (Rollings, 108ff.). French horses radically improved Osage buffalo hunting in the enormous herds that blanketed the plains all the way to the Rocky Mountains. French trade goods, including textiles, weapons, tools, and cooking and eating utensils, made their life of hunting and horticulture easier in many ways (Din and Nasatir, 22–23, 50).

The Spanish, who claimed control over the vast Louisiana Territory after the Seven Years' War ended in 1754, were not as accommodating to the Osages as the French, but the Osages continued to grow economically throughout the eighteenth century. They dominated the fur trade and successfully kept tribes from both sides of the Mississippi and to the north and south from gaining a foothold in the rich hunting grounds of the Ozarks. Eventually, with a population of 6,500 to 7,000 people, they controlled an enormous territory that stretched in places as far south as the Red River, which forms much of the present-day border of Oklahoma and Texas (Pierce, 11).

But with the arrival of the Americans in the latter part of the eighteenth century, the Osages had to deal not only with traders and adventurers, but with people who looked at the land of the Osages as ripe for settlement. After President Thomas Jefferson's Louisiana Purchase, in which the United States paid the French for the right to attempt to colonize and settle the area west of the Mississippi, the Osages were soon hurtling toward a century of radical changes.

THE TREATY ERA OPENS

The Osages signed their first treaty in 1808. That treaty created a clear line between the Osages and the settlers who were pouring into the Missouri Territory and competing with the Osages for game animals, though Osage leaders rightly complained that the line established was within sight of their villages in western Missouri (Mathews, *The Osages,* 389ff.). It also "conveyed to the United States 52,480,000 acres comprising approximately half of the present state of Arkansas and seven-eighths of the state of Missouri" (Pierce, 9). More than that, it also provided for the approval of the U.S. president in any future land sales or cessions. "This . . . reveals," according to Pierce, "the beginnings of the subtle, gradual diminution of Osage sovereignty by the federal government in ways collateral to the acquisition of the tribe's lands" (9).

White settlers would establish enough of a foothold in Missouri for the territory to gain statehood in 1821, but the Osages were frustrated not only by white settlers arriving in their territory; in addition, the Cherokee, Chickasaw, and Choctaw people, whose lands were being engulfed by the southeastern colonies of the young United States, were being offered land in the West in exchange for the land they were losing in the East (Mathews, *The Osages,* 349). "That the lands were already claimed by the Osages," writes Terry Wilson, "was conveniently ignored" (7).

As removal of these southeastern tribes, as well as those from the Ohio River valley, came to seem imminent, more and more people arrived in the land of the Osages and were frustrated to find that the land the United States had promised them was already occupied by other Indians. The "old settlers," as these Cherokees came to be called, were in constant conflict with the Osages as the groups vied for territory and resources (Mathews, *The Osages,* 408ff.). As Pierce notes, "In the two years following . . . 1817, . . . over four thousand Cherokees immigrated into the Arkansas Territory. By 1840 over 60,000 eastern Indians had settled in the Osage hunting territories" (11).[7]

The Osages signed subsequent treaties in 1818 and 1825 that drove them from the Ozarks to the plains, ceding over forty-five million acres in the process. The first Osage reservation, a 50-by-150-mile strip in what is now the state of Kansas, was the result of these treaties. The reservation stretched along the northern boundary of what would become Indian Territory. Another 25-by-50-mile rectangle of "neutral land" nestled between their eastern boundary and what would become the western boundary of Missouri. This was supposed to create a buffer between the Osages and the Cherokees, who by then were bitter enemies. As Wilson writes, "In the course of seventeen years, the United States had forced three unequal treaties on the Osages. For ceding nearly 100,000,000 acres, the tribe received $166,300 in livestock, horses, farming equipment, cash, and annuities—one penny for each six acres" (*Underground,* 8–9).

In the space of a quarter century, the Osages had gone from being able to thwart European aspirations and American expansion to being more and more dependent on the United States government. The territory that had once been theirs was more and more crowded with other Native groups and whites looking for land to settle. Yet the Osages persisted. Crowded out of their once vast domain by a series of unfair treaties, they still maintained a way of life that closely resembled what it had been a century and a half before. They still hunted near their villages for small game, planted throughout most of the year, and descended to the plains for semiannual buffalo hunts.

Mathews rises to some of his strongest prose in an extended description of this moment in Osage history. "The Little Ones," Mathews comments, "had been in contact with the Europeans since the latter part of the seventeenth century, 150 years and more, yet they would have nothing to do with his God" (*The Osages,* 582–83). Instead, they continued their annual rhythm of life, punctuated by ceremonies and changing seasons.

Compared to their new Native neighbors from the east, the Osages were completely unreconstructed. "They should have been loitering about the agencies or the forts," writes Mathews,

> sitting in rows in the sun, detached from the world. Their Nobodies should have carried Bibles and become the afflated centers of attention of the Heavy Eyebrows. . . . They should have sold their souls for the whisky and rum of the Heavy Eyebrows, and when sober and without furs, begged at the kitchen doors of the missions, the forts, and the traders' stores. They should have been living in little government-built log cabins, in the center

of their little patches of corn and beans and squash, with their rooting
hogs and their lazy dogs fighting fleas. (*The Osages,* 583)

Instead, Mathews argues, the Osages continued in the way of living on
the plains they had been developing for centuries. Mathews completes his
paean by writing,

> No one dared wear the clothing of the Heavy Eyebrows for fear of ridi-
> cule, and each morning when the morning star came up, men went to the
> high places to chant their prayers while the women stayed in their lodges
> or came out to stand in front of them facing east. Grandfather rose each
> morning bringing the light of day, in which they desired to live into old
> age, and *Wah'Kon-Tah*'s voice was still heard in the long prairie grasses,
> in the leaves of the oaks and the elms and the cottonwoods, in the patter
> of the rain and the hissing of snow; and after fasting and prayer-singing
> with earth on their temples *Wah'Kon-Tah* would speak to them through
> the owl, the pelican, the curlew, the splash of a fish, the wind over the
> prairie, the clouds he had painted. (*The Osages,* 583)

It was a moment of deep anxiety and threatened dissolution. But it was
more as well. Looking ahead to the future, change was far from over. But
Osage commitment to being Osage remained. "That is why," Mathews
writes in concluding his account of this period, "the story of the Little
Ones cannot end as it might with all other people. It is because they were
resistant that they have a long story to tell" (584).

THE OSAGES IN KANSAS

In 1854, the Osage reservation stood on the eastern edge of the newly created Kansas Territory. The once innumerable buffalo were dwindling as
overhunting by white hunters curtailed the life of Indians on the plains.[8]
And with increasing demands for white settlement in the Kansas Territory,
the Osages faced the prospect of losing even the small area they had managed to hold on to.

The situation in the Kansas Territory was as difficult for the Native
people as it had been anywhere on the continent. Reservations spanned
essentially the entire north-south boundary of the eastern side of the territory, meaning that Indian people stood directly in the way of the thousands of settlers moving westward. The land in eastern Kansas, with its

rolling hills and stands of timber, was much more desirable than the more arid lands in the west. Furthermore, railroads were more and more interested in carving out routes that would most directly connect the east and west coasts of the United States, and the Indian reservations of the Kansas and Indian territories created a barrier to those routes.[9] Interestingly, the geographical conditions that had been so advantageous for the Osages in an earlier time were now creating their greatest challenges.

Looking back with hindsight, it is easy to see that the Osage and other indigenous nations in Kansas had little chance to make permanent homes there. In spite of the fact that not a single inch of Kansas Territory was open to settlement when it was created in 1854 and all of the Native groups there had treaties guaranteeing secure boundaries for their homelands, squatters had already moved freely into Native lands, and the United States government failed to police its own citizens. The idea of squatter sovereignty, linked as it was with the Jeffersonian ideal of yeomanry, populism, and Manifest Destiny, was much stronger than any concept of the rights the aboriginal inhabitants, like the Osages or the emigrant tribes like the Shawnee, Kickapoo, or Sac and Fox, held through negotiated agreements with the United States (Mathews, *The Osages,* 624, 645–66).

Throughout most of the 1850s, the situation was chaotic, as annual reports to the U.S. Commissioner for Indian Affairs by agents for the Osages attest.[10] Squatters and land speculators would lay claim to land they insisted was outside of reservation boundaries and tribal leaders could only insist on surveys that would provide them with clear markers of where their lands began and ended (*Annual Report* 1860). For the Osages, bi-annual buffalo hunts became less and less reliable in providing hides for trade and subsistence food. Hunger, which had been all but nonexistent in times past, became a constant threat (*Annual Report* 1851, 403; *Annual Report* 1858, 139). And diseases like measles and smallpox became more and more common (*Annual Report* 1852, 106; *Annual Report* 1855, 175). Trespassing white settlers regularly stole horses and timber from the Osages, as had been the case with the Mashpees a half century before. These trespassers went so far as to set up a sawmill on Osage land to process that stolen lumber (*Annual Report* 1852, 106–7; *Annual Report* 1857, 206; *Annual Report* 1858, 137; *Annual Report* 1859, 170).

The impact was devastating. The Osage population was approximately five thousand in 1850.[11] In March 1852, both the agent and Father John Schoenmakers, a Catholic priest who started working with the tribe in the late 1840s, reported one thousand deaths among the Osage villages due to a measles outbreak followed by typhoid fever, then whooping cough (*Annual Report* 1852, 106, 109). In 1855, the agent reported four hundred deaths from smallpox, a number that might have been greater but for a significant number of vaccinations (*Annual Report* 1855, 176). The next year, over one hundred Osages reportedly died from an outbreak of scrofula (*Annual Report* 1856, 134). The 1856 and 1857 reports of Osage population place the number around 3,500 (*Annual Report* 1856, 136; *Annual Report* 1857, 206). In 1865, that number had dropped further to 2,800 (*Annual Report* 1865, 293).

As their own population plummeted, the Osages were overwhelmed by an ever-increasing population of Americans. Their agent, Andrew Dorn, reported in 1857 that "[t]he Osages complain most bitterly about the great number of people passing through their country, since the establishment of Kansas Territory, in every direction, killing and destroying the buffalo and other game, from which I apprehend a collision will take place between the Indians and our citizens, if continued under the present situation of affairs" (*Annual Report* 1857, 206).

As a solution, Dorn proposed what would become the standard action on Kansas reservations: offering to buy a portion of the current reservation, use the opportunity to resurvey Indian land, and, as Dorn suggests, "marking its boundaries distinctly with stone monuments, that all might at a glance, both Indians and citizens, know where their rights extend" (*Annual Report* 1857, 206). Such "diminished" reservations were in reality steps leading toward removal to Indian Territory. Meanwhile, squatters wantonly established homes and other buildings using Osage timber resources while officials of the U.S. government cravenly stood by. The Osages were working to maintain a space for themselves as a people, but the United States showed itself less and less willing or able to accommodate those Osage hopes.

The sectional crisis that became the Civil War only strengthened the resolve of the squatters and weakened the government in its already feeble attempts to limit the damage caused by its citizens. Kansas became a state in 1861 in large part as a political move to favor the antislavery side (Miner and Unrau, 24). Once the Civil War began and "Bloody Kansas" became a crucial place in it, the vast majority of Osages remained loyal to the Union side. Significant numbers of Osages, in fact, joined Indian regiments of the Union Army (*Annual Report* 1862, 144). Native refugees from reservations in Kansas crowded into safe areas and tribal agents relocated with them. For a time, Osage warriors patrolled the embattled southern boundary of Kansas Territory and protected these refugees from Confederate marauders (*Annual Report* 1863, 187).

The United States did not reward Osage loyalty. Instead, the Union victory created increased pressure among whites for lands to settle in Kansas. In 1865 Osages signed a treaty that was ratified by the Senate in which the Osages relinquished four million acres of their lands in an attempt to relieve some of the pressure from the continuing flood of settlers (Miner and Unrau, 98). The treaty also raised the issue of eventual removal from Kansas to Indian Territory. Osages had lived in their territory longer than anyone, but racism ran deep among the usurping settlers, who were convinced that their claim to the Osage homeland was superior to that of the Osages. By 1867, their agent reported that "four companies of 'militia' have been organized on the border by the State authority, who are threatening the Indians with 'extermination'" (*Annual Report* 1867, 325).

The Osages were experiencing the full force of Manifest Destiny. Their claim to their homelands, their hopes for the future of their grandchildren, and their stake in shaping their own destiny were withering away as they were forced to make room for squatters, timber thieves, and a corrupt colonial governing power. The Osages still sought to forge a relationship with the United States in which their integrity as a people would mean something, but their best efforts only led to betrayal. Indeed, given this cascade of events, it is easy to see why American destiny came to be thought of as manifest, given how crippled it was in its more tangible, material aspects.

With each passing season, the situation became more and more untenable as the Osages confronted life with what Mathews would later call "frontier histrionics" (663). The citizens in Kansas viewed the aboriginal Osages as unworthy of the fertile lands the tribe had reserved for itself in negotiations with the United States. The federal government did nothing when Osage horses were stolen from the reservation, but local citizens who bought the stolen property got redress from the government when the Osages sought out their ponies and took them back. Schoenmakers, in his 1867 report on the Osage mission school, said,

> Indians unaccustomed to discipline will object to stringent laws, yet the sober and better-minded Osages feel the void of suitable laws. The chiefs and some of the leading men regret that the Indian fields and produce are

unprotected against thieving neighbors, and would willingly accept laws
of their own liking. They often advise in their councils the adoption of
laws. To effect such salutary reforms government officers should strength-
en the authority of your Osage chiefs, and assist them in selecting suitable
laws. Where there is no law there is no transgression. No wonder, then,
that the Indians retaliate for the loss of their horses, this very thing being
a trait of their industry and wit. (*Annual Report* 1867, 327)

For a people whose traditions told them they had come to their homelands
long, long ago from the order of the stars, and who sought in their philosophy and their social organization to copy that order, the two decades
after 1850 were excruciating.

One of the few constants throughout that period was the buffalo hunt.
The Osages' biannual treks to the west, in fact, were the main reason their
agents believed, in the words of one, "They have made but little advance-
ment in civilization" (*Annual Report* 1867, 324). The difference between
these later hunts and the ones from the past, the agent said, was that
"[t]hey now have to go much further to secure a full supply of meat, robes,
and furs than they did a few years ago. They take all their families, horses,
etc., on the fall or winter hunt. They return to their camps in February,
and trade their robes for flour, coffee, sugar, and such articles as they need
for dress and ornaments" (*Annual Report* 1867, 325).

The hunt, though, was less and less reliable for providing a means of
subsistence. The herd was pushed westward and had its numbers reduced
by the same processes of colonization as the Natives who had built a way
of life around it. Eventually white hunters stalked buffalo from the comfort of railroad coaches and many thousands of carcasses shorn of their
hides were left to rot on the plains. But even before that, conflict with
other Western tribes sometimes kept the Osages off the plains or inter-
rupted them partway through their hunt.

By 1868, removal to Indian Territory was imminent. As many as fifteen
thousand white Kansans were squatting on their territory, and "several
Osage land towns, Wichita for example, had applied to the state for incor-
poration papers despite the absolute illegality of such an action" (Miner
and Unrau, 123). Conflict with the Arapaho made the buffalo hunt impossible. Osage leaders feared that delaying a move to Indian Territory would
mean other tribal groups would choose all the best lands. They negotiated a draft treaty that would have allowed a single railroad company to

buy their entire eight-million-acre reservation. When that treaty reached the U.S. Senate for ratification, though, the squatters and their supporters railed against its passage. Eventually, with the uproar over the Osage treaty as part of its impetus, Congress severely curtailed the treaty-making power of the executive branch (Deloria and DeMallie, 233ff.).

Throughout this wrangling, Osages were in limbo. In the fall of 1870, the Osages relinquished the last part of their once enormous domain and agreed to purchase from the Cherokees a half million acres of land in Indian Territory. This new domain, a small corner of the territory that once had been theirs, the Osages purchased in fee simple, using money they had received for earlier land cessions. Osage leaders insisted that they receive title to this land and that they would hold it in common.[12] As Pierce points out, though, the Cherokee Treaty of 1866 that created the mechanism for such sales west of the ninety-sixth meridian to other Native groups included "the ominous proviso that would prove prophetic in light of the later development of the allotment concept: 'the land [to be] conveyed in fee simple to each of said tribes to be held in common or by their members in severalty *as the United States may decide*'" (17, emphasis added by Pierce).

The move to the new reservation should have been easy given that it lay just over the Kansas border. But as the Osages made plans to move to their new home in late 1870, the Cherokees complained that part of it was east of the ninety-sixth meridian. Even after having adjusted the boundary line, the Osages were still not sure of their eastern boundary when they began arriving on the new reservation in 1871 (Mathews, 1871). It was not until late that year, when some buildings had already been erected on the eastern edge of the reservation, that the Osages found that the survey that had been done for them had, in fact, still placed their boundary three and half miles east of the ninety-sixth meridian. That land had been easily the most desirable for farming of what the Osages had initially selected, so the potential loss of it was momentous. Incredibly, they also found themselves besieged by white squatters, some of whom had moved there as soon as the site was announced, eager to take advantage of what they assumed would be favorable conditions for laying claim to Osage land (*Annual Report* 1870, 486, 491).

In 1869, the United States assigned a new agent, Isaac Gibson, to the Osages. In long annual reports to the Commissioner of Indian Affairs and on trips to Washington, D.C., to advocate on the tribe's behalf, the Quaker agent was perhaps the most eloquent the Osages ever had (T. Wilson, *Underground*, 20). Upon agreeing to the Osages' move to their Indian Territory reservation, Gibson wrote of the impression the Osages had made upon him:

> This tribe of Indians are richly endowed by nature, physically and morally. A finer-looking body of men, with more grace and dignity, or better intellectual development, could hardly be found on this globe. In judging of their moral character, some facts in their history must be remembered. They were once the most numerous and warlike nation on this continent, with a domain extending from the Gulf to the Missouri River, and from the Mississippi to the Rocky Mountains; but they have been shorn of their territory, piece by piece, until at last they have not a settled and unquestioned claim to a single foot of earth. Their numbers have been wasted by war and famine. This little remnant is all that remains of a heroic race that once held undisputed ownership over all this region. (*Annual Report* 1870, 487)

He then adds, "It is almost without precedent, yet strictly true, one great cause of their decline has been fidelity to their pledges" (487).

With all the snafus of the move yet to come, Gibson would need all his patience and the Osages would have their own endurance tested severely. In response to the bad survey and the presence of pre-squatters, Osage leaders demanded the right to purchase a significantly larger area and that all trespassers be removed. At the same time, the United States requested that the Osages make available some land to the Kaws for purchase so that they could also move to Indian Territory (*Annual Report* 1872, 227). The Osages agreed and finally found themselves with a 1,470,559-million-acre reservation (T. Wilson, *Underground*, 16). At the insistence of the Osages, U.S. military personnel swept through the reservation and cleared it of trespassers (*Annual Report* 1872, 246).

MOVING TO INDIAN TERRITORY

The first years on the reservation were, at least in part, a respite from the constant harassment of the previous two decades in Kansas. Large numbers of people continued their biannual buffalo hunts, though an impressive number stayed behind in 1872 and 1873 to take advantage of Gibson's offer to pay those who did so to build split-rail fences (*Annual Report* 1873,

216; *Annual Report* 1874, 222). The 250 or so mixed-bloods who had made the move to Indian Territory did not hunt buffalo anyway, so they were naturally inclined to take the offer. But the full-bloods who did must have peered into the future and seen that this, eventually, would be part of what their new life entailed.

The 1876 agent's report indicated a hunt with very poor results (*Annual Report* 1876, 54). The buffalo had been the center of the Osages' existence for centuries. Just a few years before they had taken 10,800 hides and traded them and other furs for $68,000 in trade goods (*Annual Report* 1874, 222). The hunt in 1876 was the last recorded by the Osages (T. Wilson, *Underground,* 24).

Their agents held out hope that the Osages would take up the plow, and a good number did attempt to grow crops. Seemingly, though, the Osages had a strong belief that crops were self-sustaining after being planted (T. Wilson, *Underground,* 20). And at least some indications show that Osage men, like many men in other North American tribes, considered growing crops to be women's work.

Gibson, a Quaker who would spend five years among the Osages, had high ambitions for his charges. He envisioned schools, a hospital, and other features of what he deemed civilization. For those who built fences and planted crops, he promised and delivered houses. For those in houses, he provided "three chairs, one bedstead, bed-tick, table, broom, washtub, washboard, six plates, cups and saucers, knives and forks, one gravy-bowl, steak-platter, sauce-dish, dish-pan, wash-basin, candlestick, two towels, and table-cloths" (*Annual Report* 1875, 278).

The early years of reservation life were an odd mix of that sort of detail—plenty of trappings of the new life the agents and government were pushing the Osages toward, but months and years when those steak platters and gravy bowls were far from full. By 1876 the buffalo herd of the plains had diminished to the point that those few who set out to hunt did so out of habit or in defiance of their new circumstances. Perhaps most insulting to the leaders of the people was Gibson's practice of using Osage annuity money to purchase food and goods to be distributed as rations to those the agent deemed worthy (T. Wilson, *Underground,* 21). Not only had Gibson turned out to be as paternalistic as other agents, but leaders complained that the quality of the food and other goods he procured was low. More important, Gibson's practice of distributing rations rather than paying out annuity monies that the Osages could spend with the traders on the reservation and in Kansas was an infantilizing slap in the face to the dignity of Osage leaders, who had been making their own choices in such matters for over a century (*Annual Report 1875*, 276). A new generation of leaders arose as the realities of reservation life unfolded. Some of these men had become educated in the Catholic mission school, adding to their communication skills and expertise in ways that would become more and more necessary to the survival of the people. They were committed to "accepting usable parts of white culture without conceding the traditional past as worthless" (T. Wilson, *Underground*, 23). Joseph Paw-ne-no-pa-she, whose name means "Not Afraid of Long Hairs" and who came to be known as Governor Joe, was one of these leaders. His father sent him to the mission school, but when he graduated, he is said to have proclaimed, "It took Father [Schoenmakers] fifteen years to make a white man out of me, and it will take just fifteen minutes to make an Osage out of myself" (qtd. in T. Wilson, *Underground*, 23). Another of these leaders, James Bigheart, also attended the Catholic schools, and was able to read English and Latin and speak Osage, Ponca, Sioux, Cherokee, French, and English (T. Wilson, *Underground*, 30).

A New Country of Constitutional Democracy

It was in the midst of this complicated context that the Osages came to frame their constitution. In the 1870s and even before in Kansas, the Osages had experimented with various forms of representational government. One of their agents, Cyrus Beede, encouraged them to elect a governor, a chief counselor, and a five-person council through which they could settle internal disputes and assist him with decisions he had to make (*Annual Report 1876*, 54). In his 1877 report, Beede noted, "The biennial election of these important officers of the 'Osage government' is a matter of great interest to the tribe. Already candidates are in the field, some eight months in advance of the election, and but for the right reserved to the agent to remove for cause, the temptation to betray all into the hands of particular friends might be hard to overcome" (*Annual Report 1877*, 92).

Beede's quotation marks around the words *Osage government* and his paternalistic evocation of his ultimate power to remove elected Osages to protect the tribe from itself epitomize the attitudes of agents and other representatives of the U.S. government toward Osage self-government. Even Laban Miles, the agent who served the Osage Agency from 1879 to 1885 and 1889 to 1893 and who did the most to provide consistent, sympathetic service to the Osages represented Osage self-government, at best, as a stepping-stone away from traditional leadership (*Annual Report* 1882, 73).

But the Osage leadership seems to have seen much more than a stepping-stone in the idea of constituting themselves as a nation. Instead, they seemingly saw a self-determined government as a way to bring order and justice to reservation life. Miles reports as much in 1881 when he writes, "They are clamorous for some simple laws for the settlement of their difficulties with one another; and for the enforcement of the same by their own officers, whom they desire to elect and have paid out of their own tribal funds" (*Annual Report,* 1881, 86). By then, Osage leaders had already sent a delegation to study the Cherokees' constitution and were three months away from meeting in constitutional convention to adopt their own.

Osages, given their history of agreements and treaties with the French, Spanish, and Americans, were familiar with the power of written documents. But they had also become familiar with the constitutional governments of the Cherokees, Creeks, Choctaws, and Chickasaws. Even in the years before moving to Indian Territory, Osages sent delegations to territory-wide meetings of Native groups to discuss the political future of the territory. Mathews, who turned Miles's agency diaries into a nonfiction novel, *Wah'Kon-Tah: The Osage and the White Man's Road,* in 1932, creates the impression that Miles was the major player behind the idea of the constitution (*The Osages,* 720ff.). But certainly Beede's earlier model of a business committee would have served the agent's needs.

Much more likely, given what actually transpired, is that James Bigheart, whom Terry Wilson calls the "prime mover" of the effort to establish a constitutional government among the Osages, used his influence among other leaders and his considerable language skills to bring about a wide consensus on the need for Osages to do for themselves what the United States would not (*Underground,* 30). That is, through constituting themselves as a nation, they claimed a status for themselves and their lands that the United States would only do in trust. Indeed, their annual requests for clear title to their lands continued to fall on deaf ears until the early 1880s, when the United States asked the Cherokees to deed the land to the United States to be held in trust for the Osages (*Annual Report,* 1885, 89).

The fifteen Osage male leaders who eventually signed the constitution seemed to clearly understand that it would put them on a different footing from Beede's ad hoc business committee. Among those fifteen are individuals whose names have continued to resonate through our history as Osage people: Bigheart, Governor Joe, Wah-ti-an-kah, Claremore, White Hair (Pawhuska), Saucy Chief, and Tall Chief. Although most of the specifics of the process of drafting and adopting the constitution have not survived in the written historical record, the constitution itself and other bits of evidence say a lot about what Osage leaders intended. From their demand for strong title and clear boundaries to their frustration with the ration system, these leaders embraced in their constitution a form of government that allowed them to see themselves as a sovereign nation.

The leaders displayed that attitude toward their constitutional government well over a decade later when their new agent remarked, "The Osages regard themselves as a nation with a big 'N,' and the government is vested in a principal chief, assistant chief, fifteen councilors, and five district sheriffs, who are elected by the people for terms of two years, respectively. . . . This government is a very real thing to the Osages" (*Annual Report* 1894, 241). Clearly, the Osages had transitioned to constitutional democracy with impressive success.

How to explain that success? Of course, any number of factors could have contributed. The fierce independence of the Osages over the course of two hundred years of dealing with European and Native encroachment on their lands surely had something to do with their strong desire to find a means through which to assert their independence in the face of American expansion. The example of the neighboring Cherokees, who in spite of their tragic past had embraced constitutional democracy and provided a model for the Osages, is also crucial. Some might aver that democratic ideals have an intrinsic empowering effect on newly enfranchised people.

I would like to suggest, though, that a major part of the answer lies not with the cultural practices the Osages were learning from outside their culture, but with the continuation of traditions they had developed over the course of centuries. In adopting their constitution, in other words, they were "moving to a new country."[13]

The form had changed, as had the conditions. The document they adopted was almost a word-for-word copy of the Cherokee Constitution, which was in its turn copied from the U.S. Constitution. But this was more than mere mimicry and the framers of the Osage Constitution took it as seriously as the leaders of the United States had in adopting theirs. As had happened all those centuries ago when the people from the stars invited the Isolated Earth People to turn away from chaos and violence, the embattled Little Ones looked deep into themselves and declared themselves to be a people. With this "move to a new country" of constitutional democracy, the Little Ones staked their claim to a future in which they would be, in the words of an African writer describing a similar history halfway around the globe, "refashioned, but strangely obdurate" (Appiah, 172).

Whatever the motivations of the framers of the Osage Constitution, I would argue that the result of their deliberations was a profound, inalienable gift to future generations of Osages. Unlike later tribal constitutions sponsored or in other ways impinged on by the U.S. government, the 1881 constitution sets out the parameters of a self-determined, self-imagined, autonomous Osage Nation. They undid the lie that Indian people were not capable of living out the challenges of modernity. No wonder, then, that the United States ended up fighting so hard against them, but what a shame. The Osage adoption of a constitution could be a proud moment in U.S. political history, a demonstration of the positive potential of American ideals even in the midst of the challenging dynamics of Indian-white relations in the nineteenth century. It became, instead, a disaster for the Osages as a people and a further mark against the U.S. experiment in democracy.

THE PULVERIZING ENGINE OF ALLOTMENT

As a document creating an independent nation holding its lands in common among its citizens, the Osage Constitution became a target for those who sought to undermine Native nations in the 1880s and 1890s. In that era, the United States turned its attention to the vast lands of the indigenous tribal nations of North America and set out to allot to individuals parcels of land that was, like the land purchased by the Osages in 1870, held communally. In 1887, President Grover Cleveland signed the Dawes General Allotment Act, which authorized the president to survey Indian lands, distribute homestead-sized plots to individual families, and open up remaining lands to white settlers. Merrill E. Gates, who presided over the Lake Mohonk Conference, a progressive "friends of the Indian" organization that supported the assimilation of Indian people, called the Dawes Act "a mighty pulverizing engine for breaking up the tribal mass."[14] Indeed, in the early 1880s, more than 150 million acres were held by Natives. By 1890, that number had been reduced to roughly 100 million, and at the turn of the century, only about 75 million acres remained in Indian hands.

The Osages, along with the tribes in Indian Territory that had migrated from the Southeast, the so-called Five Civilized Tribes (Cherokee, Creek, Seminole, Chickasaw, and Choctaw), managed to gain exemptions from the Dawes Act. However, pressure for allotment increased throughout the 1890s as Indian Territory became split between the Native republics that had been constituted there over the previous decades and Oklahoma Territory, made up of lands opened to white settlement starting with the land run of April 22, 1889 (T. Wilson, *Underground,* 37).

Throughout the decade, the United States added to the pressure for more white settlement by undermining constitutional governments like those of the Cherokees and the Osages. "By the early 1890s," according to Daniel Littlefield Jr., "not only were thousands of Americans living in Indian Territory, but their numbers were increasing daily. . . . The national press engaged in a propaganda war against the tribes and in behalf of these Americans" (11). Soon, whites outnumbered Natives in the territory.

As with allotment, the major pressure on the government to weaken the power of tribal governments came from white reform groups. Friends of the Indian groups were certainly no friends of self-determined indigenous constitutional governments. As the 1895 platform of the Lake Mohonk Conference stated:

> The [United States] possesses a supreme sovereignty over every foot
> of soil within its boundaries. Its legislative authority over its people it
> has neither right nor power to alienate. Its attempts to do so by Indian
> treaties in the past does not relieve it from the responsibility for the
> condition of government in the reservations and in the Indian Territory;
> and, despite those treaties, it is under a sacred obligation to exercise its
> sovereignty extending over the three hundred thousand whites and fifty
> thousand so-called Indians in the Indian Territory the same restraints
> and protection of government which other parts of the country enjoy.
> (qtd. in Prucha, 751)

The perversity of this platform is that it uses the growing presence of white settlers illegally squatting on Indian land to justify the U.S. government's inability to control its own citizens and hence the need to dissolve indigenous governments. Such is the twisted history of Oklahoma, a state that proclaims "Discover Native America" on its license plates but that regularly fails to acknowledge the lawlessness and injustice that led to the area becoming open to white settlement.

Overwhelmed by squatters and often unable to access the funds and the aid needed to run their own affairs, tribal governments strained for control. Failure, rather than being a learning opportunity as it had been in earlier times, added fuel to the antisovereignty sentiment. "They have demonstrated their incapacity to so govern themselves," one commission reported, "and no higher duty can rest upon the Government that granted this authority than to revoke it when it has so lamentably failed" (Prucha, 750). Completely lost in the discussion was any recognition that none of the framers of these tribal constitutions had appealed to the United States for permission to exist. The United States had not granted the Native people the right to be themselves. For the Osages, peoplehood had been constituted after their descent from the stars and was a gift of Wah'kon-tah. The 1881 constitution was a vehicle for affirming that peoplehood.

This dismissive attitude toward self-determined governments is unfortunate given the seriousness expressed in tribal constitutions. One good example is the very first article of the Osage Constitution. Compared to the U.S. Constitution, whose first article is about the fundamental power of the legislative branch, the Osages and the Cherokees needed to use their constitutions to declare their boundaries. Unlike the United States, which framed its constitution in the aftermath of its victory in the American Revolution, the Osages and the Cherokees framed theirs as a way to defend their boundaries against U.S. encroachment on U.S. terms. Further, the Osages reference allotment, reserving to the National Council the sole right to submit Osage lands to the practice of severalty. Indeed, given the growing concern over allotment in the era of the Osage Constitution, the wording of the document shows that one of its primary concerns was the protection of the Osage homeland in the face of the threat of severalty.

But the Osages do something else in the first section of that first article. After declaring Osage boundaries, the constitution says "except that portion purchased by the Kaws." The Kaws, as I have already noted, purchased their reservation from the Osages when the Osages moved from Kansas. What is remarkable about the addition of that phrase is the way it demonstrates that Osage leaders, in the midst of being hemmed in by their own boundary struggles with the United States, paid attention to the rights and aspirations of other indigenous people living in their midst

and on their former lands. It's not too much to say that the Osages found
themselves facing their own "Indian problem" and solving it very differently from the United States, which placed enormous pressure on indigenous peoplehood in that same era.

Faced with those pressures, between 1897 and 1902 the Five Civilized
Tribes gave in to allotment. In response to the growing crisis, one Osage
leader, Strike Axe, stated:

> When our chiefs sold reservations in the states the government would
> say you are all hemmed in by whites and your Great Father does not
> want you to be bothered, just come down to the red man's country where
> you will never be disturbed. The government promised me when we
> came here that we would be the fartherest west and . . . at the fartherest
> edge of Indian country and was impossible to be bothered and now you
> seem to think we are in bad shape with the whites. As you say, we have
> more whites than Indians, but where shall we go? (qtd. in T. Wilson,
> *Underground*, 40)

Increasingly, however, Strike Axe and other antiallotment leaders were
losing ground to a proallotment faction that was growing, a faction that
included a number of white men, perhaps numbering in the hundreds,
who had been placed on tribal rolls over the past decades. Some of these
men were intermarried with Osage women, while others managed to sneak
onto the rolls after long association with the tribe.

But the biggest part of that faction was made up of mixed-blood members
of the tribe. Predominantly the product of liasons between Osage women
and white traders, the mixed-bloods had begun to appear as a significant
subgroup among the Osages in the nineteenth century. In 1852, Osage agent
W. J. J. Morrow had worried about the way this tiny minority of two hundred or so among five thousand were being treated. As he writes:

> Many of the half-breed Osages manifest a disposition to cultivate the
> soil for a livelihood, and no doubt would have made greater advance-
> ment in the arts of civilization had it not been for the maltreatment they
> received from their full-blood relatives, who often kill and eat their hogs
> and cattle, and frequent their houses solely for the purpose of being fed.
> In default of being invited to eat, they unceremoniously take it wherever
> they can find it. They consume almost everything raised by the half-
> breeds, and consider it their prerogative to do so. In addition to all this,

when their annuity goods are distributed, the half-breeds are turned off without anything. At present, I am unable to suggest any plan by which the government could throw around the property of this class the protection they ask. (*Annual Report* 1852, 107)

A half century later, the mixed-bloods would find themselves in the stronger position. As the full-blood portion of the Osage population decreased over the course of the second half of the nineteenth century, the mixed-bloods grew in strength. In 1870, an estimated 250 mixed-bloods appear in reports of a total Osage population of 2,962 (*Annual Report* 1870, 483). In 1883, Gibson reported a drop of nearly half for the full-bloods, to 1,348, while the mixed-bloods numbered 333 (*Annual Report* 1883, 73) (Table 1).

In 1890, Osage full-bloods numbered 1,009 while mixed-bloods had shot up to 503. Over the course of the next decade, the mixed-bloods increased in political power and were courted by the proallotment forces of the U.S. government. Having taken many of the best lands on the reservation in the early years, when nearly all of the full-bloods were still committed to buffalo hunting, the mixed-bloods by the 1890s were a formidable presence, owning, for instance, a proallotment newspaper that could trumpet the benefits of giving in to federal demands to parcel out the reservation. In 1896, the mixed-bloods garnered "enough full-blood support to capture a majority in the National Council and to place in office their full-blood candidates for principal chief and assistant chief" (T. Wilson, *Underground,* 39–41).

By 1898, the groups had reached virtual parity, and a contested election led to an acrimonious struggle over the results. Black Dog and the conservatives managed to have themselves declared the winners of the two executive positions and a majority of the National Council. The rancor over this situation provided an ideal moment for the secretary of the interior, Ethan A. Hitchcock, to declare "that after 1 April 1900 the Osage national government would cease operations" (T. Wilson, *Underground,* 42). Osage nationalists refused to give up their government, but they could do little in the face of the power of the United States, which still held control over Osage monies in its treasury.

For six years, the Osages lived in an uneasy, chaotic time. In 1897, oil had been discovered on the tribe's land, prompting significant interest from burgeoning oil companies in Oklahoma. By 1905, between ten and fifteen thousand non-Osages were living on the reservation (T. Wilson,

TABLE 1. OSAGE POPULATION FROM ANNUAL AGENT REPORTS, 1850–1908 (ESTIMATES IN ITALICS)

Year	Full-bloods	Mixed-bloods	Total Population
1850			*5,000*
1856			*3,500*
1863			*2,900*
1865			*2,800*
1870		*250*	2,962
1874			2,872
1878	1,889	256	2,145
1879	1,872	263	2,135
1880	1,754	270	2,024
1881	1,677	285	1,962
1882	1,646	304	1,950
1883	1,348	333	1,681
1884	1,305	358	1,663
1885	1,233	385	1,618
1886	1,135	443	1,578
1887	1,078	448	1,526
1888	1,059	464	1,523
1889	1,001	497	1,498
1890	1,009	503	1,512
1891	994	610	1,604
1892	974	663	1,637
1893	928	709	1,637
1894	932	724	1,656
1895	929	753	1,682
1896	934	804	1,738
1897	912	850	1,762
1898	897	871	1,768
1899	886	879	1,765
1905	838	1,156	1,994
1908	926	1,303	2,229

Note: Numbers as estimated in annual agent reports are in italics to differentiate them from official counts. Numbers for 1878–98 come from a table in the 1898 agent report intended to show the changes in Osage population during that period. Annual agent reports in 1884 and 1885 differ from the 1898 table. The 1884 report noted 1,215 full-bloods and 355 mixed-bloods for a total of 1,570. The 1885 report noted 1,170 full-bloods and 377 mixed-bloods for a total of 1,547.

Underground, 49). Some of them were tenants on Osage farms, while others owned stores and other businesses serving the growing population. But plenty of them were simply there to try to take advantage of Osage wealth and the possible opening of surplus Osage lands after the inevitability of allotment.

By the turn of the twentieth century, the antiallotment full-bloods were a clear minority, and even the staunchest supporters of Osage nationhood knew that allotment and statehood for Oklahoma and Indian territories were coming. In 1906, Congress passed the Osage Allotment Act, which called for Osage land to be distributed among tribal members and for a Tribal Council to be elected to handle the business, social, and political affairs of the Osage people—and don't think for a moment that oil and legislation did not mix intimately. In the only victory for the traditional Osage nationalists, a provision of the 1906 Act allowed the Osages to retain ownership of subsurface rights, including oil and other minerals, communally. All three of these factors—the legislated forced allotment, the congressional creation of the council, and the communal holding of only subsurface rights on reservation land—are unique in the history of federal Indian policy (Pierce, 26–27).

A SYSTEM BUILT ON FLAWS

Through these unique moves, the United States failed to erect even the façade of an independent Osage polity. The primary flaw of the government created by the 1906 Act is its concentration of all governmental power in the hands of the holders of the original 2,229 shares of the mineral estate, who vote according to a corporate model based on shares held. Some Osages hold multiple shares, while others now hold extremely fractionated shares.

The Osages, robbed of their democracy, adapted to the tribal council system, working around the fundamental flaws of an imposed, corporate-style system, but those flaws are woven into the very fabric of the 1906 Act. Corporate interests seemingly got what they wanted, an entity that oil companies could deal with in extracting the mineral resources underneath the reservation. By and large, the council limited itself to the mineral estate, though with time the need for input into other issues became necessary (T. Wilson, *Underground,* 273–75). Unfortunately, the ultimate authority of the council has always been hamstrung by the fact that it is a creation of the U.S. Congress, elected in recent times by a small minority of Osages. Under the 1906 Act, the Osage people have no popularly elected officials. Osage shareholders, including me, elect officers who take up issues of interest to all Osage people. The Osage Tribal Council has a chief elected by its shareholders. The people as a whole have had no voice in their own affairs.

Thus, the vast majority of the descendants of those who chose constitutional democracy in 1881 have no shares and thus have not been able to vote or run for office. Those without headright interest have only been able to watch from the outside as people elected in an imposed form of government take up issues and make decisions that affect their lives.

Various Osage individuals and groups, including some members of the Osage Tribal Council, have protested this situation since at least 1917 (T. Wilson, *Underground,* 174). In 1964, a group of disaffected Osages formed the Osage Nation Organization (ONO) (T. Wilson, *Underground,* 190). ONO led the charge against the tribal council system for a generation, seeking restoration of the Osage form of government supplanted by the U.S. Congress in 1906. Though never reaching its goal of overturning the 1906 Act, ONO succeeded in paving the way for future actions (Pierce, 47).

One of the crucial actions of the ONO era was the court case *Logan v. Andrus.* Plaintiffs in *Logan* contended that the Tribal Council lacked jurisdiction to act beyond the interests of the mineral estate. The same Tenth Circuit Court of Appeals that would hear the *Fletcher* case decided in favor of the *Logan* defendants. Pierce says of the decision, "The Court of Appeals . . . revealed a remarkable lack of understanding of the concept of the sources of Indian sovereignty. For example it considered the language in an amendment to the Allotment Act which described the officers and council as the 'tribal government' as talismanic, that the mere assignment of that appellation 'resolves the question of the Council's general authority'" (46–47). This, as Pierce points out, runs against the grain of seven decades of contested practice for the council.

The litigation in *Fletcher* grew from *Logan.* Four plaintiffs, William Fletcher, Charles Pratt, Juanita West, and Betty Woody, filed suit in 1990 as representatives of a reconstituted Osage National Council. They sought "a determination of the validity of the 1881 Constitution," an issue expressly left open in *Logan,* and "a judgment declaring that the voting regulations [of the 1906 Act] are unconstitutional on their face and as applied" (Pierce,

48) based on the equal protection clause of the fourteenth amendment to the U.S. Constitution. Defendants, who included both members of the Osage Tribal Council and officials of the U.S. Department of the Interior and the Bureau of Indian Affairs, responded with separate motions to dismiss, with the council, crucially, asserting sovereign immunity against such legal action based on its congressionally mandated authority.

Judge James O. Ellison either decided against these motions or tried to bypass them and ruled in September 1992 that his court had sufficient jurisdiction "to mandate a referendum on the enfranchisement issue and provide a forum for resolution of the voting conundrum" (qtd. in Pierce, 50). Ellison did not, however, rule on the validity of the 1881 constitution or on the equal protection issue. Instead, he reached, in legal terms, a decision in equity, in effect deciding that the law as it stands was not sufficient in remedying the injustice experienced by the Osages as a people.

In response, Ellison created an Osage Commission, which established a referendum process. In 1993 two-thirds of Osage voters, including many not eligible to vote under the headright system, decided in favor of drafting a new constitution. In 1994, the Osages adopted the new constitution the commission drafted and, later the same year, elected members of a restored Osage National Council.

The restored Osage National Council was a mix of achievement and failure, which, of course, is one of the hallmarks of democratic governments. The *Fletcher* case and its predecessors are testament to the fact that elements of the tribe have never given up their fundamental belief in the Osage Constitution of 1881 and its model of citizenship. The reversal of that decision in 1997 was a devastating setback for the constitutionalists' ongoing dream of Osage self-determination. Just as important, the end of the new government put at risk all the new social programs that the National Council had created, programs that addressed needs the Osage Tribal Council had all but ignored, often for generations.

The basis of the Osage Tribal Council's successful appeal of the *Fletcher* decision was the concept of sovereign immunity.[15] Under U.S. law, federally recognized tribal governments, like federal and state governments, enjoy a freedom from being sued without their consent or an abrogation by Congress. The *Fletcher* court, in never ruling on a motion to dismiss from the tribal council an assertion that their sovereign immunity was being violated in the suit, opened the door for the successful appeal.

While sovereign immunity was the chief issue the appeals court took up, the court also ruled on other matters. It decided, for instance, that the Osages could not make changes to their form of government (as had happened in the post-*Fletcher* referendum) because the 1906 Act gave to the U.S. Congress alone the prerogative to prescribe the form of Osage government. Admitting that Congress played that role in no other cases, the Tenth Circuit announced, in effect, that the Osages were stuck with the situation that Congress had put them in in 1906 in the rush toward allotment and statehood (*Fletcher,* 1328).

The court further ruled that the 1906 Act prescribes the specific form of government for Osages (*Fletcher,* 1327). Crucially, they left open the issue of how the Osages can extend the franchise—or have Congress do so—while retaining the form of government prescribed by the 1906 Act, a strategy the current Osage Tribal Council has been attempting to follow. The Tenth Circuit judges also left open the question of whether or not the "headright restriction violates Individual Plaintiff's equal protection and due process rights" (*Fletcher,* 1329). In spite of these open questions, the court made clear its opinion that the U.S. Congress has the power to do what it did to the Osages in 1906 and retains that power to the present.[16]

The Tenth Circuit, thus, hewed closely to federal law in reversing the district court while overlooking the compelling issues of equity that Ellison took up in his decision. In doing so, the court sided with an anti-democratic minority in the face of the two-thirds of Osages who voted for a return to constitutional government. One year short of the hundredth anniversary of the United States' announcement of its unilateral abrogation of Osage constitutional democracy, the colonizers of the Osages (aided and abetted by the Osages who preferred the conditions of U.S. control) repeated their pattern of first putting themselves in position to be part of the flowering of justice among this continent's indigenes only to turn around and reimpose their own power. Except to those who place great faith in the American judicial system, this should come as no surprise. Judges sitting on a United States federal court decided in favor of the power of the United States Congress over and against the aspirations of people whose roots in the soil of this continent began with their descent from the stars in time immemorial.

The new Osage Constitution of 1994 was, like every constitution the U.S. Bureau of Indian Affairs helps write, a deeply flawed document that reflected micromanagement of the constitutional and governmental processes. Those flaws were, for many, worth living with in order to restore

Osage democracy, if only partially, and efforts at redress continue under the congressionally imposed system. But with the overturning of the reorganized government in 1997, all that, at least for the time being, became moot.

THE 1881 CONSTITUTION AND NATIVISM

Having traced out some of this complicated history, I want to briefly discuss some of the issues that arise from it. First, I am interested in coming to an understanding of the Osage Constitution through which the cultural achievements of the Osages, and by extension other tribal peoples with similar histories, are recognized, but which does not collapse into an uncritical and, I believe, ultimately unhelpful nativism. As I have considered my own response to the Osage constitutional crisis I have attempted to keep in mind Frantz Fanon's classic critique of nativism in *The Wretched of the Earth,* in the chapters titled "The Pitfalls of National Consciousness" and "On National Culture."

In these chapters, Fanon warns against the assumptions some intellectuals make about how their work affects the struggle for justice. He argues that the process through which we as scholars and writers become effective agents for change requires much more than championing native culture. "The native intellectual who comes back to his people by way of cultural achievements," Fanon argues, "behaves in fact like a foreigner. Sometimes he has no hesitation in using a dialect in order to show his will to be as near as possible to the people; but the ideas that he expresses and the preoccupations he is taken up with have no common yardstick to measure the real situation which the men and the women of his country know" (223).

Such an approach by the native intellectual—the holding up of native culture as equal or superior to that of the colonizer—becomes for Fanon an unwitting move that only serves to prompt a response of guilty sentiment (as in "Lo, the poor Indian") and makes no material difference in the struggle for real change. This is but one aspect of the strangely conditioned positionality of the native intellectual: skilled in the languages and techniques so often needed by those at the local level trying to make change, but also often thrust into the role of spokesperson or, worse, seeking out positions of leadership for which they have few of the necessary gifts. The native intellectual, according to Fanon, "wishes to attach himself to the people, but instead he only catches hold of their outer garments" (223–24).

In a paradox that even Fanon could never really resolve, intellectuals come to exist in a position where they either inappropriately draw too much attention and too many resources to their own needs, or they risk becoming little more than superficial appendages to movement toward a new future. And rather than becoming fascinated with one's own positionality or abandoning the intellectual needs of a struggle for change, Fanon suggests the intellectual should insert him- or herself into the actual lived lives of real people living in real time. This, he says, is the path toward finding, indeed creating, "the new man," and I will add, the new woman. "The native intellectual," Fanon writes, "must realize that the truths of a nation are in the first place its realities. He [or she] must go on until he [or she] has found the seething pot out of which the learning of the future will emerge" (225). That future, according to Kwame Anthony Appiah, ought to be a "postnativist" one in which we understand the fallible human dimension in which we struggle for a future.[17]

In the months and years that have followed the Tenth Circuit's 1997 decision, I have tried to understand my own responses with Fanon's critique in mind. Eventually, I have come to see myself as being part of the larger failure of the institutions of academic Native American studies to speak to contemporary Native needs. While I am not at all interested in posing as an Osage victim pointing a blaming figure at the failures of Native studies, my own attempts to respond to the real needs of my own tribal community have deepened my awareness of how much further Native studies needs to go in its development.

My conviction has become that those of us who do Native studies in the academy have focused on the programmatic possibilities on our campuses at the expense of the intellectual needs of Native communities. This problem, of course, is a deep one, and it can't be solved by complaining, whining, or creating another committee. Native studies will become sufficiently accountable to Native communities when those communities become its primary constituencies and when it is slowly working, situation by situation, to be part of remaking the Native world.

In the Osage case, merely opining on the wondrous genius of the Osage leaders who adopted the 1881 constitution without being aware of the contemporary ramifications of its continued suppression would be to walk around blinded by history. Moving toward a new vision of Native studies has meant doing those things scholars are equipped to do: delving into archives, learning the contours of Osage constitutional history, peering into the constitution's pages in search of its meanings and intentions, and developing a language by which to articulate its abiding importance to an Osage constitutional future.

I now think of the 1881 constitution as a gift bequeathed to future generations by those who developed and signed it. It is a gift that embodies the aspirations Osages have for our own peoplehood across generations and across time. It represents an attempt by our Osage forebears to give us the strongest sense we can have of who we are as a people. It seeks the surest footing for our continued existence on terms we can own as having been drawn from the wellspring of Osage reality.

Unfortunately, the most practical route toward addressing the problem of tribal membership under the system imposed by the U.S. Congress in 1906 has been to seek redress from that same Congress. The most recent Osage Tribal Council has successfully lobbied for a congressional revision of the 1906 Osage Allotment Act that recognizes the right of the Osages to determine their own membership and form of government (U.S. Public Law 108–431). The rights of shareholders to the financial benefits of the mineral estate are not infringed upon in this new legislation, which was signed by President George W. Bush on December 3, 2004. This new legislation goes so far as to claim that it "reaffirms" the inherent sovereign rights of the Osages to self-determination, though it does not mention the primary historical document of Osage self-determination (the Osage Constitution of 1881), much less why the U.S. government abolished self-determined Osage democracy in 1900.

Still, many Osages believe that their aspirations can be served by this new legislation, including some nonshareholders who have expressed gratitude toward Congress and President Bush for finally giving them an opportunity to feel as though they are really Osages. Others, especially those who understood their peoplehood to derive from much older sources, are committed to making the most of the opportunity whatever else they believe about how it came about.

The 1881 Osage Constitution has not been rendered meaningless by this turn of events, but its place within the political reality of Osages remains on the margins so long as the U.S. Congress maintains its role as the primary legitimator of Osage peoplehood. Even so, the constitution can play a significant role in contemporary Osage life, providing conceptions of the foundations of what it means to be modern Osages that the U.S. Congress has never affirmed—a sense of how tribal people can draw on their own strengths in meeting the challenges of modernity, an uninterrupted link to the strongest and most vital political and cultural wellsprings of the Osage past, and a clear and unambiguous statement of Osage intentions to exercise their rights as a people in this world. The constitution, of course, could also become with time less and less known as new generations articulate their sense of what it means to be Osage, even if it continues to be invoked as something vaguely important to our political past.

Either way, it should remain a living gift, not an heirloom to be venerated. Through it Osages would be wise to seek not a magical link to a mystical past, but an Osage-envisioned path to a self-determined future. And it is far from a perfect gift. Like all leaders, the Osage framers were products of their time and it reflects their own limits. To offer just one example, in 1884 the Osage National Council showed its fallibility by passing a law that declared that "the negroes residing within the Osage Nation shall be ordered to get out" (Fitzpatrick, 95). To be postnativist is to recall and resist such imperfections. It is to come to grips with the ease with which we can all be blind to justice, even when we ourselves are so much in need of a measure.

In this way, the Osage Constitution of 1881 and documents like it demand status within contemporary discussions of Native American literature. Leaving such a document to the historians, lawyers, and political scientists risks missing the beauty of the linguistic transaction that occurred when those Osage leaders worked through the creation of this text, which would forever represent their best attempt to negotiate the Osage encounter with modernity. They created not only a document, but a vision. They practiced a form of what I have called "intellectual sovereignty." Indeed, one of the several iterations of that concept, Scott Lyons's idea of "rhetorical sovereignty," sums up the way Osage leaders asserted control, in Lyons's terms, over their own communicative needs.

This adds one more reason that the development of Native American literature and criticism should be an inclusive enterprise in which a broad range of written and oral Native expression can be considered. "Can one fracture Native literature," Jace Weaver asks, "and segregate orature as a more 'pristine' Native literary type? Or isn't there still something 'Indian' about it regardless of its form or the language in which it speaks?" (*That the People*, 24). Along with fitting almost ideally into Weaver's definition of "communitist" literature, which places the highest priority on the active pursuit of preserving and promoting community, the Osage Constitution also helps demonstrate the efficacy of not drawing too thick a line between oral and written, traditional and modern.

The Osage Constitution sits at a critical nexus of Osage experience and the modern world. Following Homi Bhabha, it might be tempting to find it a text of colonial mimicry. Yet, it mimics a Cherokee text that was by 1881 at least two generations removed from the Cherokees who developed it from the U.S. Constitution. Further, it was, for Osages, clearly a vehicle for furthering what they thought of as a way of life and being that was very much Osage. "The postmodernists might laugh at claims of prioritizing insider status," Womack writes, "questioning the very nature of what constitutes an insider and pointing out that no pure . . . Native point of view exists" (5).

For many Osages, though, the Constitution was a gift bequeathed to the future with theorizing and agonizing that was as profound as any contemporary piece of literary criticism. "We might remind ourselves," says Womack, "that authenticity and insider and outsider status are, in fact, often discussed in Native communities, especially given the historical reality that outsiders have so often been the ones interpreting things Indian. Further, it seems foolhardy to me to abandon a search for the affirmation of a national literary identity simply to fall in line with the latest literary trend" (5–6).

In such a search in the Osage context, the constitution becomes the first important document in the history of Osage written literature. Womack calls for

> a literary criticism that emphasizes Native resistance movements against colonialism, confronts racism, discusses sovereignty and Native nationalism, seeks connections between literature and liberation struggles, and finally, roots literature in land and culture. This criticism emphasizes unique Native worldviews and political realities, searches for differences as often as similarities, and attempts to find Native literature's place in Indian country, rather than Native literature's place in the canon. (11)

The Osage Constitution provides an excellent Osage starting point for just that sort of criticism.

The Osages have been fortunate to have produced a number of successful writers, including John Joseph Mathews, Kenneth Jacob Jump,

Louis Burns, Carter Revard, George Tinker, Rennard Strickland, Dennis McAuliffe, Maria Tallchief, Elise Paschen, and Charles Red Corn. The genealogy of Osage writing looks different, however, when the framers of the Osage Constitution are included. Osage writing in this reading is no longer something mastered first by mixed-blood elites (i.e., Mathews), while the traditional people wait generations for similar achievements on their side. Instead, writing in English is a technology that our best and brightest traditional leaders, at a portentous moment in history, embraced as a means toward the future.

This brings us full circle to Whitman. Walt Whitman's speculations on the future of American democracy in "Democratic Vistas" are in many ways a classic articulation of the nativist point of view. In his confidence in what he figures the "native stock" of the continent, Whitman displays a famous disregard for the potential of Africans, Asians, and Osages, for that matter, to participate in the sweeping breeze of democracy (522). When Whitman says, "America has yet morally and artistically originated nothing," we see him as a product of his time, unable to see the moral and artistic achievements on this continent that predated the arrival of Europeans on these shores (530). At the same time, though, his "Vistas" allow us into the mind of the intellectual deeply engaged in the question of a national future. It is in these moments of insight that he shines a light on the intellectual processes of the Osages and other indigenous people.

For how can we help but think of our own time when he says of his, "Never was there, perhaps, more hollowness than at present, and here in the United States. Genuine belief seems to have left us. The underlying principles of the States are not honestly believed in (for all this hectic glow, and these melodramatic screamings), nor is humanity itself believed in" (510). Whitman's vistas are places from which he gains perspective over the largeness of the landscape and the longness of history. From them, though he admits he can only see the broadest outlines, he also sees what is not so clear from a closer view. In one of the most lyric passages of the essay he writes:

> There is, in sanest hours, a consciousness, a thought that rises, independent, lifted out from all else, calm, like the stars, shining eternal. This is the thought of identity—yours for you, whoever you are, as mine for me. Miracle of miracles, beyond statement, most spiritual and vaguest of earth's dreams, yet hardest basic fact, and only entrance to all facts. In

such devout hours, in the midst of the significant wonders of heaven and earth . . . creeds, conventions, fall away and become of no account before this simple idea. Under the luminousness of real vision, it alone takes possession, takes value. (529)

An air of tragedy hangs in these glorious words as we stand and consider what we can see from the democratic vistas of the Osage constitutional crisis. Here we have the same yearning for clarity of vision, simplicity of purpose, and philosophical innovation in the midst of respect for the way that beauty becomes manifest in history and tradition. Whitman's words are a reminder that, in spite of the history of betrayal the Osages have experienced, a vision worth pursuing remains.

It is this vision of the Osage framers that puts their achievement on a par with the nonfiction writing of William Apess before them. Like him, the framers sought to achieve in writing something that would help them forge a path to a more just future. In doing so, they put their experiences on the line as they inscribed themselves on paper. As important, they, like Apess, found themselves needing to lead, and they found in writing an important aspect of their leadership. In his manifesto on Native independence, Taiaiake Alfred looks forward to a new generation of leaders, who "will be able to interact with the changing mainstream society from a position of strength rooted in cultural confidence. These leaders will practice a new style of Native politics that will reject the colonial assumptions and mentalities that have allowed state domination to continue" (133). This reading of Osage leadership and the constitution that derived from it suggests that just such a new generation emerged well over a century ago for the Osages. The challenge, then, is to figure out how to follow their lead.

Yet for all the genius of Osage leadership, Whitman could no more recognize among the Osages the impulses he outlined in "Democratic Vistas" than did the United States policy makers, who finally undid the Osage and other experiments in democracy. Our stories, our abilities, and our rights to reach high toward the stars from which we came did not, seemingly, enter Whitman's mind. For I cannot believe the Osage experience would have ever registered for him when he wrote,

I can conceive a community, today and here, in which, on a sufficient scale, the perfect personalities, without noise meet; say in some pleasant western settlement or town, where a couple of hundred best men and women, of ordinary worldly status, have by luck been drawn together, with nothing extra of genius or wealth, but virtuous, chaste, industrious, cheerful, resolute, friendly, and devout. I can conceive such a community organized in running order, powers judiciously delegated. (536)

Perhaps the Osage attempt to live out their conception of the sort of community Whitman imagined would never have succeeded, given the constraints of the historical situation that Native nations found themselves in by the turn of the twentieth century. What a shame, especially for those of us who care about democracy and the crucible in which it currently exists, that we'll never know what would have happened, though many Osages still dream of making of that vision as much as can still be made. It would be a story worthy of the American ideals that persist in so many people's minds, rather than a telling reminder of just how often those ideals have failed.

CONCLUSION

Understanding the crisis of Osage democracy requires coming to grips with the complexities of history as it has been lived over the past century. In doing so, the challenge for the intellectual is not simply to celebrate and lionize the Osage past, but to present and interpret our present realities in all their complexity. Fanon's critique, in this reading, is not so much a guide for how to engage in committed intellectual work as a challenge to confront the existential realities from which such committed work needs to emerge. It is an invitation to understand the ways our current intellectual world is failing our most important constituencies and a means for moving toward a new vision of who we are as scholars and what Native America can be intellectually.

Such responses help those who seek to recover the sense of sovereignty and self-determination embodied in both the philosophical traditions of tribal nations and their emerging literatures—with that literature being defined broadly enough to include such things as constitutions, novels, poems, newspapers, translations, and contemporary songs. Only by taking Osage literature in its fullness can we understand how it is that the constitutional process of the Osages links us as a people to, for instance, the popular aspirations that prompted the French Revolution in the eighteenth century, the slave uprisings in nineteenth-century Haiti, the revolutionary struggles in Bolivia and other parts of the Americas, the ongoing anticolonial struggles in Asia and Africa, the 1994 peace accords in that part of the Mayan world that exists inside the borders of Guatemala, and the continuing struggles for indigenous autonomy in New Zealand, Australia, and around the world.

At the same time, we must continue to understand each of the small parts of this history and process as occupying its own integral psychic, cultural, and spiritual space. Near the end of his essay, Whitman speaks to the dynamics of the Osage crisis and, as important, to the intellectual needs of the communities that scholars in Native American studies have so often declared themselves committed to. As he writes, "Thus we presume to write, as it were, upon things that exist not, and travel by maps yet unmade, and a blank. But the throes of birth are upon us" (527).

3

The Work of Indian Pupils: Narratives of Learning in Native American Literature

*A*s the 1880s were drawing to a close and the Osages were nearing the end of the first decade of their experiment in constitutional democracy, the print shop of the Santee Normal Training School, which educated Dakota and other Native people in the late nineteenth century, produced a leaflet describing the history and philosophy of the school. The leaflet was a single sheet of paper 7½ x 4 inches, printed on both sides and folded twice to create six panels (three on each side). The cover identifies the leaflet as a "souvenir," which indicates it was something visitors to the school could read and then take away as a reminder of what they had seen.

I imagine stacks of these leaflets in a reception area outside the principal's office. Perhaps a secretary, some other staff underling, or specially designated Dakota students passed them out to people coming through for a tour, an inspection, or some other official visit. The leaflet is dated 1888–89, which indicates it was probably one in a series of such souvenirs. Opening the cover, the first page reports on the history of the school, saying, "The Santee Normal Training School, now under the charge of the American Missionary Association, was . . . started nineteen years ago, in 1870, though its beginnings were still back of that. It was established for the purpose of raising up teachers, preachers, interpreters, and business men for the Dakota or Sioux nation." The leaflet goes on to discuss normal and manual training (or teacher and industrial training) as the basis for the school's philosophy, with teacher training, religious instruction, and more complicated subjects, including physiology and philosophy, making up important aspects of what the school taught. It goes on to describe the school's work in a classically Christian missionary manner, saying, "The great object of our work is to prepare a native agency that shall work as leaven for the regeneration of their own people."

Religious training, according to the pamphlet, was central to preparing that leaven, as "Indians are so thoroughly controlled in all their ideas and customs by their heathen religion that no change of life is possible except through a change of religion. Their religious philosophy makes their idea of life so wrong that nothing but the true religion can set them right." The curriculum listed on one of the backside panels includes instruction in biblical history and theology, but also tends to civil religion. United States history and civil government are included in the curriculum, and a Dakota translation of the preamble to the U.S. Constitution takes up the other back panel.

That use of a Native language marks an important difference between the Santee School, a missionary enterprise, and the Carlisle School, founded in 1879 in Carlisle, Pennsylvania, by Richard Henry Pratt, and later schools modeled after it, which were government operated (Child, 1ff.). Part of Pratt's famous educational philosophy was to prohibit the use of Native languages, creating a linguistic distance from students' home communities to parallel the physical distance that was already enforced by being at the boarding school. Schools like Santee, which predated Carlisle, operated closer to the homes of their students and some saw Native languages differently. At Santee, simultaneous instruction was given in Dakota and English so that graduates of the school would be, according to the pamphlet, "competent instructors among their own people."

But that difference aside, by 1889 schools from Santee to Carlisle to Chemawa in Oregon had become crucial components in an era of Indian policy in which Native youth were targeted to be instruments of transformation as many of their tribes entered full-scale into modernity. School time for these students was split between very basic academics and industrial training. For the girls and young women, industrial training meant learning domestic work—keeping a house, cooking, sewing, and the like. For the boys and young men, agricultural work was primary, with blacksmithing, carpentering, shoemaking, and printing being other more specialized options (Lomawaima, 4ff.).

The boys and young men in the print shop make the Santee souvenir a compelling item of material print culture. Virtually all publications from

STUDIES PURSUED.

Arithmetic—Advanced	41
" Intermediate	51
" Primary	83—175
Biblical Theology	24
Botany	26
Civil Government	6
English Composition	169
Geography	68
History—Bible	27
" United States	43—70
Methods of Teaching	11
Music—Instrumental	13
" Vocal	162—175
Physiology and Hygiene	112
Reading—English	174
" Dakota	49
Writing	139

INDUSTRIAL WORK—BOYS.

Blacksmith Shop	32
Carpenter Shop	53
Shoeshop	28
Farm	88
Printing Office	15

INDUSTRIAL WORK—GIRLS.

Sewing, Cutting and Fitting, Cooking, Laundry Work and Housekeeping	83

This little leaflet is the work of Indian pupils.

PREAMBLE

OF THE

Constitution of the United States

IN THE DAKOTA LANGUAGE.

WOIÇIÇAĜE WOOPE KIN.

United States en unkoyatepi kin, odakonkiciyapi sanpa suta unkaĝapi kta, woowotanna kin eunhdepi kta, unkoyatepi en wowaŝbadan unyuecetupi kte, ataya wowinape okihiunkiciyapi kta, wicookiciwaŝte unkaĝapi kte, qa tawaiçiyapi wowaŝte kin unkiyepi qa unkicincapi on tinsa unhdubapi kta e on etanhan, United States America etanhan kin makoce kin en, woiçiçaĝe woope kin de eunhdepi qa unyusutapi.

We, the People of the United States, in order to form a more perfect union, establish justice, insure domestic tranquility, provide for the common defence, promote the general welfare, and secure the blessings of liberty to ourselves and our posterity, do ordain and establish this Constitution for the United States of America.

Souvenir

SANTEE

Normal Training School

AMERICAN MISSIONARY ASSOCIATION

INDIAN SCHOOL.

SANTEE AGENCY, NEBRASKA.

A. L. RIGGS, A. M., *Principal.*

1888-89.

A WORD ABOUT THE SCHOOL.

The Santee Normal Training School, now under the charge of the American Missionary Association, was definitely started nineteen years ago, in 1870, though its beginnings were still back of that. It was established for the purpose of raising up teachers, preachers, interpreters, and business men for the Dakota or Sioux nation. In raising the standard of higher education for the Indian, our progress has necessarily been slow. We have had to plant the very idea of the thing in the Indian mind and carefully tend its growth. We find our success in the revolution that has taken place in the ideas of this people, who are now anxiously seeking educational advantages; and our pupils are already filling places of usefulness as artizans, teachers and preachers among their own people.

INDUSTRIAL EDUCATION.

In a certain sense industrial training is at the very foundation of our work. It is not incidental or accidental but fundamental to our theory of education. We believe in it as a condition to true self-knowledge, and as the necessary avenue to the knowledge of the world without. And, furthermore, we regard manual training and industrial occupations as the best means for that discipline of mind and will which gives the fibre of high moral character. Hence, with us, industrial education does not mean merely teaching "how to make a living," but rather "how to enter into life." And our aim in all occupations, in the house, the farm, or the shops, is to make all subserve this end.

NORMAL TRAINING.

Our school is a normal training-school in the double sense of being loyal to the normal or natural laws of education, and as a training-school for teachers. The great object of our work is to prepare a native agency that shall work as leaven for the regeneration of their own people. Hence, while we plan to fit them as individuals for citizenship with us, we are also careful to maintain their common interest in, and sympathy with their own race. This gives law to our methods and makes it needful to use two languages—the English and the vernacular—in order to make them competent instructors among their own people. Were it not required on this account, there is yet no other way so good for giving an idiomatic knowledge of English as by the study of the comparative grammar of these languages.

A MISSIONARY SCHOOL.

Indians are so thoroughly controlled in all their ideas and customs by their heathen religion that no change of life is possible except through a change of religion. Their religious philosophy makes their idea of life so wrong that nothing but the true religion can set them right. Hence the hope of their regeneration does not lie in education or in civilization, but in the Gospel and Spirit of Jesus the Christ. Education and civilization are of use only as instruments of this gospel. Our aim, therefore, is to bring everything into a religious atmosphere, and make Christianity the ruling power of life. And we confidently expect our pupils to become, in one way and another, missionaries of the new life they find. Nor are we disappointed.

HIGHER EDUCATION FOR INDIANS.

Higher and lower are only comparative terms, depending on the standard by which we compare. Though our programme of studies is not high as compared with schools in our white communities, yet it means a great deal to be able to teach Indians understandingly the elements of geometry, algebra, physiology, physical geography, natural philosophy, and mental science.

Souvenir from the Santee National Training School, Santee Agency, Nebraska, 1888–89.

the boarding-school era, both large and small, were published in the schools' print shops by young Native workers. In the case of the souvenir, however, the work of those who did the printing is interestingly elucidated.

The souvenir is printed in two colors, with the main text in black. On the cover, which takes up the right-hand third of the exterior side of the single sheet, the word *Souvenir* appears in red in a fancy type underscored with a fancy design. All three panels of the outside of the document feature a thin red border. In the bottom left-hand corner of the exterior side, in two lines of tiny type and red ink, are the words, "This little leaflet is the work of Indian pupils."

The phrase is an intriguing one. At first glance, the young printers themselves might seem like the writers of this small phrase, as if they injected a bit of Native agency into a document that otherwise spoke for the students and about them, but kept their own voices muffled (like so much of what came out of Indian boarding schools in the late nineteenth century). It's tempting to imagine one of the older boys secretly setting the type of the phrase, then sneaking it into the rest of the red-ink press run—a daring moment of a young Native student making himself part of the history of Native nonfiction writing. Or, if that seems too far-fetched, imagine that the boys and young men in the print shop somehow asked their supervisor to allow them this presence in the document.

Neither of those scenarios seems likely. The prose in the phrase, short though it may be, lingers a bit too long in the realm of the precious to have come from the mind of a Santee student. Much more likely, the phrase is the work of an English teacher or perhaps a print shop manager. At best, those students in the print shop who could read were probably happy to see themselves and their work highlighted in this small way.

Regardless, it is still interesting to consider what this small document from the Santee School provokes in a broader discussion of education, intellectual history, and Native literature. In similar fashion to the way Apess moved toward the leading edge of modern American print culture and the public discourse it engendered, the printers at Santee and other schools found themselves encountering one of the hallmarks of modernity, the printing press, even as they were wrapped up in broader negotiations over how American Indian people would relate to modernity. This chapter is an engagement in that larger discussion about education for modernity and the ways that an appreciation of its pervasiveness impacts Native intellectual and literary history. I start by looking at this little document from the Santee School because it provides a different lens through which to see American Indian articulations of educational experience. It provides a starting point for thinking about a range of historical and contemporary narratives, most of them nonfiction, that provide a way to move toward a greater understanding not just of what Native experiences of education have been, but what those experiences have meant and continue to mean to Native communities.

THE TRAJECTORY OF NATIVE EDUCATION

Modern educational experience has been a pervasive feature of Native American life for the past three centuries. For all its importance, though, education has rarely been the focus of Native academic discourse outside its own specialized area. For instance, Russell Thornton's recent edited volume on the status of Native American studies, *Studying Native America: Problems and Prospects,* includes little specific evaluation of educational discourse. Part of this, no doubt, comes from resistance among some Native scholars against subtle and not-so-subtle pressures to be funneled into educational schools and teacher training programs.

As Jorge Noriega says, "Tellingly, of those Indians completing a college education, well over half have been tracked into programs leading them to pursue 'educational vocations' through which they will usually dispense more of the same to younger Indians" ("American Indian Education," 389). This is part and parcel of what Noriega identifies as a basic impulse of colonial schooling. "Education," he writes, "has been the mechanism by which colonialism has sought to render itself effectively permanent, creating the conditions by which the colonized could be made essentially *self*-colonizing, eternally subjugated in psychic and intellectual terms and thus eternally self-subordinating in economic and political terms" (374).

A lot of terrific Native scholars have done important work from within educational programs. But one of those scholars, Karen Gayton Swisher, argues that white educators' control of the discourse in those programs has limited the ability of Native scholars to limn the depths of their own educational existence. As Swisher argues, "The voices that communicate intergenerational meaning are missing from this literature. How can an outsider really understand life on reservations, the struggle for recognition, sovereignty, economic development, preservation of language and culture?" (86).

This chapter takes up what Swisher calls for when she says, "Indian professionals have a role and responsibility in defining what is best for us in Indian education" (88). Scholars of Native literature have an important part to play in Swisher's call as the history of Native writing is, among other things, a history of Native education. Looking at the sweep of that history, I am interested in furthering an intellectual agenda that centers on Native leadership of Native educational programs.

Doing so requires an understanding not just of the boarding-school system, which is at the center of historical studies of Native education, but of the trajectory of Native education, from its origins in traditional communities to its present manifestations. Looking at various texts that represent Native educational experiences across this spectrum, I will argue here that only an approach that recognizes the synchronicity of educational experiences across time makes sufficient sense of who Natives are and where Natives have been as students and teachers.

I will start with a discussion of the boarding-school era and the policies that led to it, then move to the present, arguing along the way for a new agenda in educational and literary scholarship that encompasses the fullness of who Natives have become, not just as students but as leaders (teachers, professors, professionals) who have emerged on the other side of the educational process. Native-authored texts provide a rich, under-utilized resource in that process.

These Native texts are, in an important way, the backbone of Native American literature. Rarely does a Native author come to his or her vocation without at least some reflection on the educational process that led to his or her taking up the challenge of becoming a writer. This is why Native educational texts are a microcosm of Native literary history. The movement from nonfiction autobiographical accounts of education to more recent fiction, poetry, and essays helps strengthen the case that nonfiction has been at the center of the development of a Native American written literary tradition.

Tracing how that tradition has grown from its nonfiction roots to the diversity of genres in this contemporary era is an important feature of this chapter. But I am in no way suggesting that the schools somehow created a literary tradition in a sort of quid pro quo. All of these writers brought something to school with them that helped them invent themselves as writers, whether that was a background in the sort of traditional life that inspired the Osage Constitution or a determination to overcome the hurdles of oppression so evident in Apess's writing.

Thus, more than looking at what researchers have typically taken up in considering education, I am interested in expanding the boundaries of what Native writers talk about when they invoke education. As Maori scholar Linda Tuhiwai Smith points out, most educational research among indigenous people "has been crisis research," seeking reasons for the failure of indigenous people, for instance, to graduate from high school and college at higher rates (174).

While some are hesitant to take on the educational establishment by calling for indigenous writers to tackle the topic of education, Smith avers that the problem has been that Western knowledge is based on an a priori assumption that indigenous knowledge is, by definition, suspect. "The objects of research," she says, "do not have a voice and do not contribute to research or science. In fact, the logic of the argument would suggest that it is simply impossible, ridiculous even, to suggest that the object of research can contribute to anything" (61).

Schools, as Smith argues forcefully, have been the primary loci in propagating that point of view. Thus, problems occur even when programs and disciplines try to reorient themselves to indigenous forms of knowledge. "Attempts to 'indigenize' colonial academic institutions and/or individual disciplines within them," she says, "have been fraught with major struggles over what counts as knowledge, as language, as literature, as curriculum and as the role of intellectuals, and over the critical function of the concept of academic freedom" (65).

Rather than add my voice to the considerable chorus of those who detail the faults of Western-style education for Native people, I will suggest in this chapter that Native educational history is best regarded not as a problem to be solved, but as a journey that we are in the middle of. As travelers on that journey, Natives inherit wisdom and foibles from the experiences of those who have gone before. That journey has been, as I will describe here, one of devolution, not just from traditional tribal forms of education to Western ones, but from somewhat benign institutions like the Santee School, which recognized, albeit in an inscribed way, Native potential to a national system of boarding schools that operated with the assumption that Native learning was something to be wiped away and replaced by docile manual skills. Indeed, an important feature of the argument here is that manual training as it developed in the Pratt era specifically undermined earlier educational efforts, both traditional and colonial, that saw the importance of training Native learners to be leaders.

Vine Deloria argues that thinking through issues of education is central to the fortunes of Native people. He suggests that recovering traditional models of Native education is crucial, not because they are a magic bullet that restore some vague notion of cultural pride, but because "the way the old people educated themselves and their young gives a person a sense that education is more than the process of imparting and receiving information, that it is the very purpose of human society and that human societies cannot really flower until they understand the parameters of possibilities that the human personality contains" ("Knowing and Understanding," 139).[1] Education, in this reading, is less about curriculum and more about probing the depths of the philosophical terrain of what it means to be a Native learner in the contemporary world.

As Emerson and Whitman provided counterpoints in the first two chapters, here I have used another non-Native author, W. E. B. Du Bois, for the same purpose. One of the interesting features of Native educational discourse in the boarding-school era is the near complete lack of Native voices insisting on higher education for Natives. Addressing the issue in the present brings in such voices, including Deloria, Swisher, and Smith. But Du Bois's work allows me to highlight what that earlier lacuna has meant for Native discourse.

For Du Bois, whose seminal work, *The Souls of Black Folk* (1903), appeared in the heyday of the boarding-school era, higher education was the "central problem" of African American life and Du Bois's critique of the status quo in African American education is the engine that drives *Souls.* As he writes in his *Souls* essay, "The Training of Black Men," "I sit with Shakespeare and he winces not. Across the color line I move arm in arm with Balzac and Dumas, where smiling men and welcoming women glide in gilded halls. From out of the caves of evening that swing between the strong-limbed earth and the tracery of the stars, I summon Aristotle and Aurelius and what soul I will, and they come graciously with no scorn nor condescension. So, wed with Truth, I dwell above the Veil. Is this the life you grudge us, O knightly America?" (87). This is but one example of how Du Bois attempted to elevate the discussion of African American education in a way unparalleled at that time in Native writing.

Du Bois's voice joins the others in considering the past and future of the educational and intellectual journey of Native America. These voices testify to the fact that, wherever Native people are going, we have to learn how to get there. That, in the end, is why Native leadership of Native discourse is so important. As Linda Tuhiwai Smith says, "To resist is to retrench in the margins, retrieve what we were and remake ourselves" (4). To get there is to learn.

BOARDING-SCHOOL LIFE

The printer boys at Santee were just some of the many young Native men around the country who learned printing as a trade as part of their educational experience. At Santee, their other choices were to work in the blacksmith shop, carpenter shop, or shoe shop, or on a farm. Girls and young women worked at sewing, cutting and fitting, cooking, laundry, and housekeeping. Of all these, the print shop provided the most elaborate mechanical education.

The print shop workers at the more famous Carlisle School in Pennsylvania provide an example of how those who ran the schools regarded their charges. The *Indian Helper,* a weekly publication that reported school news to interested people around the country, announced to its readers each week that it was "printed by Indian boys, but edited by the Man-on-the-band-stand, who is not an Indian."[2] The paper also included a standing offer to send "a photographic group of the 13 Carlisle Indian Printer boys, on a card 4½ x 6½ inches, worth 20 cents when sold by itself" to anyone who purchased five ten-cent subscriptions to the paper. No doubt, whoever wrote "This little booklet is the work of Indian pupils" had the same thing in mind for the Santee souvenir as the editor of Carlisle's *Indian Helper* did; the effort to highlight the young men in the print shop seems designed to prompt people to feel some extra connection beyond the printed words to what was happening in Indian schools.

The relative ease with which people like Marianna Burgess, the Carlisle teacher behind the Man-on-the-band-stand persona, could draw attention to the work done in boarding-school print shops was convenient given that such work also represented the most advanced training a student at an Indian boarding school was going to receive. The newspaper, program, or report in the hands of a reader was itself the evidence of pedagogical success, even more so than what the document actually said. Technical acumen and manual dexterity were prized above rhetorical skill or creative use of the written word. As a short piece in Burgess's *Indian Helper* comments proudly in 1891,

> Martin Archiquette, Charlie Dagenett, Yamie Leeds, and Levi St. Cyr are printers and could have set up and printed their own graduating essays. Yamie and Levi could have copied theirs upon the typewriter. This knowledge of business was obtained while taking the regular school course. Are not these superior advantages? If dependent upon their own exertions for a living now, each one of the boys mentioned could earn a comfortable living at the trade he has partially acquired. Schools where the knowledge of a useful trade may be acquired while gaining the book knowledge necessary to take one through life respectably are few and far between. Let us be thankful that we are in such a place and make the very best use of the chance that is now ours! And let us stay long enough to get an abundant supply of useful knowledge and experience. (12 June 1891)

Clearly, Burgess and her cohorts at schools across the continent thought of their students almost exclusively as needing trades and vocations.

But what about the boys in the print shop themselves? What did they think of their work? Imagine a young Santee student sounding out the phrase "Indians are thoroughly controlled in all their ideas and customs by their heathen religion." I would like to think that at least sometimes two or three young men sneaking stolen cigarettes on a break discussed the things they printed, laughing at the simplified ways their teachers thought of them, coming up with their own descriptions of the inadequacies of the new world they were learning to be part of, or remembering fondly things learned at the feet of grandmothers, uncles, and older brothers. Mostly, though, I imagine the industrial smell of wet ink on newsprint and the whirring repetition of drums spinning, churning out copy after copy of souvenirs, newpapers, class materials, and whatever else the school's print shop manager found to keep the shop and the boys busy.

The worth of the Santee souvenir is in the way it provides a window into what is an immense history of Native American education. That history is daunting for many reasons, but perhaps mostly because it seems so simple to judge and also so difficult. Native American histories of going to school include some of the most straightforward accounts of the worst and most violent experiences of colonization—a simple look at the graveyards at off-reservation boarding schools attests to the killing power of homesickness set against an ideology of eradicating all traces of Indianness from a young person's life.

At the same time, making a tempting comparison of the boarding-school experience to Hiroshima, concentration camps, or slavery pushes the limits of comparison. Nothing good, after all, comes from exploding a nuclear bomb, creating a place to exterminate an unwanted population, or enslaving people and forcing them to work. The history of Native education has included elements of these other oppressive historical situations, especially confinement and forced labor. But the fact that this most central experience of Native history happened inside schools, institutions that many people saw and still see as necessary to the future of Native people, gives the history of Native education a character that cannot be reduced to these other moments in history.

The federal government of the United States first took responsibility for indigenous education in the early part of the nineteenth century, when it appropriated money to establish schools for tribal groups that did not already have them (Lomawaima, 2). Prior to that, of course, individual schools, almost all of them connected to Christian churches, had worked on the project of Native education. The history of American Indian writing in North America, in fact, dovetails with one important moment in that history—the founding of Dartmouth College in New Hampshire.

Eleazar Wheelock, who founded Dartmouth, had originally planned to start a school for New England Indians. His protégé, the Mohegan writer Samsom Occom, had been a student of Wheelock's in his younger days and eventually worked alongside his mentor in starting a higher educational enterprise. Occom, in fact, made a long trip to England to raise money for the school. When Occom returned with £12,000, Wheelock welcomed him with the news that plans had changed and the goal of Dartmouth would now be the education of the sons of white New Englanders rather than Indians (Weaver, *That the People*, 50–51).

Though a mythology of Dartmouth as a place for the education of Native youth has persisted throughout the school's history, Occom's worry that Dartmouth would become primarily an institution for the white sons of New England was well-founded, and very few Natives passed through its halls until the 1970s (Garrod and Larimore, 8). Indeed, Occom's work as a writer has arguably been more important to history than his role in Native education (Weaver, *That the People*, 50ff.).

Wheelock's was just one of many failed experiments in Indian education. Harvard and William and Mary, at least in their early years, were committed to educating Native youth, but those commitments faltered after a very few years (Carney, 24–31). But schools, in spite of these prominent failures, played a crucial role in Native history. As Delores Huff argues,

> Indians were defeated not by military force . . . but by politically restructuring the institution of education to mold a colonial ethos. Colonialism that imprisons young minds with the concept of "racial/ethnic inferiority" is much more tyrannical than brute force. Labeled as "pacification," the education developed by missions and the Indian service encouraged young Indian people to lose confidence in their own leaders and their own people and view their history and culture as second-rate. Ultimately, this form of colonialism chipped away at Indian culture, making it more and more difficult for each succeeding generation to lead autonomous and pro-active lives. (1)

These colonial institutions stand in contrast to the efforts among individual tribes to create, or at least control, their own educational systems in the nineteenth century. The Choctaws and Cherokees are the most prominent examples, with the neighborhood schools of the Choctaw and the Cherokee Male and Female Seminaries standing as early examples of institutions formed by tribal nations that took up the reins to provide formal education for their own youth.[3]

Yet it is the schools founded in the latter part of the nineteenth century, like the Santee School, that have deservedly garnered the most attention in contemporary discussions of Native education. While the era of boarding-school education had its roots in the mission schools of a much earlier generation, the crucial turning point in that era came in 1879 with the establishment of Richard Henry Pratt's Carlisle School in a former army barracks at Carlisle, Pennsylvania.

FOUNDING CARLISLE

In the aftermath of the Red River War of 1874–75, the U.S. Army took custody of thirty-three Cheyennes, two Arapahoes, one Caddo, twenty-seven Kiowas, and nine Comanches the U.S. Government identified as "Indian activists and offenders to be incarcerated and treated as prisoners of war" (Mann, 40). "Included in the group" of seventy-two enemy combatants, says Henrietta Mann, "were eighteen innocent Cheyennes, who were arbitrarily and randomly cut from the end of a line of men because darkness fell before the end of the selection process could be completed" (40). Among the group were also the wife and daughter of one of the Comanche chiefs and a Cheyenne woman, "*Mo-chi,* Buffalo Calf Woman, the wife of Medicine Water, who was charged with having struck a white pioneer in the head with an axe" (40).

At Fort Sill, in Indian Territory, Lieutenant Richard Henry Pratt, who had previously commanded a black cavalry regiment, became these prisoners' jailer. Making their way to the nearest railhead in Kansas, Pratt escorted the prisoners through Fort Leavenworth, Indianapolis, Nashville, Atlanta, and Jacksonville (Mann, 41).[4] Weaver points out the political motivation of these incarcerations, making them an integral part of the history of the United States' practice of jailing war prisoners without the benefit of a trial or legal hearing. In an act of defiance, one of the Cheyenne leaders, Grey Beard, "jumped from the speeding train carrying them to incarceration. The locomotive was halted. Grey Beard was hunted down and shot as he fled," never having been found guilty of anything, accused only of defending his homeland (Weaver, *Turtle Goes to War,* 42). According to Mann,

Viewed from the Cheyenne perspective, this exile was a disaster; banishment or isolation was the sentence for intratribal murder, the most extreme . . . behavior in their social structure. Thus, symbolically, this separation sundered their very social fabric. The men and the woman had committed no crime in their cultural context to warrant such harsh punishment. As their prophets had predicted, the strange white man had even stranger concepts that were anathema to the The People's way of life. (40–41)

The prisoners were transported all the way to the Atlantic coast of the United States to Fort Marion in St. Augustine, Florida. Impossibly far away from his charges' homes, Pratt did not have to worry about any sort of breakout. More important, these prisoners became hostages to ensure the good behavior of the people left behind.

Pratt instituted military discipline in the prison and promoted the use of English among the prisoners. His wife, Anna Mason Pratt, and former teachers from the local community offered classes. The prisoners became known around the United States, drawing attention from representatives of the Smithsonian Institution and from reformer Harriet Beecher Stowe, who wrote two articles about them (Mann, 41). As Mann argues, these prisoners "adapted to Pratt's routine and ideology. They were forced to become bicultural, but in so doing maintained a strong tribal identity" (42). Mann points to the tradition of "ledger painting," which grew from the Fort Marion experience, in which some of the prisoners produced works of art on the one type of canvas they could access—blank pages of ledger books.

Those pictures are precursors to later marketable works of Native art, and this beginning of an art movement is one of three modern traditions of contemporary Native America in which Fort Marion played an important role. The second is the rise of the intertribal sociality that later helped produce American Indian powwow culture. People from different tribes at Fort Marion shared songs and their situation provided a forum for developing the ethic of respect for particularity and sameness that remains an ideal of intertribal gatherings and organizations. Intertribalism, importantly, stands in marked contrast to Pan-Indianism, which seeks to blend and homogenize Native cultures.

The off-reservation boarding-school ideology is the third phenomenon that grew from Fort Marion. Pratt's prisoners demonstrated to their jailer that Native people had the ability to learn English, as well as the other skills he believed it would take for them to achieve success in the new world that was coming to them. In 1878, the prisoners gained their release. Most of them returned home to their communities, but a significant number stayed in the East to continue their schooling. Pratt, now a believer in the idea of giving English instruction and industrial training to Natives, recruited forty-nine students from the Dakota Territory to join a group of seventeen former Fort Marion prisoners at the Hampton Institute in Virginia for further educational training (Lindsey, 28ff).[5]

Hampton is a private school that was founded to train African Americans. Interestingly, one of the people Pratt's charges encountered at Hampton was Booker T. Washington, who went on to become perhaps the most influential African American leader of his time and the great rival to Du Bois. Washington became "house father" to the Native male students and associated with them closely for a year.[6] In *Up from Slavery,* Washington displays affection and admiration for his charges and refers to these Native students as being "perfectly ignorant" upon their arrival at Hampton (80).

The students themselves, however, didn't seem to share this point of view. As Washington notes, "[T]he average Indian felt himself above the white man, and, of course, he felt himself far above the Negro, largely on account of the fact of the Negro having submitted to slavery—a thing which the Indian would never do" (80). Washington picked up on something that many white observers missed—that many of these young Native people came to school from strong political communities where they grew up leading self-determined lives in the homelands of their ancestors. But vis-à-vis their relationship to the United States, Natives had arrived where Du Bois says in *Souls* that African Americans had also arrived, at a time in which "[t]he industrial school was the proffered answer to [the] combined educational and economic crisis, and an answer of singular wisdom and timeliness." Du Bois, significantly, goes on to ask the crucial biblical question of those advocating training for such a life of toil: "Is not life more than meat, and the body more than raiment?" (77).

Pratt's prisoners-turned-students found themselves in Fort Marion, then at Hampton, because of their leadership against white encroachment. As learners under Pratt, though, they were deemed fit only for the basics of Western knowledge. Leadership was not something Pratt expected of them. They had run into an ideology similar to the one Du Bois rails against when he says, "[W]e daily hear that an education that encourages aspiration, that sets the loftiest of ideals and seeks as an end culture and character rather than bread-winning, is the privilege of white men" (78). The resulting curriculum, according to Du Bois's comment on Hampton, had a "manner and tone that would make Socrates an idiot and Jesus Christ a crank" (qtd. in Lewis, 353).

Hampton would continue educating young Indian people until 1923. Pratt's recruits and those who followed later attended a separate Indian school, using the same facilities as the African American students. Pratt was enthusiastic about the results, but not about the sharing of facilities, and created a freestanding school at Carlisle, Pennsylvania, for Indian students from around the country (Lindsey, 38ff.). Unlike Hampton and other African American educational institutions, Carlisle was not to be run as a private institution, but as a government one.

In his autobiographical text, *My People the Sioux*, Luther Standing Bear claims to have been "the first Indian boy to step inside the Carlisle Indian School grounds" by virtue of his marching through its gate first when he, among the first group of students to come from the train station two miles away from the school, arrived from Dakota country (133). Standing Bear's autobiography, including its long section on Carlisle, is one of the most interesting texts from the era, nearly all of which are nonfiction. As the son of a Lakota chief, Standing Bear's experience with Western-style education echoes that of the children of Native leaders whose parents sent them to school as a gesture of good faith in negotiations with colonial powers. As such, in his work he is ideally placed to speak to the realities of Carlisle.[7]

According to Standing Bear, the first days at Pratt's new school were anything but organized. Furniture had not yet arrived, classes would not begin for a time, and mostly the students wandered around the grounds, still in the clothes they had worn on their journey from the West. Standing Bear recalls being both less comfortable and more hungry at Carlisle than he had ever been back home; indeed, until mattresses—that students had to fill with straw themselves—and other bedding arrived, students had only the blankets they had traveled with for warmth (134–36).

But soon, all the hallmarks of Pratt's pedagogy would be evident. Early on, teachers arranged for students to take on Western first names that they would assign them from lists on blackboards (137). And even before Western-style clothes arrived, the students went one by one to have their long hair cut by local barbers. Standing Bear at first welcomed the idea of joining the older boys in this, saying, "I began to feel anxious to be 'instyle' and wanted mine cut, too." But soon the actual experience changed his mind. "When my hair was cut short, it hurt my feelings to such an extent that the tears came into my eyes. I do not recall whether the barber noticed my agitation or not, nor do I care. All I was thinking about was that hair he had taken away from me" (141).

Gertrude Bonnin, who wrote under the name Zitkala-Sa, writes in her autobiographical fiction of the experience of a young Dakota woman from a much more modest background than Standing Bear at school in the East, trying in vain to hide from scissors-wielding schoolmasters intent on cutting her hair. After being hunted down and strapped to a chair, she says, "I cried aloud, shaking my head all the while until I felt the cold blades of the scissors against my neck, and heard them gnaw off one of my thick braids" (56).

This fictional young woman, who had begged her mother to be allowed to attend the school in the East based on promises of its great beauty and its abundance of red apples, found the foreign, regimented world of boarding school far from the idealized alternative to home that she had imagined. For her, with her Dakota upbringing, shorn hair was a sign of mourning or cowardice. Thus, as hers was being cut, she says, "I lost my spirit. Since the day I was taken from my mother I had suffered extreme indignities. People had stared at me. . . . And now my long hair was shin-gled like a coward's. In my anguish I moaned for my mother, but no one came to comfort me. Not a soul reasoned quietly with me, as my mother used to do; for now I was only one of many little animals driven by a herder" (56).

For both Standing Bear and Bonnin's protagonist, the experience of having their hair cut short made them realize that they were young people in the position between the expectations of their parents and the designs of those educators in whose hands their lives were placed. In spite of her misgivings, the mother of Bonnin's young protagonist thought of educa-tion as recompense. "The palefaces," Bonnin shows her thinking, "who owe us a large debt for stolen lands, have begun to pay a tardy justice in offering some education for our children." But she also thinks, "I know my daughter must suffer keenly in this experiment" (44).

Standing Bear recalls that his father had taught him to be brave enough to die for the Dakota people. "But my father had made a mistake," Standing Bear writes. "He should have told me, upon leaving home, to go and learn all I could of the white man's ways, and be like [him]. That would have given a new idea from a different slant; but Father did not advise me along that line. I had come away from home with the intention of never return-ing alive unless I had done something very brave" (141). Leaving aside the obvious fact that Standing Bear and the other students were quite brave in facing the new experience of being in boarding school so far from home, Standing Bear identifies here one of the most important points that can be made from the history of Native education.

That is, when Native parents sent their children to Carlisle, or a few years later to Chilocco in Indian Territory, Chemawa in Oregon, or to the other off-reservation boarding schools that would be the dominant form of school for indigenous children for over four decades, they knew they were sending their children to learn how to live and work according to the new realities that the overwhelming presence of whites demanded. Mann quotes one of her Cheyenne elders on the supposed efficacy of Western education:

> Perhaps this education the White Man talks to us about is not all bad. We need to understand the Veho [literally, white man]. We have to live with him. We have to deal with him. If our children go to his school they [will] learn his language; they will know how he thinks. They will become our eyes, our ears, our mouths. Through the children we will listen, and we will speak. Thus we can better protect our ways, our culture as it has come down to us through many generations. (44)

Certainly this echoes the sentiment of the vast majority of Native parents, who imagined that their children would return home better equipped to help their tribal nations make the incremental changes that would ensure their survival as distinct peoples.

STUDENTS OR HOSTAGES?

Pratt and the other progressive educators who actually did the adminis-tering and teaching had something else in mind. They were interested in the quickest path to the most complete transformation possible for young Native students. And that kind of complete transformation, as Pratt ar-gued, required distance:

> I suppose the end to be gained, however far away it may be, is the com-plete civilization of the Indian and his absorption into our national life, with all the rights and privileges guaranteed to every other individual,

the Indian to lose his identity as such, to give up his tribal relations and to be made to feel that he is an American citizen. If I am correct in this supposition, then the sooner all tribal relations are broken up; the sooner the Indian loses all his Indian ways, even his language, the better it will be for him and for the government and the greater will be the economy to both. Now, I do not believe that amongst his people an Indian can be made to feel all the advantages of a civilized life, nor the manhood of supporting himself and of standing out alone and battling for life as an American citizen. To accomplish that, his removal and personal isolation is necessary. One year in the midst of a civilized community where, whichever way he may turn he can see the industrious farmer plowing his fields or reaping his grain, and the industrious mechanic building houses or engaged in other manufactures, with all the realities of wealth and happiness which these efforts bring to the farmer and mechanic is worth more as a means of implanting such aspirations as these you desire for him in his mind than ten years, nay, than a whole life time of camp surroundings with the best Agency school work that can be done. (Utley 1964, 266, qtd. in Lomawaima, 5)

Whether in long quotations like this or in the short phrase most often associated with him—"Kill the Indian and save the man"—Pratt was the great apostle of eradicating from students every available trace of Native identity and replacing it with a facsimile of whiteness.

Pratt and his apologists generally stressed the abstract and the cosmetic—civilization, identity, a change of clothes—in the propagation of their pedagogical ideals. What has become more and more obvious by now is the extent to which the totality of being of the Indian students at Carlisle and other off-reservation schools was part of the experience. Standing Bear, for instance, was one of the most successful of Pratt's students and he actively recruited other young people from his tribe to make the long journey to Pennsylvania to be Carlisle students. He was hand-selected to work at Wanamaker's department store in Philadelphia, marched in the Carlisle band, and later actively sought and received the rights of citizenship that Pratt pushed for. Yet even he, in discussing the experience of being at Carlisle, writes, "That was one of the hard things about our education—we had to get used to so many things we had never known before that it worked on our nerves to such an extent that it told on our bodies" (159). While it perhaps goes without saying, without a robust concept of experience, it is difficult to see how the force of this and so much else that Native educational narratives say can register effectively.

If the radically new things they were learning were not enough, many students, especially those from tribes that had only recently negotiated peace with the United States, had to deal with the fact that their presence in the keep of the U.S. government was a guarantee of their families' behavior back home. This had been true of the schools close to home; as Mann says of the Cheyenne students in reservation boarding schools,

> [t]he Indian child became the control mechanism, as [Agent] Miles articulated: "I would respectfully represent that there is no other means so effectual in holding restless Indians in check as to have their children in school." Judging from his statement, it appears that the children were not being educated so much as they were being held hostage. (33)

Mann refers to those Cheyennes and Arapahoes who later attended Carlisle as "students held hostage for the good behavior of their people" (56). Standing Bear, exemplar that he was, expresses a similar sentiment in writing, "Sometimes we felt that we were in a very tight place, miles away from our homes, and among white people, where we felt that at the least show of trouble we would all be killed; but we were always ready" (160).

Suffice it to say, in these situations one of the last things on the minds of teachers, matrons, and administrators was the kind of learning that would pave the way for Native students to gain an understanding of their place in the contemporary world and how their history had led them to that place. Indeed, the primary work of the schools for which Carlisle was the flagship was producing the food, clothing, and other goods it took to keep operations going. Young people in boarding schools spent fully half of each day toiling in the fields and working in dairies, sewing their own clothes, cleaning the facilities they used, and making their own shoes. As Vine Deloria says of the schools, "Actual learning was minimal; these institutions resembled reformatories where culturally deficient inmates struggled to achieve a measure of respectability. Classes were held only in the mornings; the afternoons were devoted to work, hard work, and relentlessly boring routine work" ("Burden," 163).

By most accounts, the students had little choice of vocation. Standing Bear, who was clearly a candidate to learn at a higher level, spent years working as a tinsmith in spite of his desire to spend more time learning in the classroom. As he writes, "I was getting along very well. I made hundreds of tin cups, coffee pots, and buckets. These were sent away and issued to the Indians on various reservations. After I had left the school and returned home, this trade did not benefit me any, as the Indians had plenty of tinware that I had made at school" (147).

Standing Bear's narrative is an apt example of devolution in Native education. Just a generation before, a student with Standing Bear's talent might have attended a school like Santee and come to the attention of educators like Alfred Riggs and perhaps made his way to high school and college. Though Standing Bear had a much different family background, he might have followed more closely the writerly career path of an earlier Sioux writer, Charles Alexander Eastman.[8]

Eastman's Odyssey from the Deep Woods

Eastman, who at birth was named Ohiyesa by his traditional Dakota family, was brought up in camp life and raised to become a warrior. His father, Many Lightnings, was one of the 303 Sioux who in 1862 were sentenced to hang for defending their homeland against white encroachment (Eastman, *Deep Woods*, 3). U.S. President Abraham Lincoln pardoned Many Lightnings and 263 others, condemning 39 men to die in the largest mass execution in U.S. history (Weaver, *Unforgotten Gods*, 2). One more of these condemned men gained a reprieve before the hanging and local newspapers reported that the 38 who hanged sang a death chant on the gallows, not realizing that they, in fact, were singing a Christian hymn.

Many Lightnings, in the midst of continuing conflicts between the Sioux and settlers in Minnesota in the early 1860s, traveled to Canada and converted to Christianity, in the process changing his name to Jacob Eastman (R. Wilson, 16). While still a young man, he returned home and took his family, including Ohiyesa, to join a group of Sioux converts who were seeking to build a new life in imitation of the settler culture that was increasingly edging traditional Native societies off the plains. Ohiyesa became Charles and soon embarked on one of the most remarkable educational careers recorded in Native intellectual history (R. Wilson, 20).

After a short stint in a local day school, the young Eastman proceeded to none other than the Santee School to learn from its combination of white and Sioux teachers under the direction of superintendent Alfred M. Riggs, who was still superintendent years later when the souvenir that opened this chapter was printed (*Deep Woods*, 40).

As Eastman's father put it, "You will be taught the language of the white man, and also how to count your money and tell the prices of your horses and of your furs" (*Deep Woods*, 17). Along with learning in the classroom, Eastman worked hard. He sawed wood to make extra money and had to take his turn hauling water from the Missouri River to the school almost two miles away.

Eastman went on to Beloit College, Knox College, Dartmouth, and then to medical school at Boston University. As he writes of his move to school in New England, "I went on to Dartmouth College, away up among the granite hills. . . . This was my ambition—that the Sioux should accept civilization before it was too late! I wished that our young men might at once take up the white man's way, and prepare themselves to hold office and wield influence in their native states" (*Deep Woods*, 65). Interestingly, for Eastman taking up the white man's way meant progressing as far as possible through the educational system as his talent would allow him. This is what his father had pushed him to do and it is what he achieved.

Eastman's experiences of education seem at times incredibly trying, including his arrival at Beloit in the immediate aftermath of the Sioux victory at Greasy Grass (Little Big Horn) over General George Armstrong Custer and his troops. When Eastman got to campus, he reports hearing one student yell to another, "Hurry up! . . . We have Sitting Bull's nephew right here, and it's more than likely he'll have your scalplock before morning" (*Deep Woods*, 52–53). Similar assumptions about his relationship to Sitting Bull plagued him for years as he made his way through white America, including the train ride to Dartmouth in 1882.

Eastman describes himself during his years at Dartmouth as "a sort of prodigal son of old Dartmouth" (*Deep Woods*, 68). A better description, though, might be that Eastman found himself wrapped up in the same rhetoric of novelty and ancientness with which Apess contended. His response was very different from the directness with which Apess often met such rhetoric. Eastman often wrote in a way that made Indian people seem responsible for their own troubles, and he often obscured the real reasons for Indian problems behind a misty veil. For instance, he describes how "[t]he New England Indians, for whom [Dartmouth] was founded, had departed well-nigh a century earlier, and now a warlike Sioux, like a wild fox, had found his way into this splendid seat of learning" (*Deep Woods*, 68).

He doesn't discuss how it was that New England tribes had come to the situation they were in. His novelty stands in relation to their ancientness, and he doesn't question their "departure." "Though poor," Eastman says, "I was really better off than many of the students, since the old college took care of me under its ancient charter. I was treated with the greatest kindness by the president and faculty, and often encouraged to ask questions and express my own ideas" (*Deep Woods,* 62).

Eastman's class made him captain of its football team and they apparently enjoyed him distracting their classes with his dissertations on Native knowledge:

> My uncle's observations in natural history, for which he had a positive genius, the Indian standpoint in sociology and political economy, these were the subjects of some protracted discussions in the class room. This became so well understood, that some of my classmates who had failed to prepare their recitations would induce me to take up the time by advancing a native theory or first hand observation. (*Deep Woods,* 68–69)

At one and the same time, Eastman would have his readers believe that white Dartmouth students were sage enough to appreciate his articulations of ancient Dakota knowledge and that he was also precocious enough to use his novelty to help them avoid doing their homework.

Eastman was a remarkable person who lived through a remarkable time. Gerald Vizenor says of him, "Eastman endured the treacherous turn and transvaluations of tribal identities, the simulations of ferocious warrior cultures, the myths of savagism and civilization, federal duplicities, assimilation policies, the rise of manifest manners, and the hardhearted literature of dominance" (*Manifest Manners,* 50). Eastman declares at the end of *From the Deep Woods,* "I am an Indian; and while I have learned much from civilization, for which I am grateful, I have never lost my Indian sense of right and justice. I am for development and progress along social and spiritual lines, rather than those of commerce, nationalism, or material efficiency. Nevertheless, so long as I live, I am an American" (195).

In this declaration he embodies the fundamental tensions and seeming contradictions that he and others of his era experienced. The fact is, Eastman, Standing Bear, Bonnin, and others wanted what the schools they attended offered. Yet they also wanted to have a stake in their own destiny. As Malea Powell says in her astute analysis of Eastman's *Deep Woods,* "At the same time as Eastman acknowledges that Indians are the objects of a Euroamerican gaze," as in his presumed association with Sitting Bull, "he also establishes himself as having the ability to look back. . . . Although many may buy his book to read about Indians, there will also be an Eastman reading back at his readers" (421). The book becomes a way of entering the discussion, of gaining a place at the table.

Attempting to put the work of Eastman and his generation in a context that makes sense of these tensions, Vizenor asks, "What did it mean to be the first generation to hear the stories of the past, bear the horrors of the moment, and write to the future?" (*Manifest Manners,* 51). These questions resonate in the present, and it's telling to note that not a single Native writer mentioned thus far in this chapter, nor any other I have yet been able to think of from before this most recent generation, presents an account of even one white teacher or mentor who encouraged him or her to become a writer.

NONFICTION AND NATIVE LITERATURE

Examining the conditions at the schools and proclaiming the schools' policies and those who enforced them to be the embodiment of evil is not enough. It is important to see that the experiences that the ideology behind the off-reservation schools gave rise to are real. Though Bonnin fictionalized her narratives of boarding-school life, all these writers relied on the techniques of nonfiction to represent their experiences as Native students. Nonfiction, in this reading, is important in and of itself, and it is not waiting for short stories and novels to arrive and make Native literature more literary. Nonfiction as nonfiction deserves to be regarded as constitutive of the Native written literary tradition.

This is not a minor point of fact. It speaks to the way that scholars and students have envisioned Native literature. The written expressions of Eastman, Bonnin, and Standing Bear are chronicles of their experiences and responses to the times and conditions in which they found themselves. That their work often transcended the conventions of the genres in which they wrote testifies to the wonder of their intellectual and literary achievements. As Powell writes of Eastman, "In *using* dominant discourse, Eastman marks himself as a subject within it, not just as a victim subject to it. In doing so I hear him imagining a new Indian-ness" (425). Eastman and the others wrote as witnesses to that process. Their works persist as gifts of intelligence and artistry. To assume otherwise is to hamstring written Native literature as an innocent outgrowth of Native literacy and to view Native writers as writing merely because they could.[9]

The things that happened to Native young people that Native authors record in their work happened in a way that was different for those in a previous generation, and these texts by Standing Bear, Eastman, and Bonnin provide important witness to those experiences. Margaret Archuleta, Brenda Child, and Tsianina Lomawaima maintain that "Indian boarding schools were key components in the process of cultural genocide against Native cultures, and were designed to physically, ideologically, and emotionally remove Indian children from their families, homes, and tribal affiliations" (19).

Yet, they also point out that boarding-school experiences prompted a range of responses, from people who were extremely grateful for the chance at an education to those who developed a deep sense of rebellion. And, of course, those hundreds who died while away at school are compelling witnesses to that era. This is especially true of those who died from diseases like tuberculosis, which school administrators saw as a defect in Native constitutions, rather than as a highly contagious disease (Archuleta, Child, Lomawaima, 39). These victims certainly paid the ultimate price in the educational process.

Scholars seeking to understand the history of Native education have turned a crucial corner over the past decade. Whereas in the past researchers have focused on the official record of the schools and the policies that created them, more recently we have seen an insistence on uncovering the voices of students themselves. Lomawaima's history of the Chilocco Indian School, *They Called It Prairie Light,* relies on the oral histories of students who lived at the Oklahoma boarding school, mostly in the 1920s and 1930s. Child's study of the Flandreau Indian School, *Boarding School Seasons,* makes use of archival correspondence, mostly between the parents of boarding-school students and their children. These are important books that bring the voices of students into the center of the discussion on boarding schools.[10]

In the remainder of this chapter I am interested in going one step further in understanding that student voices are central not just to understanding boarding schools, but to understanding other aspects of Native educational life. Comparing those experiences to the Holocaust, Hiroshima, slavery, and imprisonment, as I have already indicated, is tempting. What I would like to suggest is that the boarding-school experience does not need the metaphor of some other group's experience to validate it, but is in and of itself irreducible to any other experience.

The boarding-school experience has become the sine qua non of Native educational experiences. But the boarding schools are one important chapter among many that represent a larger history of Native education. Most important, the boarding-school era is not a discrete moment in history that is now over. Along with the fact that some of these schools are still open, I contend that boarding-school experiences continue to affect Native learning (Archuleta, Child, Lomawaima, 20). Boarding-school trauma is, according to Duran and Duran, generationally cumulative:

> After so many decades of abuse and internalizing of pathological patterns, . . . dysfunctional patterns at times became very nebulous. . . . The dysfunctional patterns at some point started to be seen as part of Native American tradition. Since people were forced to assimilate white behaviors—many of which were inherently dysfunctional—the ability to differentiate healthy from dysfunctional became difficult (or impossible) for the children who were to become the grownups of the boarding school era. Therefore, many of the problems facing Native American people today—such as alcoholism, child abuse, suicide, and domestic violence—have become part of the Native American heritage due to long decades of forced assimilation and genocidal practices implemented by the federal government. (35)

Contemporary Natives, then, carry the boarding-school experience into the classroom with them, and it often colors the way Natives think about education. It is, in the end, indicative of the rest of the contemporary educational experiences of Native people and provides the experiential bedrock for understanding what it now means to be Native learners and leaders, and to be in school.

RETHINKING EDUCATION

Native education, of course, did not begin in the mind of missionaries or other colonial ideologues, but has its roots in the farthest reaches of history and has developed over centuries. As Mann writes of her own people, "Cheyennes over time had developed sophisticated concepts of education to prepare their children for satisfying lives in an adult world" (15). Adopting contemporary language from her own training in education, Mann says, "Innovative teaching strategies that Cheyennes employed over the centuries were the open classroom or open school, team teaching, modular scheduling, individualized instruction, competency or performance-based education, humanistic education, and life-long learning" (15). Stuart A. Tonemah extends this discussion to gifted and talented Native students, arguing that "[f]rom the earliest memory of tribal people . . . there have been gifted and talented people among us. . . . These people . . . were identified early in their lives and nurtured by parents and tribe. They were taught in an environment in which they learned by example, learned at their own pace, learned by discovery, and learned from grandparents and uncles and aunts with whom they shared a symbiotic relationship" (3).

The history of Native education, Mann argues, has its roots in tribal traditions of bringing up young people to be productive members of tribal communities. She is the author of the first of three long quotations I want to use here to show how Native educational narratives lend themselves to what Edward Said calls "contrapuntal reading," which for Said "must take account of both processes, that of imperialism and of resistance to it, which can be done by extending our reading of the texts to include what was one forcibly excluded" (*Culture and Imperialism*, 66–67). Said goes on to say, "Each text has its own particular genius, as does each geographical region of the world, with its own overlapping and interdependent histories of conflict. . . . In reading a text, one must open it out both to what went into it and to what its author excluded" (67).

Mann's reading of traditional education stands in relation to Ngugi wa Thiong'o's description of what colonialism has done to traditional life. Together, these two authors provide a counterpoint that helps makes sense of the words of one Carlisle student who became an apologist for the school's ideology. As Mann argues in the first quotation by these three authors:

The Cheyenne education system had a holistic and well-developed curriculum. Philosophy, history, and language were incorporated into the oral tradition. As the tribe moved over the plains, the young people learned the geography of the land. Courses in biology and science were offered in which the students learned the ways of animals and the uses of plants and herbs. They also had practical courses in mathematics and geometry, learning to count by the number of poles it took to put up a tepee or lodge. Young men learned to survive on the hunt in bachelor survival courses. Young women gathered vegetables, prepared food, and made clothing in home economics classes. Education was not separated from life, but was intertwined with it. (15)

Mann here reaches toward an understanding of history in which the starting point is not the importation of Eurocentric ideology, the end of a ruler, a prohibition on the use of one's language, or the feeling of children being stolen from the embrace of their parents. Instead, education is something that permeates life and has done so for the length of Native memory.

The perspective that Mann presents does more than recover a longer Native intellectual history of pedagogy. It also provides a different sort of footing for discussing the history of education that Natives inhabit. Natives can fruitfully understand themselves as inheritors of what Ngugi has called the detonation of a "culture bomb" in our midst. As he writes:

> The oppressed and the exploited of the earth maintain their defiance: liberty from theft. But the biggest weapon wielded and actually daily unleashed by imperialism against that collective defiance is the cultural bomb. The effect of a cultural bomb is to annihilate a people's belief in their names, in their languages, in their environment, in their heritage of struggle, in their unity, in their capacities and ultimately in themselves. It makes them see their past as one wasteland of non-achievement and it makes them want to distance themselves from that wasteland. It makes them want to identify with that which is furthest removed from themselves; for instance, with other people's languages rather than their own. It makes them identify with that which is decadent and reactionary, all those forces which would stop their own spring of life. It even plants serious doubts about the moral rightness of struggle. Possibilities of triumph or victory are seen as remote, ridiculous dreams. The intended results are despair, despondency and a collective death-wish. Amidst this wasteland which it has created, imperialism presents itself as the cure and demands that the dependent sing hymns of praise with the constant refrain: "Theft is holy." (3)

Schools, in this reading, have been the detonation zone of culture bombs, detonation zones that continue to be with us.

How else to explain Dennison Wheelock's award-winning untitled essay, which appeared in the *Indian Helper* in 1887? Wheelock, an Oneida student at Carlisle, was a leader of the marching band and one of the most prominent students in his era at Carlisle. In response to the question, "Is it right for the government to stop the teaching of Indian languages in reservation schools?" Wheelock writes: "I think the Indian languages is *[sic]* one that few person who wish to live as human beings can use." In contrast to Ngugi, Wheelock has the following to say about his and other Native students' languages:

> It is a language that is of no use in the world and should not be kept any longer. You can't express a wise idea with the Indian language in a way that would be wise and you can't make a law with it, and you can never make a speech as well and as good, as you would with the English language. Why? because the Indians never made laws, never saw so many things to talk about as the white men see, and do not do much thinking for the future, and talk mostly by signs, and thus they have only a few words in their language.
>
> It has only the words of every day use, and does not have any, I call "hard words."
>
> The Indian language is not only a disgrace to the Government for being in it, but it is also the cord that pulls down the race who have been bound by the same cord to ignorance and barbarism for centuries.
>
> The Government has been slow to see this.
>
> It has now seen, and will it leave them as they are and not lend a hand to their doleful cries?
>
> The people of the country choose the men who are in Congress to rule, and make laws for the country and they have made a law which has long been a matter of necessity. . . .
>
> Now, which will the Government undertake to do and which would be the quickest way to civilize the Indians, to teach the 60,000,000 of white people the Indian language or teach the little handful of Indians, the English language[?]
>
> In trying to teach the Indians in their own language, I would really repeat the words used by P. O. Matthews, an Indian, in describing his lecturing tour through the country that it was like a goose trying to stand on its wing.

Clearly, Wheelock had learned to filter his ironies and contradictions, and his rhetoric is as tortured as Ngugi's is eloquent. In Wheelock's years at Carlisle, he had been taught that expressing himself in his own language was akin to a goose using its wings as feet.

But this essay is not the entirety of the story. Wheelock went on from Carlisle to become an attorney, make his way home to Oneida, and work there and other places on land transactions. Along with his professional achievements, he (and his numerous siblings and other contemporary relatives) left a generational legacy of an extended family that has continued to be part of the ongoing life of the Oneida as a native nation.[11]

Regardless, the facts of Wheelock's future do not erase the jarring impact of his student essay. That essay shows that Pratt's ideology had succeeded, though not totally. A picture of Wheelock speaks nearly as powerfully as the essay, especially if read contrapuntally. In the photo, Wheelock stands as a walking contradiction in a bandleader's uniform, the musical version of the rhetoric of his essay. Wheelock peers at the camera pensively, looking away, his ears standing out from his closely shorn head of hair, his uniform spiffy and neat. In one hand he holds a cornet, in the other his baton (Archuleta, Child, and Lomawaima, 60).

The counterpoint comes from the later history of marching bands at the boarding schools, which were a natural outgrowth of the military discipline of nineteenth-century schools. Standing Bear reports that band music was part of the earliest days at Carlisle. He tells of how the music teacher outfitted the boys with horns, then played her own. "Then she motioned to us that we were to blow our horns," Standing Bear writes. "Some of the boys tried to blow from the large end. Although we tried to do our best, we could not produce a sound from them. She then tried to talk to us, but we did not understand her. Then she showed us how to wet the end of the mouthpiece. We thought she wanted us to spit into the horns, so we did. She finally got so discouraged with us that she started crying" (149).

The bands at Carlisle and other schools got much better. As Rayna Green and John Troutman argue, Indian school bands became popular in surrounding communities and around the country. "They were popular not only because of their talents, but, to the consternation of many boarding school officials, because of their exotic appeal to non-Indians, due at least in part to the 'Indianist' compositions that were circulating in American popular music" (67). Administrators may have envisioned "Stars and Stripes Forever" and other patriotic fare, but the appeal of "Indian Love Call" and other such gestures toward the Native players was hard to ignore.

Read in isolation, Wheelock the rhetor or bandleader seems to be every inch a victory for colonialism. Read with the counterpoint of recoverable alternatives from Native traditions and the subsequent developments at the schools, Wheelock becomes a marker at the most difficult stage in a process that is still unfolding. In many ways, what the marching bands and other musical groups became were much more in line with what Native leaders and parents hoped for when they sent their children off to school. The schools were an alternative to "an unrelentingly grim life filled with prayer, plow, and pen . . . a life that Indian students, often recruited to mission and federal schools at the point of a gun, hated and rejected" (Green and Troutman, 64). A number of boarding-school students, in fact, went on to successful musical careers.

If music created opportunities for Indian students to simulate Indianness by playing romanticized "Indian" songs by white composers, art eventually became a means through which students found a haven in which their indigenous ideas and identity were actually encouraged in the midst of other, more assimilative processes. In 1906, Winnebago artist Angel DeCora left her successful design career in New York City to open the Department of Indian Art at Carlisle and she adds to the growing counterpoint that emerges in Native educational narratives.

DeCora had been a student at Hampton, then graduated from Smith College before studying fine art in Philadelphia and Boston (Archuleta, 87). She taught at Carlisle for nine years before leaving with her husband, Lakota artist and football star William "Lone Star" Dietz, for Washington State University, where he became head coach of the football team. DeCora reflected on her arrival at Carlisle:

> An Indian's self-respect is undermined when he is told that his native customs and crafts are no longer of any use because they are the habits and pastimes of the crude man. If he takes up his native crafts he does it with the sense that he has "gone back to barbarism." On taking up the work at Carlisle I found one of the necessary things to do was to impress upon the minds of my pupils that they were Indians, possessing native abilities that had never been recognized in the curriculum of the Government schools. (Archuleta, 89)

For the pedagogical ideology of the boarding schools, this was a marked change, of course, one that was ahead of its time but would be regularized only in the 1930s with the creation of the Indian Arts and Crafts Board under Indian commissioner John Collier. Music and art created space within the schools for a sanctioned alternative to the totalized space that Pratt and other educators initially designed. To take Said's insight to its natural conclusion, that which had been excluded can also reemerge, becoming all the more evident for its earlier absence.

Thus, a contrapuntal reading contextualizes an essay like Wheelock's and points out how even he, in his participation with the Carlisle band, was part of the movement toward a different future from the one he writes about in his essay. The Wheelock who wrote in 1887 did so at what can be thought of as the apex of Pratt's educational ideology. It was simultaneously the low point in the devolution of Native education.

The boarding schools would remain into the twentieth century, and some continue to operate even now. But, as Lomawaima argues, students made the schools their own, providing their own counterpoint to the music they were assigned to play:

> The richness, complexity, and variety of memories of boarding-school life convey to us an important message about the history of Native American education. Indian people at boarding schools were not passive consumers of an ideology or lifestyle imparted from above by federal administrators. They actively created an ongoing educational and social process. They marshaled personal and shared skills and resources to create a world within the confines of boarding-school life, and they occasionally stretched and penetrated school boundaries. In the process, an institution founded and controlled by the federal government was inhabited and possessed by those whose identities the institution was committed to erase. (167)

Students like Wheelock were part of creating that world. Make no mistake. I like to imagine the printer boys at Carlisle seeing the printed praises of Wheelock's exploits and resenting him and the administrators who extolled him with every turn of the drum of their printing press. But all of these students, from those sneaking a smoke behind the print shop to those trying desperately to please their teachers, are part and parcel of Native educational legacy.

By the 1930s, Indian clubs began springing up in the schools and students learned about one another's tribal music and dances in the same classrooms where every vestige of their cultures had once been prohibited (Archuleta, Child, and Lomawaima, 78). Marching band members dressed up in Indian-themed clothes and jewelry. As likely as not, Wheelock's counterpart in the 1940s would wear a feathered headdress to lead the band. I would like to think that Wheelock, in a later generation, would have just as gleefully indulged in donning that headdress.

Reading Native narratives of education helps provide an integrated sense of the development of indigenous people and is a reminder of the synchronicity between the experiences of those who have gone before and those who go to school today. That sort of reading provides a glimpse of the challenges that continue to confront Natives as modern people. These are not only challenges that pit modernity against tradition, but ones that call for the creation of new forms in response to new conditions. This seems to be part of what Lomawaima means when she argues that Native students made the schools their own.

Thus, not only is it imperative to recover traditional styles of Native education, but it is also necessary to think through the legacy of how Native students created new traditions of education in the midst of adapting to the challenges of modernity. In his memoir of going to boarding school, for instance, Francis LaFlesche describes a world in which Native students learned in classrooms, but also late at night after "lights out," when they would tell stories and jokes (14). It was in moments like the one LaFlesche describes that boarding-school students were most able to express their agency and thus participate in the forging of their own future. Their nighttime chorus was a counterpoint to all else that happened through the day.

LIVING THE LEGACY

LaFlesche, like other authors of the boarding-school era, used nonfiction as a primary vehicle for representing student experiences, an important continuation of the North American Native writing tradition. More recent authors have turned to fiction to contribute to this same intellectual legacy. These works are worth considering because of the way they show the educational story to be longer and larger than the boarding-school era. These contemporary authors demonstrate that many of the themes Standing Bear, Eastman, and Bonnin explored continue to define Native educational experiences.

Near the end of the historical novel *Fools Crow,* for instance, James Welch's title character goes on a journey in which he has a vision of the future. That vision comes in the midst of a deep crisis for Fools Crow's Pikuni (Blackfeet) people. As the novel opens, white settlers are overrunning their territory, smallpox and other diseases are wreaking havoc, and the buffalo they rely on are dwindling. Welch describes young men like Fools Crow as being at the nexus of this crisis, as many of them grow frustrated at their new circumstances, prompting some to listen to the siren song of adventure in the border towns that had sprung up on the edges of their territory. Fools Crow thinks back on earlier times, when the traditional Pikuni way of life had held sway and he was making his way successfully in it: "I was powerful then ... my luck was good. But what good is your own power when the people are suffering, when their minds are scattering like horses in the four directions?" (314).

At the end of the novel, Fools Crow travels several days and finds himself at the home of Feather Woman, a figure from Blackfeet tradition who spends each daybreak mourning her husband and son. The future vision that Fools Crow has there appears on a yellow skin that Feather Woman gives him. The vision is truly awful. He sees the Pikuni people ravaged by smallpox and chased by the U.S. military. "He had seen the end of the blackhorns," Welch writes, indicating the buffalo, "and the starvation of the Pikunis. He had been brought here, to the strange woman's lodge in this strange world, to see the fate of his people. And he was powerless to change it" (358).

Then, Fools Crow's vision changes and he hears "the sound of children laughing" (343). On the yellow skin, he sees

> a long white building with four of the Napikwan square ice-shields on each of the long sides. . . . He . . . saw faces through the ice-shields, and they were young and open with laughter. Outside, there were other children, running and playing, laughing. The girls wore long dresses and high-topped shoes. They held hands and danced around and around in a circle. The boys, in white shirts and short pants, chased each other. (358)

Amidst this laughter, Fools Crow sees another group of children. They are dark-skinned and they are watching the others. Their clothing and hair is similar to the other children, but they are not part of the fun the other children are having. "Around the building and the ground the children played on," Welch writes, "stood a fence made of twisted wire and pointed barbs. Beyond the fence there was nothing but the rolling prairie" (358–59). A woman with a bell beckons the children to come back into the building.

This vision of school completes Fools Crow's larger vision of the fate of his people. This fate awaits Pikuni youth behind the four walls of Napikwan schools. "I grieve for our children and their children," Fools Crow tells Feather Woman, "who will not know the life their people once lived. I see them on the yellow skin and they are dressed like the Napikwans, they watch the Napikwans and learn much from them, but they are not happy.

They lose their own way" (359). Feather Woman comforts Fools Crow by telling him that the children will learn through hearing stories of how "their people were proud and lived in accordance with the Below Ones, and the Underwater People—and the Above Ones" (360). But Fools Crow can only think of the punishment and misery that lies in store for his own and future generations.

Fools Crow's vision and the sense of mourning it provokes in him foretells the dual sadness of the world of school that awaited future generations. On the one side would be an educational system designed by foreigners, with someone else's needs in mind, and the experiences of Native children would be demoted in a larger scheme in which abstractions like civilization would matter more than the lives of young people. On the other side are all the things those young people trapped behind barbed wire would never learn from their aunts, uncles, and grandparents, the sorts of things one comes to know by living in the camp setting. Feather Woman tells Fools Crow the truth that Lomawaima points out, that within this new situation Pikuni children would create their own new world.

Perhaps the most remarkable aspect of Welch's story is the manner in which Welch represents Fools Crow as looking into the future and thinking about his progeny to come. Almost any present-day Indian person can describe what it is like to search for some semblance of the world of their ancestors in narratives and photos of the past. Welch beautifully offers a vision in which those same ancestors are thinking of, even agonizing over, those to come.

Louise Erdrich, in her novel *Love Medicine,* takes Fools Crow's vision one generation into the future in her characterization of the brothers Eli and Nector Kashpaw. Their mother, Margaret, "had let the government put Nector in school, but hidden Eli, the one she couldn't part with, in the root cellar dug beneath her floor. In that way she gained a son on either side of the line. Nector came home from boarding school knowing white reading and writing, while Eli knew the woods" (19). In their twilight years, Eli would remain sharp to the world around him while his brother Nector suffered from Alzheimer's disease, a seeming indication of how their early years continued to follow them.

Leslie Marmon Silko highlights the same differences in educational approaches in her masterful book *Storyteller.* The book traces out the various ways that storytelling has been an art that breathes life into tribal people. She begins her written version of storytelling with an account of her Aunt Susie, who had gone away from her home at Laguna Pueblo to Carlisle around 1896, then continued her studies at Dickinson College, also in Carlisle. Silko portrays her aunt, who was married to her father's brother, as someone who had

> come to believe very much in books
> and in schooling. She was of a generation,
> the last generation here at Laguna,
> that passed down an entire culture
> by word of mouth
> an entire history
> an entire vision of the world
> which depended on memory
> and retelling by subsequent generations. (5–6)

Susie's stories, and her manner of telling them, inflects much of Silko's compendium of stories. And Silko traces even the most modern sorts of stories, including bizarre ones involving weird sex and evil intentions, to an earlier ethos of story at Laguna (24). Yet, in the midst of this continuity, Silko points to the same disruption that Welch does in Fools Crow's vision. As she writes of Aunt Susie,

> She must have realized
> that the atmosphere and conditions
> which had maintained this oral tradition in Laguna culture
> had been irrevocably altered by the European intrusion—
> principally by the practice of taking the children
> away from Laguna to Indian schools,
> taking the children away from the tellers who had
> in all past generations
> told the children an entire culture,
> an entire identity of a people. (6)

Silko's Aunt Susie was a bridge between generations. She had more than survived at Carlisle; she had thrived. Or at least she seemed to, given the fact that she went on to college, then returned home to teach among her Laguna people.

But Silko includes two pieces toward the end of *Storyteller* that are reminders of that dual sense of loss. She writes of her grandfather, who graduated from Sherman Institute, a boarding school in Riverside, California, saying, "While he was at Sherman, he became fascinated with engineering and design and wanted to become an automobile designer" (192). In an earlier generation, such ambition would have been possible; Ely Parker, the Seneca who was the first Native Commissioner of Indian Affairs, for instance, started his professional career as an engineer (P. Deloria, *Playing Indian,* 83). But, as Silko says of her grandfather's later story, schools like Sherman were vocational schools, and the teachers there trained her grandfather to be a store clerk. Upon returning home, he opened his own store. "He never cared much for storekeeping," Silko writes, "he just did what had to be done. When I got older I was aware of how quiet he was sometimes and sensed there was some sadness he never identified" (192).

She comes to understand that silence through his subscriptions to *Motor Trend* and *Popular Mechanics,* which Silko's grandfather read to keep track of the latest in the automotive industry he once dreamed of working in. "In 1957," Silko writes, "when Ford brought out the Thunderbird in a hardtop convertible, Grandpa Hank bought one and that was his car until he died" (192). People like Grandpa Hank were the dark-skinned children of Fools Crow's vision, realizing that the schools were not going to be a gateway to a more settled future, but another obstacle to be overcome in the creation of a new world.

What accentuates experiences like Grandpa Hank's even more is the clear sense Silko gives of not just the stories he missed by being in school, but the other things he could not learn except when he was back home. "A Geronimo Story," the next to last short story in *Storyteller,* provides a compelling alternative to the kind of education Grandpa Hank received. In the story, a young man from Laguna named Andy is allowed to go on an expedition with Laguna men who are scouting for the U.S. military.

Their goal was to find Geronimo, who was reportedly in the area threatening white settlers. Andy's uncle, Siteye, the best of the Laguna scouts, has a broken foot and would not have gone along, but "'Shit,' he said, 'these Lagunas can't track Geronimo without me'" (212). Needing someone to go along to saddle his horse, he chooses Andy. The story that follows is a Native bildungsroman, as Andy follows Siteye and learns lessons about the past, the present, and the future. Andy narrates the story later in life, seemingly after having left Laguna to attend school. As if to underscore the educational stakes that Silko writes against, the white officer in charge of the expedition is named Captain Pratt.

Early in the story, Siteye lets Andy know that Geronimo is almost certainly not in the settlement to which they are heading. Still, Siteye sees the learning opportunities the trip will provide for his nephew and says, "It will be a beautiful journey for you. The mountains and the rivers. You've never seen them before" (214).

Andy's geography lesson was not just one of appreciating beauty, but of understanding that this was a journey into an area the Laguna people had known for countless generations. During a break from riding, Siteye takes an opportunity to tell Andy about hiding places their ancestors had nearby. "In little caves they left pottery jars full of food and water. These were places to come when somebody was after you. . . . I suppose the water is all gone now . . . but the corn might still be good" (217). Siteye highlights for Andy that Laguna knowledge and traditional ways of learning are alive, a means of responding to new dangers with older strategies. At the same time, Siteye indicates that danger is nothing new at Laguna.

Upon entering unfamiliar mountain territory, Siteye rides mainly at the front of the group. "Captain didn't know the trail. . . . Siteye told me later on he wasn't sure either, but he knew how to figure it out" (218). This is the essence of the style of education Silko writes about in "A Geronimo Story." As Andy subsequently says, "Since I was a child my father had taught me, and Siteye had taught me, to remember the way; to remember how the trees look—dead branches or crooked limbs; to look for big rocks and to remember their shape and their color" (218).

This is exactly what Siteye had done, so he could now guide the group in the right direction. "I've only been this way once before," he tells Andy, "when I was a boy. Younger than you. But in my head, when I close my eyes, I can still see the trees and the boulders and the way the trail goes. Sometimes I don't remember the distance—things are closer or farther than I had remembered them, but the direction is right" (218). Andy uses this moment to think back on the journey to that point: "I closed my eyes and tested my vision of the trail we had traveled so far. I could see the way in my head, and I had a feeling for it too—a feeling for how far the great fallen oak was from Mossy Rock springs" (218). Siteye then tells Andy how he had once even used a distinctive old rattlesnake as a landmark, following it back to its hole near a trail from which he had strayed. Siteye and Andy live at different life stages during an era of transition: Siteye's childhood was one of relative freedom in the years before the advent of close confinement, while Andy lived in an era in which going away to school was all but inevitable.

By the end of their day together on the trail, the group reaches their destination, a place called Pie Town, so called, according to the adult Andy, for the excellent pies one of the women there made (219). Andy's education continues there as he sees the treatment the Laguna scouts receive from the white settlers who are afraid of Geronimo. The scouts have been summoned at a moment's notice because a white Army officer, Major Littlecock, came upon an abandoned campsite and decided it belonged to Geronimo.

When Andy finishes feeding and watering the horses, he finds the scouts relegated to the kitchen to eat their dinner. Filling up his plate with roasted meat and beans, he is disappointed not to find any pies. Later, when Major Littlecock joins the scouts and Captain Pratt in the kitchen, Andy sees the tyranny of expectations in action. Littlecock, who had previously soldiered among the Crow and the Sioux, is disappointed to see the Laguna scouts in Indian clothes, rather than in their wool military uniforms, which they say they wear only in the wintertime.

Then, Captain Pratt suggests to the Major that the scouts sleep in the kitchen. The major responds that regulations prohibit using civilian quarters. "The women," he said, "you know what I mean" (221). Then, turning to the scouts, he says, "You boys won't mind sleeping with the horses, will you?" (221). Silko writes, "Siteye looked intently at the Major's face and spoke to him in Laguna. 'You are the one who has a desire for horses at night, Major, you sleep with them'" (221). The scouts laugh at the joke, which Pratt claims he cannot translate, and the Major leaves embarrassed. Later, when the scouts have settled in the barn and they have expressed their disgust for Pie Town, Siteye says, "I am only sorry that the Apaches aren't around here. . . . I can't think of a better place to wipe out. If we see them tomorrow we'll tell them to come here first" (221). As the men laugh at Siteye's joke and their circumstances, Andy is reminded of another of his uncle's lessons: "Anybody can act violently—there is nothing to it; but not every person is able to destroy his enemy with words" (222).

Late that night, before going to sleep, Andy asks his uncle, "You've been hunting Geronimo for a long time, haven't you? And he always gets away" (222). Silko continues, "'Yes,' Siteye said, staring up at the stars, 'but I always like to think that it's us who get away'" (222). Siteye's response resonates at several levels, the most obvious meaning being the scouts not getting caught by their prey.

But his response is also one that reaches toward a different sort of getting away. In this vein, getting away relates to the theme of escape that runs through *Storyteller* and other writings by Silko. Getting away means gaining perspective on a wider world than the one the reservation, with its regulated life, offered. The journey to Pie Town allowed Siteye to show his nephew an earlier Laguna geography that had become circumscribed by settlement. It allowed him to give Andy a cross-cultural understanding of the people whose history was impinging on and confining his own. It was a continuation of an older form of education, even as it prepared Andy for the world he would inherit. Looking ahead to the boarding school that seemingly awaited Andy, perhaps he would take the form of repartee and camaraderie he experienced on the trail and replicate it late at night in a boarding-school dormitory.

The next day, the scouts accompany Major Littlecock and his soldiers to the camp that had set off the Geronimo scare. Briefly looking over the site and rolling a cigarette, "Siteye lit the cigarette and took two puffs before he walked over to Captain Pratt. He shook his head. 'Some Mexican built himself a sheep camp here, Captain, that's all.' Siteye looked at the Major to make sure he would hear. 'No Geronimo here, like we said'" (222). All the Major could do was say, "Accept my apology for this inconvenience, Captain Pratt. I simply did not want to take any chances" (222–23).

The scouts decide to use the opportunity to hunt deer and end up with an impressive amount of meat and skins to take home with them to Laguna. Silko describes their experience as they approach home:

> "Here we are again," I said to Siteye.
>
> We stopped. Siteye turned around slowly and looked behind us at the way we had come: the canyons, the mountains, the rivers we had passed. We sat there for a long time remembering the way, the beauty of our journey. Then Siteye shook his head gently. "You know," he said, "that was a long way to go for deer hunting." (223)

The journey had been about more than deer hunting, of course. The story functions as a reminder of what Mann argues for—the efficacy of traditional education and the importance of understanding modern education in its context.

Andy's getting away confirms lessons he had been learning all of his life, while exposing him to a wider world that would be more and more impossible to ignore. His getting away, like Aunt Susie's to Carlisle and Dickinson College or Grandpa Hank's to Sherman, would lead back home. *Storyteller,*

Fools Crow, and *Love Medicine* present fictional visions of the losses that colonial educational ideology have imposed on Native communities. These narratives are bridges between that time and our own. At their best, these works allow contemporary Indian people to peer backward and meet the eyes of those on the other side of the bridge as their ancestors peer into the future, wondering who and what their progeny will be.[12]

COMPARING EXPERIENCES

Vine Deloria invokes something like this bridge metaphor when he says of contemporary education, "[S]ome of the brighter Indians are now emerging on the other side, having transversed the Western body of knowledge completely" ("Higher Education," 153). Higher education, as Deloria points out, plays an important role in that transversal. Yet higher education has not often been the topic of Native writing.[13]

As a college professor, I have had the privilege of working with hundreds of Native college students over the past decade. Watching their struggles and achievements, I am convinced of the need for the articulation of Native voices on higher education to complete the educational bridge the narratives of boarding-school students helped start. As Deloria contends, the present challenge is to integrate institutional aims with traditional forms of knowledge: "A solid foundation in the old traditional ways enables students to remember that life is not scientific, social scientific, mathematical, or even religious; life is a unity, and the foundation for learning must be the unified experience of being a human being" ("Knowing and Understanding," 142).

Though nuanced differently, Deloria here takes up some themes that Du Bois brought to African American discourse on higher education a century ago. As Du Bois writes in describing his vision of southern universities,

> [T]he final product of our training must be neither a psychologist nor a brickmason, but a man. And to make men, we must have ideals, broad, pure, and inspiring ends of living—not sordid money-getting, not apples of gold. The worker must work for the glory of his handiwork, not simply for pay; the thinker must think for truth, not for fame. And all this is gained only by human strife and longing; by ceaseless training and education; by founding Right on righteousness and Truth on the unhampered search for Truth. (*Souls,* 72)

In considering the challenge of integrating Native educational discourse into contemporary Native intellectual work, that contemporary Native discourse needs to self-consciously develop the sort of discourse that was common among African American writers a century ago. Among many important differences between African American and Native American experiences, the boarding-school era for Natives did not produce anything resembling the discourse on higher education among blacks.

Some Native voices of critique exist in that era, though none of them are as vociferous as Du Bois. Henry Roe Cloud, an alumnus of both the academic program and the print shop of the Santee School and who in 1910 became the first Native American to graduate from Yale, spent a lifetime working to establish schools and programs to promote higher education for Native youth.[14] But he is an exception in a discourse in which higher education is rarely a topic.

This absence of viewpoints that counter the mainstream of Native intellectuals points toward a dynamic that has been part of Native written intellectual discourse since the 1660s, when Occom (an acquaintance and correspondent, by the way, of Phillis Wheatley's) began his intellectual work. That is, Native written discourse has not featured a back-and-forth between opposing points of view, but a coming together of similar voices striving toward the same goal. Staking out a position has not prompted the staking out of an oppositional position as in the spawning of the Niagara Movement or the later emergence of Garvey as a foil to Du Bois and the NAACP. In Native history, opposing points of view have existed in every generation, but often they are hard to find; they are the voices of those holding tenaciously to Native independence in discrete Native homelands, voices that value orality over literacy. Rarely, except in U.S. government proceedings, do those voices come down to us with the clarity of the Eastmans and Bonnins on the other side.

The previous example of Erdrich's representation of Margaret Kashpaw sending one son to school while keeping the other at home illustrates this dynamic. This was not the line between ignorance and knowledge or between degradation and uplift, but between learning to meet the demands of modern society and learning those things that had been part and parcel of Ojibwa tradition for countless generations. Nector comes home outfitted for life as a night watchman and a clerk. Eli retains an older knowledge in the face of the promises of modernity. An important difference, though, is that those like Nector are much more likely than the Elis of the Native world to have left a paper trail documenting their experiences.

Standing Bear managed to straddle that line and is in certain ways the Native author easiest to compare to Du Bois. After Carlisle, Standing Bear returned to the Dakotas and worked as, among other things, a teacher, a rancher, a store clerk, and a performer in Buffalo Bill's Wild West Show. When he wrote his first book in 1928, he promoted the benefits of learning to live in white culture while demonstrating the capabilities of Native people who are given opportunities.

Five years later, at the end of his 1933 book, *The Land of the Spotted Eagle,* Standing Bear was much more critical. He writes,

> The white man does not understand the Indian for the reason that he does not understand America. He is too far removed from its formative processes. The roots of the tree of his life have not yet grasped the rock and soil. The white man is still troubled with primitive fears; he still has in his consciousness the perils of this frontier continent, some of its fastnesses not yet having yielded to his questing footsteps and inquiring eyes. (248)

The problem with America, according to Standing Bear, is that "[t]he man from Europe is still a foreigner and an alien. And he still hates the man who questioned his path across the continent" (248).

Somewhere in those five years, Standing Bear's stance had changed. He began advocating, as strongly as anyone ever had, that American Indian students should reap the benefits of having American Indian teachers, which, of course, requires teacher education—a form of higher education. As he writes, "Every problem that exists today in regard to the native population is due to the white man's cast of mind, which is unable, at least reluctant, to seek understanding and achieve adjustment in a new and significant environment into which it has so recently come" (248–49). Native teachers were key to what he saw as the development of "a native school of thought" (255).

Standing Bear foresaw Native teachers teaching Native students, who would be "doubly educated" in creative arts, traditional religion, and philosophy, on the one hand, and modern duties and professions on the other. As Standing Bear argues,

> Every reservation could well be supplied with Indian doctors, nurses, engineers, road- and bridge-builders, draughtsmen, architects, dentists,

lawyers, teachers, and instructors in tribal lore, legends, orations, song, dance, and ceremonial ritual. The Indian, by the very sense of duty, should become his own historian, giving his account of the race—fairer and fewer accounts of the wars and more of statecraft, legends, languages, oratory, and philosophical conceptions. (254)

Standing Bear, by then regarded by some as a chief himself, had traveled a long path toward this vision of education. One can only wonder how much sooner he might have articulated this vision if he had had access to even the minimal normal teaching training, which would have given him conceptual tools for working through these philosophical and peda-gogical issues.

Though Standing Bear does not include poets in his list of vocations, poetry provides one example of taking up the challenge of higher edu-cation that Deloria, Du Bois, and Standing Bear articulate. Gloria Bird reflects this when she says of Native literature, "[W[e have a native lit-erature produced in English that is written for an English-speaking au-dience and that incorporates a native perception of the world in limited ways" (*Reinventing the Enemy's Language,* 25). While encouraging efforts to produce literature in Native languages, Bird advocates the continued use of English as a means toward Native liberation. "There is hope," she writes, "that in 'reinventing' the English language we will turn the process of colonization around, and that our literature will be viewed and read as a process of *de*colonization" (25).

Various Native poets have given voice to Native educational experi-ences. Louise Erdrich's "Indian Boarding School: The Runaways" in her collection *Jacklight* is a prominent example. The poem is a rich explora-tion of boarding-school consciousness that invokes the agency and resis-tance of Native students. "Home's the place," Erdrich writes, "we head for in our sleep" (11).

But poetry has limned other important aspects of Native education, and is perhaps in no case more moving than Roberta Hill's paean to her Carlisle-era grandmother, Lillie Rosa Minoka-Hill in "Philadelphia Flowers."[15] The poem describes Hill's visit to the site of the Philadelphia medical school her grandmother graduated from in the early twentieth century, becom-ing only the second Native woman to earn an M.D. "I was tracking my Mohawk grandmother / through time," she writes. "She left a trace / of her belief somewhere near Locust and Thirteenth" (Whiteman, 62–63).

She encounters an impoverished person selling flowers on the street. "You stopped me," Hill says, "shoving flowers toward my arm." The flower seller says, "At least, I'm not begging." Hill reaches for money. "I wanted those flowers," she writes,

> iris, ageratum, goldenrod and lilies–
> because in desperation
> you thought of beauty. I recognized
> the truth and human love you acted on,
> You had to keep your pride, as I have done,
> selling these bouquets of poems
> to anyone who'll take them. (63)

In the midst of trying to make a spiritual or emotional connection to the physical place where her grandmother struggled to follow a higher educational calling, fresh flowers lift Hill from the bricks and concrete of the city and she sees her own poetic vocation in the beauty of the flowers. She has not followed in her grandmother's footsteps to become a medical doctor. But the poem affirms her sense that poetry can be a healing force and represents its own high calling—a calling that requires the same dedication to learning and growing as any other. "After our exchange," Hill writes, "grandmother's tracks grew clearer" (63).

"Philadelphia Flowers" becomes for Hill a way to bridge her grandmother's experience with hers, and she finds synchronicity across time. That synchronicity, though, comes at a time of new challenges. In the final section of the poem, she describes an increasingly polluted environment and says, "Sometimes you get angry enough / to question." Through language, she diagnoses the toxicity of the physical world and prescribes "learning how this continent's / getting angry. Do you consider what's in store for you?" (64). The poem is a warning, but it is also a call to learn new ways to fight against those forces that threaten all life on this continent. It evinces the past even as it points to the future. And it is a reminder to look for the power of fresh flowers along the way.

As Hill explores the meaning of education at its highest forms in the Western institutional setting, William Hurtado de Mendoza, in a poem originally written in Quechua, returns to the roots of Native learning under colonialism. In "A Learning Song," Mendoza takes up the position of teacher and describes colonialism as imbricating itself onto the consciousnesses of indigenous people from their earliest experiences. Before anything else, he writes, "You had already learned / that obedient Yes" (45). In the second part of the poem, though, Mendoza promises as an indigenous teacher that "As of today and tomorrow / through this song I'll teach you / to shout NO, to refuse" (47). He goes on to repeat the first two lines, adding that he will teach students "to rebel," "to become a giant," and "to bloody the sky" (47). He ends this poem about learning to resist the continuing assault on indigenous consciousness with "As of today and tomorrow / through this song I'll teach you / to turn to yourself" (47).

Like Hill, Mendoza calls not just for a critique of educational systems, but for finding ways to create alternatives to those systems. These poems are evidence of the power poetry has in addressing these issues. Indeed, Standing Bear's call for a Native school of thought is all the more powerful when those most able to understand the transformative power of language hold a prominent place in it.

The resources for thinking through these issues are clearly considerable. The literary and intellectual witness of Native people in education is vast and growing. Yet this is a discourse that remains distressingly underdeveloped. That underdevelopment, especially regarding higher education, goes back to that period from the turn of the twentieth century to the Great Depression when Standing Bear wrote.

Calling Native educational discourse behind the curve of African American higher educational discourse at that point in time is certainly on the mark. If we measure where African American discourse on higher education had come three decades after *The Souls of Black Folk,* Native Americans were lagging. Native students attended college only sporadically. Just five higher educational institutions offered scholarships for Native students (Szasz, 135). While many higher education institutions could trace their origins to a major concern for Native education, only two, Bacone in Oklahoma and Pembroke State in North Carolina, focused on Native higher education (Carney, 82ff.).

In important ways, though, Standing Bear was exactly in step with Du Bois in understanding the function of higher education in the specific situation of a tribal people coming into modernity. Du Bois, in addressing alumni of his alma mater, Fisk University, in 1933, said, "Once upon a time some four thousand miles east of this place, I saw the functioning of a perfect system of education. It was in West Africa, beside a broad river. . . . There under the Yorubas and other Sudanese and Bantu tribes, the education of the child began almost before it was could walk" ("The Field and the Function," 51).

Du Bois goes on to say of African tribal education, "There could be no education that was not at once for use in earning a living and for use in living a life. Out of this education and out of the life it typified came, as perfect expressions, song and dance and sage, and ethics and religion" (51). This was an ideal to Du Bois at the moment, even if it was all but impossible to replicate in the confines of modern education. He argued that he had seen that ideal reflected at Fisk, at Harvard, and at the University of Berlin. In each case, the institution was highly aware of its main purposes and the specific circumstances in which it operated—the approach of the universal from the context of the particular. That approach could be problematic, especially in cases like Berlin, where national superiority and others' inferiority were topics as much as human limits, but Du Bois saw no way toward larger truths other than the embrace of a people by themselves where they are.

For Du Bois, no one ever merely founds a university. Instead, a university begins where it is, whether it is French, American, or African American. Like Standing Bear, he saw clearly the limiting confines of industrial education and instead sought a path that would embrace the actual conditions of people, even as it would also embrace the resources, capabilities, and talents of those people. Doing so, of course, required a belief in the capability of those people to reach toward new knowledge.

Standing Bear's and Du Bois's vision was one that has been shared, if sometimes only in bits and pieces, by thousands of leaders, like Standing Bear's father, who looked at the present and wondered about the possibilities of the future. In Native America, perhaps the strongest result of that vision has been the tribally controlled college movement in Canada and the United States. Those colleges and universities have articulated an educational mission that seeks to support the process of someone becoming who they are as Diné, Lakota, Comanche, Ojibwa, and Cheyenne, at the same time they are becoming better able to participate in and understand the contemporary world of which they are a part.

Native American higher education, then, has not so much lagged behind African American models as it has been on a different, sometimes convergent journey. From intact if embattled traditional cultures, Native people have emerged into a new century as legacies of the risks that parents and leaders made along the way, risks that endangered the present in the hope that the future would provide a forum for promoting and professing that which progressives like Pratt saw only as backward detritus.

Perhaps, as Native people continue to move forward in the challenge of understanding themselves in the midst of an ever more complicated world, W. E. B. Du Bois and other African Americans from then and now will become crucial voices illuminating the path behind and ahead. And perhaps Native voices will, likewise, help fill in the gaps of conversations never completed and alternative realities not yet explored.

CONCLUSION

This reading of Native educational narratives has highlighted the centrality of educational experience to Native literature and Native life. Contemporary Natives are inheritors of a complex legacy of educational policy, practice, oppression, and resistance. Starting with their nonfiction, then progressing through fiction and poetry, Native authors have encountered and explored the existential edges of Native lives of learning. In the process they have pointed not only to the past, but to the future. These narratives help elucidate the outlines of a future in which, as Delores Huff says, "In its ideal form, the institution of education is a potent liberating force, the highway to autonomy, a means by which individuals actualize and shape a productive . . . future" (1).

As such, Native discourse on education deserves highest priority. Doing so requires that we understand how "despite policy vacillations and attempts to coercively assimilate The People through education . . . they have remained a distinctly identifiable people with a living history" (Mann, 185). Articulating that living history and continuing contemporary efforts on the trail that Native authors have blazed is among the most important work Native scholars can do. As Powell points out, one reason to attend to Native writing on education is because, through these writers, "we have a language, a system of participation, a rhetoric," with which to articulate further work (428).

Native educational narratives demonstrate the extent to which Native people have come to a self-understanding of their own educational experiences and have demonstrated the importance of Natives leading the way into their own future. Patricia Monture-Angus puts it this way:

> I have thought a lot about what education is. For me, what education must be about is inclusion and not exclusion. It must be about giving each and every one of us our own good voice. Some of us are going to be the speakers, some of us are going to be the artists, some of us the teachers

and spiritual people. We each have a beautiful gift given to us by the Creator. What our education system should be doing is helping us to live those beautiful gifts rather than asking us to set them down and be like everybody else.[16]

Fittingly, regaining control of Native education is a matter itself of learning. Everyone interested in being part of this living history as it continues to unfold needs to bring to the process their own willingness to learn and relearn.

Along the way, perhaps we can find new ways of re-asking ourselves the question Du Bois posed a century ago: "What does it feel like to be a problem?" For Natives, as for Du Bois, being a problem has meant being an educational problem. Certain sorts of Native responses to the Du Boisian query may sometimes be hard to find, but more than a century after Du Bois asked his question, I will say this: American Indians don't appear to have any intention of stopping being a problem any time soon.

4

Momaday in the Movement Years:
Rereading "The Man Made of Words"

$\mathcal{T}$he educational ideology that swept through Native American communities from the beginning of the Progressive Era in the United States set the stage for twentieth-century Native American life. Due to disease, military conquest, and the increasing degradation of reservation life, says Russell Thornton, "Native American population of the United States, Canada, and Greenland" combined, which had been seven million in 1492, "reached a nadir of perhaps 375,000 around 1900."[1] In the American popular imagination, the idea of Indians vanishing was pervasive.

The twentieth was a century of deep loss in terms of land, culture, knowledge, and other resources. The fictional vision that James Welch has his character Fools Crow receive, of his people ravaged by smallpox, chased by the U.S. military, and with few buffalo left, indeed reflects what was to come. Thousands like Silko's Grandpa Hank, who had wanted to become an automobile designer, would sacrifice their dreams and aspirations to the diminished opportunities afforded in their place. Families like Erdrich's Kashpaws would raise children on either "side of the line," in traditional and modern ways, but generally life on both sides was tremendously difficult.

This chapter focuses on Kiowa writer N. Scott Momaday's intellectual contribution to the twentieth century. Specifically, I will look at one of Momaday's nonfiction works, his "Man Made of Words" essay, and consider how it fits into the history of other nonfiction I have discussed thus far. In doing so, I want to historicize Momaday's essay in its own moment, in the context of previous Native nonfiction, and consider how Momaday's literary achievement has been an integral part of how Native Americans have responded to the challenges of the twentieth century.

"The Man Made of Words" was Momaday's contribution to the First Convocation of American Indian Scholars, a signal event that occurred in March 1970. Momaday's address was one of three keynotes at that gathering. In this chapter I work through what it means that these seminal words of Momaday's were part of the program of the convocation. What does it say about Momaday's work and the time in which he publicly delivered it that the political watershed years of the early 1970s and the literary watershed of that same time came together at that moment? I will argue that Momaday's call to understand the intimate links between language, literature, and experience provides a way to understand the intellectual stakes of that moment and, further, to realize the literary and intellectual vision of the Native nonfiction tradition.

The argument here is one I build in multiple stages, including a quick run through some of the most prominent moments in twentieth-century Native American public history, a biographical sketch of Momaday, a discussion of the author's literary career, a description of the meeting at which Momaday delivered his address, an exposition of the address itself, an analysis of critical approaches to Momaday's fiction, a discussion of a recently published essay of Momaday's that is contemporary with "The Man Made of Words," an account of an event from the history of 1970s activism that connects to Momaday's work, and, finally, a return to the last sections of "The Man Made of Words." This rather complex progression grows from the paucity of works that address either Momaday's nonfiction as nonfiction, or the ways in which his early work is coterminous with the watershed era in which he emerged as a writer. Though Momaday is still, to my way of thinking, an exceptional figure in Native intellectual history, his essay in my reading demonstrates the extent to which his early work is very much part and parcel of the time in which he wrote it.

As Momaday's career attests, along with being a time of loss, the twentieth century was a time of remarkable achievement. Almost from the start, exceptional Native individuals had an enormous impact on mainstream public consciousness. Maria Tallchief, whose eponymous ancestor was a signer of the Osage Constitution, became one of the most famous ballerinas in the world. She was George Balanchine's muse during perhaps his most creative years and was the first truly great American ballerina.

Her sister Marjorie, though not as well-known to the American public, was just as accomplished a ballerina, working most of her career on European stages.[2]

Jim Thorpe, the Sac and Fox multisport athlete whose bronze image graces the entry area to the Pro Football Hall of Fame in Canton, Ohio, was named the Associated Press's greatest athlete of the first half of the twentieth century and many believe he was overlooked in not being accorded the same honor for the full century. His 1912 Olympic sweep of gold medals in both the pentathlon and decathlon remains unequaled. As an All-American in football at Carlisle, a professional baseball player, and the first president and biggest draw of the professional football league that would become the National Football League, he cut a wide swath through American sports history in the first decades of the twentieth century.[3]

Many other Native athletes had distinguished careers in the first half of the twentieth century, including baseball players Lou Sockalexis and Albert Bender, a baseball Hall of Famer who was one of the best pitchers of the early decades of the twentieth century.[4] Louis Tewanima won silver medals in the ten-thousand and five-thousand meter races at the same 1912 Olympics as Thorpe.[5] William "Lone Star" Dietz, the spouse of Carlisle art education innovator Angel DeCora, was a successful college and professional football coach.[6]

Will Rogers, the Cherokee humorist and actor who was the first person to make a coast-to-coast American radio broadcast, was perhaps the most famous person in the world at the height of his career.[7] Jay Silverheels, Dan George, and Will Sampson followed in the Hollywood tradition Rogers helped establish.[8] So did hundreds of Native extras and small part players who injected an Indian presence into the American film industry's representation of Natives, even if most of the major roles went to non-Native actors in dusky makeup and dark contact lenses.[9]

No Native has ever again achieved the fame of Rogers, but recent generations of actors, including Graham Greene, Tantoo Cardinal, Irene Bedard, and Wes Studi have built impressive resumés.[10] As important, Native filmmakers, including Shelly Niro, Beverly Singer, Victor Masayevsa, Sandra Osawa, Randy Redroad, and Chris Eyre (all of whom have multiple film credits) have implanted the idea in the film world that Native people can and should take charge of writing, directing, producing, and performing their own filmic representations.[11]

The Native twentieth century was not just about individuals making a mark in the public eye; it was also a century of significant events in which Native people played a central role. The Navajo Code Talkers of World War II, who used their native language to develop an unbreakable code that confounded the Axis powers in the Pacific, are one of the most dramatic examples. Their work on behalf of the Allies is the most prominent example of a history of profound dedication and sacrifice that Native members of the U.S. military undertook throughout the twentieth century.[12]

Other significant events were more focused on Natives restoring a measure of their political independence. In the early 1970s, for instance, Taos Pueblo regained 85,000 acres of its land, including Blue Lake, a sacred site.[13] Around the same time, Oglala patriots and members of the American Indian Movement took part in the 1973 siege at Wounded Knee, a seventy-one-day takeover of a reservation hamlet that was covered in the media in a way unprecedented before or since (Smith and Warrior, 194–268).

Many signal events were tragic. Complementing the story of the Code Talkers is the rise and fall of Ira Hamilton Hayes, the Pima Marine who helped raise the flag on Mount Surabachi during the battle for Iwo Jima in World War II (as memorialized in the famous statue in Washington, D.C.). Hayes was feted as a hero around the United States, then was unable to find a place for himself in postwar America. He died, essentially a street person, drowning in a few inches of water after passing out in a drainage ditch near Sacaton, Arizona, on the Pima Reservation (Bernstein, 49–51).[14] Perhaps even more poignant is the story of how Thorpe, having won four gold medals at the 1912 Stockholm Olympics, was stripped of those medals and publicly humiliated when the Amateur Athletic Union discovered he had played semiprofessional baseball one summer. The AAU eventually restored his amateur status in 1973 and the International Olympic Committee returned the medals to his family posthumously in 1983.[15]

Conversely, many stories were inspiring, perhaps none more than that of Billy Mills, the Lakota runner who was a surprise winner of the gold medal in the 10,000 meters at the Tokyo Olympics in 1964. Mills, who stumbled partway through the race, kept his feet and managed to come back to win the race. It is regarded by many as the greatest upset victory in Olympic history. Mills has since made countless motivational speeches, including many to young Indian people, delivering the message that they can overcome whatever disadvantages they face and achieve their dreams. Stories like Mills's stand at the apex of a century of inspiring stories that defy the stereotypes of Native Americans as dissipated, primitive, and in crisis.[16]

Most inspiring stories like this barely pierce the public consciousness or are quickly forgotten. Charles Curtis is remembered as Calvin Coolidge's vice president, but not usually as an enrolled member of the Kaw Tribe of Oklahoma, the only person of color to hold national elected office in the United States.[17] Dan George (1970) and Graham Greene (1990) lost Best Supporting Actor bids at the Academy Awards, but Cree songster Buffy Sainte-Marie took home an Oscar in 1982 for cowriting "Up Where We Belong" (from *An Officer and a Gentleman*).[18]

Sainte-Marie had been phenomenally successful as a folksinger in the heyday of folk in the early 1960s. She insisted on addressing Native politics in her music and supplied a Native presence to millions of children in her regular appearances on *Sesame Street* in the 1970s (Churchill, Hill, and Hill, 42–43). Around the same time as her emergence, Mohawk musician Robbie Robertson was leading The Band to legendary status, eventually becoming Bob Dylan's electric backup band. His recent work has focused on Native themes.[19]

These are events and careers that happened in plain sight. But certainly no one but the participants were present at the first known operation by an all-Native American surgical team or the vast majority of similarly re-markable moments of Native achievement that took place during the past century (Alvord and Van Pelt, 48). As Paul Chaat Smith asserts, the twen-tieth century was a time when "almost any Indian who painted or wrote, attended a university, played the violin, or flew a plane, in at least a small way made history. It was a political act simply to be human in the con-temporary world" ("The Meaning of Life," 32). Along the way, countless people have been the first person in their families to graduate from high school or college, the first person from their tribal nation to graduate from this or that college or graduate school, or the first to become a professional race car driver.

House Made of Pulitzer

N. Scott Momaday's achievements as an author and scholar figure promi-nently into this history of Native accomplishment. The son of a Kiowa man and a Cherokee woman who met each other at Haskell (a direct descen-dant of Carlisle), he was raised on various reservations in the Southwest, where his parents worked in Bureau of Indian Affairs schools. A gifted student of literature and language who is both a master of creative writing and a credentialed literary scholar, Momaday emerged in the late 1960s and early 1970s as a major figure in American literature and the single most visible American Indian literary author of the twentieth century.

Along the way, Momaday has contributed to a larger discussion of the category of experience in indigenous intellectual history. Momaday is a different sort of figure than Apess, inhabiting as he does a much less precarious space in his time than did Apess. Momaday is a culmination, in many ways, of the development of a public intellectual voice that Apess contributed to so mightily in his time. Momaday, further, does not come to us in the way of the framers of the Osage Constitution. Instead, his classical training in the Western tradition, coupled with his abiding sense of the importance of indigenous traditions, provokes a turn toward a mature literary expression that continues to grow. And rather than being like the Native students seeking a voice, Momaday self-consciously crafts his work, which is highly developed in terms of the more formal aspects of literature.

Experience, in Momaday's work, becomes a realm of language and ethics wrapped in the richness of words. "Language," Momaday has written, "is the context of our experience" ("Man Made of Words," 87). His career has been a reflection on the connection between language and experience. In this way, he brings into full flower the intellectual project Apess had helped bring to blossom a century and a half before.

Momaday's first novel, *House Made of Dawn,* was a literary sensation. Telling the story of a young man from a fictionalized Jemez Pueblo who runs from his own past and from the murder of an albino man to the down-and-out Indian community of Los Angeles in the 1950s, the novel carved out a new geography for Native American literary representation. The gritty, hard-edged novel eschews the kind of ethnographic description so common to books that attempt to elucidate tribal stories.

Perhaps the only Native American novel to come so close to explicating the social, political, and sexual realities of the Indian world is John Joseph Mathews's 1934 novel, *Sundown.*[20] But even compared to the most accomplished Native novels preceding it, *House Made of Dawn* is clearly in an aesthetic world far beyond. In 1969, *House Made of Dawn* won the Pulitzer Prize for fiction, making Momaday the first (and still only) Native American to win that prize.

Over a third of a century has now passed since Momaday's novel created that literary sensation. Looking back, the phenomenon effectively eclipsed the nonfiction tradition that had been central to the Native tradition of writing since at least the eighteenth century. It remains, arguably, Native American literature's finest moment, the font from which legitimacy in the academy and American mainstream publishing houses has flowed. Native nonfiction, especially regarded in hindsight, had seen moments of great success, but *House Made of Dawn* gave Native literature a leg up on gaining literary respectability. Native fiction, of course, was already emerging, but the success of *House Made of Dawn* certainly helped pave the way for more novels and some great careers (including, most prominently, those of James Welch, Leslie Marmon Silko, Louise Erdrich, and Gerald Vizenor). Native poetry found a niche in the post–*House Made of Dawn* gaps and some deeply talented writers benefited (including Simon Ortiz, Joy Harjo, and Ray Young Bear).

Courses in English and other departments and programs became places for Native authors to sell books or have a teaching career. Soon, criticism followed, most of it to this day focusing primarily on genre writing in fiction, poetry, or autobiography, or taking up issues of the relationship between oral and written literatures. Relatively little attention has been paid to Native nonfiction writing outside of autobiography, in spite of the centrality of nonfiction to the history of Native writing and the continuing nonfiction output of Native authors. In taking up Momaday's nonfiction from the era of *House Made of Dawn,* I am interested in this last chapter in revisiting the moment of eclipse and presenting an alternative way of thinking about the past, present, and future of Native writing, an alternative that preserves the tradition of nonfiction while including all forms of Native written expression.

"An Indigenous Book"

Momaday would surely have cut a wide swath through Native intellectual history even without the Pulitzer and probably without *House Made of Dawn*. He was of a generation of Native scholars who led the charge into the American academy in the 1950s and 1960s. On the cusp of his great fame, he was already doing important things insofar as he was one of the first Native scholars to achieve tenure in the University of California system.

According to his archival correspondence from that time, in 1966 Momaday took a sabbatical from his position at the University of California–Santa Barbara to spend a year in Amherst, Massachusetts. While there, Momaday was offered a position at the University of Massachusetts–Amherst, an offer Santa Barbara responded to with the counteroffer of an advanced associate professor position. Momaday accepted the counteroffer—which commanded a salary of $12,700—and returned to Santa Barbara. Not only had he achieved tenure in just four years, but his advanced position, he told his great friend and mentor, the poet Yvor Winters, was one that generally took ten years to achieve.[21]

In that same letter to Winters, Momaday reveals something of the milieu of those times in talking about having dinner with a Navajo student named David Redhorse, who attended Amherst College. Momaday enjoyed the dinner in part because, he said, "We both believe in witches and medicine men." Redhorse, who had come to New England to attend a prep school program for Native students that Vine Deloria Jr. had set up as part of American Indian Scholarships, apparently told Momaday a story of recently seeing an old woman shape-shift into a coyote.[22] As Momaday writes to Winters:

> The thing that makes this such a memorable experience for me is this: it was given me for the truth by an Amherst freshman who, before coming here, was at Lenox prep school for two years. His hair is raven black and shoulder length. He was wearing a king's ransom in silver and turquoise— and an Ivy League blazer with a blue button-down and a black silk tie. He tells me he has a younger brother who is aiming for Oxford.

There, in the heart of New England, two centuries after its Puritan obsessions would have made doing so impossible and 130 years after William Apess could hardly scratch out a living for himself and his family, Momaday and this young Navajo could talk about medicine men and witches over a genteel supper.

The story is a reminder of the context of the times. While Momaday has come to define the wave of literature that began after 1969, he was also someone of stature in the emerging world of Native scholarship. Thanks to Deloria's efforts, some dozens of young Indian people found their ways to prep schools in the Northeast. It is important to remember how little space exists between a simple supper like this one in Amherst and the explosion of activity that occurred in the next few years. Yet the dinner Momaday describes was itself a radical departure from what had been true just a decade earlier. The student's combination of blazer, turquoise, and shoulder-length hair testifies to how the changes in broader U.S. society were occurring in their own way in the Indian world.

Given the fullness of that context, Momaday as a literary figure becomes more difficult to relegate to being primarily a novelist. It was, after all, twenty years after *House Made of Dawn* that Momaday published another novel, *The Ancient Child.* Before *House Made of Dawn,* Momaday had already published a revision of his dissertation, a biographical sketch and the collected poems of American poet Frederick Goddard Tuckerman (whose most famous poem is "The Cricket").[23] He had also published a retelling of Kiowa stories, first called *The Journey of Tai-Me,* in a limited fine edition, then titled *The Way to Rainy Mountain* as a trade book. After *House Made of Dawn,* he published two books of poetry, *Angle of Geese* and *The Gourd Dancer,* and a memoir, *The Names.* He also has enjoyed success as a visual artist and has been a playwright, children's book author, and essayist.[24]

Of Momaday's many books, one would be hard-pressed to name a masterpiece. It is easy to argue that *House Made of Dawn* is the most significant, but each of the first three books (*Journey* and *Rainy Mountain* counting here as essentially the same book) made formal and aesthetic innovations that have helped define the boundaries of contemporary Native American literature. *Rainy Mountain* is a hybrid work that contains retellings of old Kiowa tales, historical narrative, and autobiography. The University of New Mexico Press, which published the book, could not even find readers to give the work a fair reading as an imaginative work. Instead, readers dismissed it as being of no value for understanding the Kiowa world.[25]

House Made of Dawn has been as formally important for the development of the Native American novel as Richardson and Fielding were for the development of the English novel. While many first novels by even the finest of Native authors feel as though the genre has outpaced the youthful talent of the writer, in Momaday's first novel he already seems in command of the prose. Momaday brings the deeply conservative demands of oral traditional material together with the opposite impulses of modern realism that he deploys in the novel.[26] As Ian Watt argues in *The Rise of the Novel,* his classic study of the emergence of the novel in English, "The novel is the form of literature which most fully reflects [an] individualist and innovating reorientation. Previous literary forms had reflected the general tendency of their cultures to make conformity to traditional practice the major test of truth" (13). Importantly, Momaday succeeds not only in producing a novel about American Indians, but in bringing these two opposing literary traditions into the same story.

In both of these first two books, Momaday self-consciously under-stands himself to be crafting material from different literary modes and making of them literary works that are remarkable both for their contrasts and their seamlessness. In *Rainy Mountain,* Momaday makes a home for the oral tradition by personalizing Kiowa stories and by self-consciously becoming an interpreter of them.

With *The Names,* Momaday entered into new formal and aesthetic space. The book calls itself a memoir and it is studied most often as an autobiography. These are certainly fair descriptions, but the book is more. The stream-of-consciousness sections are reminiscent of James Joyce's *Portrait of the Artist as a Young Man.* But again, as in the case of *House Made of Dawn,* Momaday appears to be interested in doing more than writing himself into the great traditions of modernism. *The Names* is not the story of a man preoccupied with the alienation and meaninglessness of modernity. Instead, it tells how "a man's life proceeds from his name, in the way that a river proceeds from its source."[27] Of the story that follows Momaday writes,

> In general my account is an autobiographical account. Specifically it is an act of the imagination. When I turn my mind to my early life, it is the imaginative part of it that comes first and irresistibly into reach, and of that part I take hold. This is one way to tell a story. In this instance it is my way, and it is the way of my people. When Pohd-lohk told a story he began by being quiet. Then he said *Ah-keah-de,* "They were camping," and he said it every time. I have tried to write in the same way, in the same spirit. Imagine. They were camping.

Momaday, in this passage, claims for his work not so much the kind of hybrid space of *Way to Rainy Mountain* or *House Made of Dawn.* Instead, we see the fruition of a brief comment Momaday had made years earlier to Winters. In January 1968, not long after returning to Santa Barbara after his sabbatical in Amherst, Momaday wrote to Winters, "Lately I have been thinking of a nonfiction book, an evocation of the American landscape, informed by autobiographical elements and a history of the Kiowas."[28] Momaday continues by saying, "I don't know, it's just a thought at this point. But I want to write an indigenous book."

Momaday, then, seems intent on developing what would become in *The Names* a literary form not so much centered on the clash of cultures, but on something that would allow him to educe from Native American traditions an innovative written form. In this, he echoes Richardson, who in 1741 wrote to a friend that, with *Pamela,* he "might possibly introduce a new species of writing" (Watt, 208).

Momaday's comment about an "indigenous book" is a provocative one that prompts a host of questions, the most obvious ones being at once generic and formal. Generically, it is interesting to note that Momaday attempts to make the particular innovations of indigeneity not in the novel, but in a memoir; this prompts the ripe suggestion that Momaday is, in effect, taking hold of the autobiographical tradition in Native American writing and laying claim to it not in its "as-told-to" ethnographic mode, but with the modern hallmark of individual authorship and originality. Though he was not self-consciously doing so, Momaday makes a move not unlike the ones Apess made after *A Son of the Forest,* when he defied in his own ways the tyranny of expectations and the rhetoric of ancientness and novelty.

This approach is brought out in even more stark relief when coupled with the formal aspects of oral traditional storytelling with which Momaday crafts his memoir. Again, the contrasts, even contradictions, between the modern and the indigenous blur. Momaday's emergent aesthetic lacks the rough edges so often attributed to hybridization, or worse, the grotesque dimension associated with contemporary notions of cyborgs, notions that Sean Teuton says are "insulting terms which connote parroting of and genetic breeding with the dominant culture" (205).[29]

The Names is a marvelous book that will no doubt garner much attention from literary historians and critics in decades to come. Rather than continuing this foray into its intricacies, though, I am interested in turning my attention to some of Momaday's articulations of his emerging aesthetic, which occurred in the years between the publication of his first two books and *The Names.* Specifically, I am interested in working through some of the issues that arose for Momaday then and that continue to occupy scholars about what Momaday calls "the relationship between language and experience" ("Man Made of Words," 49). In so doing, I want to draw a frame around a critical space in which we can make sense of this nonfiction essay, a frame that will help explain Momaday's remarkable aesthetic achievements and the period in which he realized them. In short, I am interested in what it meant then and what it means now for Momaday to be in his time, "The Man Made of Words."

Native Intellectualism in the Movement Years

Few gatherings of American Indian intellectuals have rivaled the Convocation of American Indian Scholars, convened on the campus of Princeton University in March 1970. The proceedings of that gathering, published by the Native-run Indian Historian Press (San Francisco), were entitled *Indian Voices: The First Convocation of American Indian Scholars.* Cahuilla historian Rupert Costo and his wife, Jeanette Henry Costo, ran the Indian Historian Press, published a journal named *The Indian Historian,* and ran the American Indian Historical Society. The couple, along with Beatrice Medicine, Alfonso Ortiz, Edward Dozier, Joseph Senungetuk, Fritz Scholder, and Robert Kaniatobe made up the event's steering committee (*Indian Voices,* 1).

The convocation took place against the backdrop of what was becoming the most extraordinary moment of political mobilization in twentieth-century American Indian history. Just months earlier, eighty students from California campuses had taken over the abandoned prison island of Alcatraz, garnering headlines and the attention of Indian people around the country.[30] Yet, in spite of the fact that some of the zealous defenders of Alcatraz and later historians would see that action as somehow the ur-protest of the movement years, protest politics was hardly new to the Indian world.[31]

Youth had become a focus in Native America in the 1950s, and the early 1960s had seen the emergence of a Native American youth movement, especially on college campuses. American Indian Development, a group in Colorado, sponsored workshops that brought American Indian students to the campus of the University of Colorado for classes to prepare them for leadership in Indian communities (Smith and Warrior, 40ff.). Some of the students who were part of these workshops were also involved in the Southwestern Regional Indian Youth Council (SRIYC), which organized young people for similar purposes in New Mexico, Arizona, and Oklahoma.[32] In 1961, SRIYC students decided to take their group national and founded the National Indian Youth Council (NIYC).

NIYC was led by Clyde Warrior (whom I earlier compared to William Apess) and Mel Thom. These two young men countered the dominant early 1960s image of young Indians as passive and shy. Together, they represented the voices of Indian youth on the boards of national organizations and worked to spread the reach of NIYC (Smith and Warrior, 42ff.).

The Youth Council became one of the first Native organizations to garner headlines when it joined with Indian fishermen in the Pacific Northwest to protest for Native fishing rights.[33] The Youth Council had an air of intellectualism about it, especially in the figure of Warrior. He seemed cut from the mold of the best of anticolonial figures from Africa and Asia, and his biting analysis of the positionality of American Indians relied on a stark look at the real possibilities for the social and political future of Native communities. He was an inspiring figure who helped young Indian people, especially those like him, who came from traditional backgrounds and who were expected to become leaders back home. His untimely death from alcoholism at age twenty-eight spoke not only to his personal demons, but to the protracted space in which the Native political imagination of the 1960s had to exist (Smith and Warrior, 36–59).

Reservation-based politics were soon rivaled by events in American cities. In the 1950s, American Indians made their way in record numbers to large cities like Los Angeles, San Francisco, Chicago, and Denver as part of the Bureau of Indian Affairs' relocation program (Smith and Warrior, 7). Promising training, jobs, and housing, relocation was twinned with the federal policy of termination, through which the federal government sought to end its responsibilities for individual tribes, bringing an end to what was still known as "the Indian problem."

In the cities, economic and social conditions drew urban Natives into organizations and community centers. Virtually ignored by the federal government, many urban Natives turned to protest politics to air their grievances. Urban Indians, as they came to be known in the era, picketed BIA offices in places like Denver and Minneapolis. In 1968—a year in which so much happened politically in the United States and around the world—the American Indian Movement (AIM), which would become the most famous of all the Native organizations in the cities, was founded in Minneapolis (Smith and Warrior, 127ff.). Committed to patrolling their neighborhood to intervene between police and Indians, who often found themselves the targets of harassment and arrest when nearby bars closed, AIM soon developed a national reputation and a set of local chapters in places like Milwaukee and Denver.

By 1970, the image of the urban Native protester, threatening direct action and speaking in a political language that borrowed from the broader antiwar and civil rights movements of the 1960s, was a given. Over the next four years, the protest movement continued to grow. Takeovers, occupations, and demonstrations became part of the American Indian world. Five years before, radical activists from the Indian world had appeared at national and regional Indian meetings as a colorful fringe, selling or giving away their pamphlets and broadsides from behind folding tables. In 1970, those same people led organizations and succeeded in gaining a place on the programs at national meetings, where they previously had been relegated to lobbies and foyers.

While the growing swell of Native protest politics was the most visible part of the agenda of the Indian world in 1970, a lot else was going on as well. Having cowritten a book of narrative history about the era and the importance of protest politics, I would never minimize the role of demonstrations and other expressions of radicalism in the early 1970s. However, it is crucial to understand these protests in the context of everything else that was happening in the Indian world in those years.

Protest was just one part of the 1960s and 1970s watershed in the Indian world. Most important to my argument here is that in higher education, Natives were finding their ways to colleges in increasing numbers. Whereas sixty-six Natives graduated from college in 1961, over thirty thousand would be enrolled in higher education by the middle 1970s (Deloria, "Burden," 184). The War on Poverty had brought an increasing level of funding to reservation social programs, and the growing ranks of Native college alumni created a group of people who could take the reins of those programs. College graduates added to a discernible stratum of Native professionals who were becoming lawyers, doctors, dentists, nurses, teachers, and administrators. Indian professionals were still something of a rarity, and even today may still not be numerous enough to represent an identifiable class in the way that African Americans, for instance, have such a class. But long-held hopes that Native people could direct the programs affecting Native life were now coming to fruition.

A CONVOCATION OF ONE'S OWN

It was the development of an educated, professional class among Natives that made Momaday's keynote at the Convocation of Indian Scholars possible. Of the event, Rupert Costo said in *Indian Voices,* "The Convocation was conceived, organized, and directed entirely by Native Americans. No Federal or other governmental agency was involved in any part of the preparations, organization, or conduct of the Convocation. No political organization, social agency, or church was involved in any way" (vii). After talking about the various panels, keynote addresses, and other sessions that occurred over the course of four days, Costo called the event "a milestone in the history of the Native Americans, and indeed it was a milestone in the history of this nation. The event proved beyond doubt that leadership exists among the Native American people, for all the purposes of education, administration, economic development, and the general betterment of the American Indian" (vii). For the first time, something akin to Du Bois's vision for African Americans was possible for Natives.

Even controlling for an element of self-aggrandizement in Costo's glowing review of this event (for which he himself was the major organizing force), this exceptional gathering deserves a prominent place in the annals of Native intellectual history. The gathering was held in Princeton because of Professor Alfonso Ortiz's academic appointment there.[34] Along with him, the other keynoters were Vine Deloria Jr., still riding the wave of popularity from his best-selling manifesto, *Custer Died for Your Sins,* and Momaday, so recently having broken through onto the national literary scene.

Other presenters included Beatrice Medicine on Red Power, Fritz Scholder on Native arts, Roger Buffalohead on Native studies programs, and former Bureau of Indian Affairs Commissioner Robert Bennett on economic development. Many who were there as participants went on to make a significant impact on Indian affairs, including Samuel Billison, Herb Blatchford, George Crossland, Philip Sam Deloria, William Demmert Jr., Adolph Dial, John E. Echohawk, Gloria Emerson, Charles Loloma, Chris McNeil, D'Arcy McNickle, Simon Ortiz, Ann Rainer, Jack Ridley, Joe Sando, Buffy Sainte-Marie, James West, and Richard West Jr. Thirty-one Native artists, including Blackbear Bosin, Allan Houser, Yeffe Kimball, and Momaday's father, Alfred, appeared in an exhibition concurrent with the convocation (*Indian Voices,* 383–90).

Highlights of the proceedings included Richard West, founding director of the Smithsonian's National Museum of the American Indian and then a law student, asking Alfonso Ortiz about differences between Native and Christian conceptions of nature and human domination (A. Ortiz, 18–19). In another moment, Vine Deloria Jr., McNickle, Demmert, Blatchford, and Bennett exchanged thoughts regarding the direction of federal Indian policy (Deloria, "Implications," 99–102).

The proceedings are filled with a sense of the importance of all these people participating with one another in a new kind of intellectual engagement on behalf of their constituents in Native communities. Momaday, who eschewed the kind of politics associated with the more radical Native American studies programs, seemed completely engaged in this different sort of intellectual endeavor.[35] Deloria, still years from heavy involvement in the vagaries of academic programs, was likewise engaged. And Costo, a figure with a reputation for being difficult and insistent on only his vision of things, seemed happy that this event had somehow become larger and more vibrant than his already expansive conception of it.

Looking back now with the benefit of over three decades of distance, it seems clear that Momaday's work from the movement years shows the need to envision a new, more robust sense of Momaday as a figure in Native literary and intellectual history. His work has suffered from his reputation of being somehow apolitical and disengaged from the immediacy of the politics of the early seventies. What I would like to argue from the perspective of his presentation at the convocation, though, is that Momaday in his work seems not so much to avoid politics as to be political in a different, deeper way than what was possible at the time.

What is compelling about Momaday's presentation is the extent to which in "The Man Made of Words" he is able to encapsulate in such a small space so much about American Indian literature and the indigenous imagination. The essay has philosophical aspects to it, revealing Momaday's deep learning and classical training. At the same time, it introduces nearly all of the important themes of the field of literature that Momaday was leading to prominence in the early 1970s. The strands Momaday presents in "The Man Made of Words" are concentrated ruminations on preoccupations that appear throughout his later work. As he states in a later essay on Jorge Luis Borges, "If words are the intricate bonds of language, and if the spoken word is the first part of this ancient design, this construction that makes of us a family, a tribe, a civilization, we had better understand how and why—and perhaps first of all, *that*—we exist in the element of language" ("A Divine Blindness," 87).

WORDS AND EXPERIENCE

Momaday begins "The Man Made of Words" with a discussion of an old Kiowa woman, Ko-sahn, who "spoke and sang to me one afternoon in Oklahoma. It was like a dream. When I was born she was already old; she was a grown woman when my grandparents came into the world." She had, in fact, been alive in 1833, when on a November night the sky was filled with falling stars, an event implanted in the Kiowa memory. Momaday, in writing about Ko-sahn and life as a Kiowa in the nineteenth century, says that he "had projected myself—imagined myself—out of the room and out of time. I was there with Ko-sahn in the Oklahoma July. We laughed easily together" (50–51).

Having entered Ko-sahn's world through writing about her, Momaday then turns the tables. Looking back over what he had written and questioning whether his words "had anything whatsoever to do with meaning," Momaday fixes on the name Ko-sahn. All at once, he writes, "everything seemed suddenly to refer to that name. The name seemed to humanize the whole complexity of language" (51).

Then, Momaday repeats the name Ko-sahn and the old woman, dead now for over a hundred years, "stepped out of the language and stood before me on the page." In amazement, Momaday indicates to her that he assumed she had died. "No," she answers him, "You have imagined me well, and so I am. You have imagined that I dream, and so I do. I have seen the falling stars" (51).

In his essay, Momaday wonders aloud, as most readers might, how the appearance of Ko-sahn could be happening. "You are not actually here," he says, "not here in this room" (51). She answers:

> Be careful of your pronouncements, grandson. . . . You imagine that I am here in this room, do you not? That is worth something. You see, I have existence, whole being, in your imagination. It is but one kind of being, to be sure, but it is perhaps the best of all kinds. If I am not here in this room, grandson, then surely neither are you. (51)

Not long after, Ko-sahn "receded into the language I had made. And then I imagined I was alone in the room" (52).

This story of Ko-sahn is integral to Momaday's consideration of the imagination and the role of literature in "exert[ing] the force of language upon the unknown." As he contends, "We are what we imagine. Our very existence consists in our imagination of ourselves. Our best destiny is to imagine, at least, completely, who and what, and *that* we are. The greatest tragedy that can befall us is to go unimagined." Momaday here stakes out what he calls "admittedly a moral view . . . but literature is itself a moral view, and it is a view of morality" (55–56).

In most of his writing, Momaday steers clear of being overtly didactic and prescriptive, so this idea of literature and morality being tightly woven together is subtle. Yet what Momaday points toward is the idea that morality is something that is seated deeply within human experience and is, like literature, prompted and provoked by the presence of human imagination. Language, within this view, plays a primary role. As Momaday says elsewhere, "To be careless in the presence of words, on the inside of language, is to violate a fundamental morality" ("Native Voice," 16). This locating of morality in our experience of language, according to this reading of "The Man Made of Words," is Momaday's response to the politics of his own time.

What draws me to Momaday's presentation at the convocation is the way it undermines what has become received wisdom both about Momaday and the time period. The watershed years of 1969 to 1973 have come to be best known for spectacular actions like Wounded Knee. American Indian intellectuals have often been identified politically based on where they stood vis-á-vis those political actions. That judgment would make Momaday a quietist or a conservative, hardly the type to be manning a bunker at Wounded Knee or even making public pronouncements in support of militancy. What seems unfortunate about such definitions is not so much that people like Momaday didn't, in fact, support militant politics (they didn't), but that the more complex contours of politics in the 1970s Indian world are obscured by too narrow a focus on the Indian world as a place where a particular kind of radicalism defines the political parameters of that world.

Momaday, in fact, grew up surrounded by the apparatus of federal Indian policy and had, from an early age, an intricate knowledge of the history of colonization in the Indian world. His parents, Alfred Momaday and Natachee Scott Momaday, worked in Bureau of Indian Affairs schools throughout his childhood and he became as acquainted with life at Jemez Pueblo, where they worked for many years, as any outsider could (*Names,* esp. 117–61). While much has been made about how much his knowledge of Jemez culture comes through in *House Made of Dawn,* not nearly so much has been written about how that same novel reflects the political realities of the Indian world.[36] The novel's protagonist, Abel, after all, goes to Los Angeles to take part in the BIA's Relocation Program, a program designed to take people away from their reservation homes for new lives in American cities. Millie, the woman who tries to help Abel in Los Angeles, works for the BIA as a relocation officer.

Momaday's knowledge of policy stands in contrast to his use of ethnography in *House Made of Dawn*. As Larry Landrum points out, Momaday's use of ethnography has long been a point of contention in Momaday criticism, one implication being that Momaday somehow lacks authenticity or authority because of his use of such texts (764). Interestingly, Momaday's archival work seemingly does not include any quotation from policy sources or political histories. It does not, I would argue, because Momaday did not need to crib off such sources to understand the political canvas upon which he writes.

A short digression into some of the critical arguments *House Made of Dawn* has prompted is instructive for developing this reading of "The Man Made of Words." *House Made of Dawn* is perhaps the preeminent novel that brings together the aesthetics of the modernist novel and Native American ceremonial traditions. In it, Momaday achieves a suffusion of two radically different traditions. As Landrum argues, "More than simply adapting Native American culture to modernist creative strategies, *House Made of Dawn* evokes typical modernist practices only to craze the mirroring effects of their insularity" (776).

Landrum is certainly on target in refusing to choose between Momaday the ethnographer and Momaday the modernist. But I will go further and contend that too much attention to these two themes can make it easy to forget the ways that *House Made of Dawn* is a novel reflecting not just Abel and his culture, but also Abel's worldliness. It is, thus, a novel in need of a more robust sense of how politics, through federal Indian policy, fits into the complex of existential realities of Native life. In such a reading, war veteran Abel not only becomes alienated from his familial and tribal past, but is more accurately someone who faces a life proscribed by the faceless character of federal policy.[37]

MOMADAY AND NATIONALISM

Simon Ortiz comes as close as any commentator on *House Made of Dawn* to bringing together all of its constituent parts. He does so rather succinctly in his essay, "Towards a National Indian Literature: Cultural Authenticity in Nationalism." As part of his overall project of linking modern Western literary forms, Native history, and "oral tradition, which includes prayer, song, drama-ritual, narrative or story-telling, much of it within ceremony—some of it outside of ceremony—which is religious and social," Ortiz argues that Native expression "speaks crucially about the experience of colonization" (9, 10).

Written literature plays a role in this process. "In every case where European culture was cast upon Indian people of this nation," Ortiz writes, "there was similar creative response and development. . . . It can be observed that this was the primary element of a nationalistic impulse to make use of foreign ritual, ideas, and material in their own—Indian—terms" (8).

House Made of Dawn, in Ortiz's reading, is primarily about how Abel can "keep integral what is most precious to him: the spiritual knowledge which will guide him throughout his life as it has guided those before him" (10). In the novel, Momaday says that the people of Walatowa

> do not hanker after progress and have never changed their essential way of life. Their invaders were a long time in conquering them; and now, after four centuries of Christianity, they still pray in Tanoan to the old deities of the earth and sky and make their living from the things that are and have always been within their reach; while in the discrimination of pride they acquire from their conquerors only the luxury of example. They have assumed the names and gestures of their enemies, but have held on to their own, secret souls; and in this there is a resistance and an overcoming, a long outwaiting. (58)

This long outwaiting, Ortiz argues, "is what proves to be the element which enables Abel to endure prison, city life, indignities cast upon him, and finally it is what helps him to return to himself and run in the dawn so that life will go on" (11).

For Ortiz, who comes from a living Pueblo tradition, Momaday writes Abel as someone who learns over the course of the novel to come home not just to a culture, but to a culture of "resistance against forces that would destroy life. It is by the affirmation of knowledge of source and place and spiritual return that resistance is realized" (11). Ortiz's reading is liable to the criticism that he has not sufficiently recognized the complexities of the interplay between culture, politics, and identity under the sign of modernity. This is especially true given that Ortiz deploys the language of nationalism and authenticity, bugbears of contemporary criticism.

Yet Ortiz is no wild-eyed proponent of an unsophisticated essentialism. He belongs in the company of Ngugi and Aimé Césaire as a writer who has plumbed the depths of the colonial experience and found in language—his own use of it as well as others'—responses to the existential realities that colonialism imposes. Ortiz finds among Native writers "the acknowledgment . . . of a responsibility to advocate for their people's self-government, sovereignty, and control of land and natural resources; and to look also at racism, political and economic oppression, sexism, supremacism, and the needless and wasteful exploitation of land and people" (12).

Ortiz's reading suggests that Abel's story is one in which he learns through his experiences to come home and take up his part in the "long outwaiting." Abel's grandfather, Francisco, spends the entire novel living out his own version of this process of resistance, hoping for Abel to finally return home to learn his part in the process. The novel, then, becomes a sort of dual bildungsroman, one that fails as Abel is unable to find a place in the Army or the city and one with the potential to lead Abel to a better life as he finally takes up his part in the political culture to which he had been born.[38] Momaday, for Ortiz, gives voice to those who have made "a persistent call by a people determined to be free; it is an authentic voice of liberation" (12). Teuton echoes Ortiz's reading when he writes that Momaday "chronicl[es] the process through which an American Indian can recover his relationship to his homeland. In *House Made of Dawn,* Abel does not innately 'sense' a spiritual connection to lands he barely remembers" (182–83). Instead, according to Teuton, "Abel fails again and again, until he eventually, through social engagement and social practice, learns, through the instruction of his grandfather and others, the way to his homeland" (185).

Ortiz and Teuton provide examples of what Landrum sees as a distinction between readings by "Eurocentric critics [who] do not have their cultural identities at stake," and Native critics, "whose subject position is not (or not only) professional competence but cultural *being*" (781). Jason W. Stevens illustrates Landrum's point in his rather misguided recent essay on Momaday's identity, "Bear, Outlaw, and Storyteller: American Frontier Mythology and the Ethnic Subjectivity of N. Scott Momaday." In the midst of an essay on the presence of Billy the Kid and other frontier myths in Momaday's fiction, Stevens fixates on Momaday's identity, charting what he supposes is Momaday's inner consciousness through examining his public statements.

"Momaday," Stevens argues, "has struggled throughout his career to define a tenable ethnic persona. His notion of his own ethnicity has wavered between his understanding of an authentic body of traditional knowledge on one hand and his development of a stylized, modern posture on an-other" (601). Stevens's formulation of identity, though, hinges on catego-ries of authenticity that sound more like the fantasies of someone whose knowledge of what it means to be a contemporary Native is cursory at best. Momaday, he writes, "did not . . . grow up within the Kiowa tribal tradi-tions on which his works draw, and he admits knowing very little of the Kiowa language" (601).

So for Stevens, to be authentically Native is (a) to grow up "within . . . tribal traditions" and (b) to know more than a very little of a tribal lan-guage. This is, of course, ridiculous, relegating the vast majority of con-temporary Natives to a nonspecified, but seemingly non-Native identity. Ortiz would be one of the few contemporary Native writers to satisfy Stevens's criteria, but he would be open to a fall from grace for his self-admitted early writings, in which he did not specify the Indianness of his fictional characters.[39]

Imagine a scholar today making the argument that W. E. B. Du Bois's "notion of his own ethnicity wavered" because he was light-skinned and did not grow up in the South. Du Bois, of course, was open to criticism from various corners in his own time on these issues, but I have difficulty believing a serious contemporary scholar would take up the position of those critics.

Stevens is but the most recent example of a scholar who is more than willing to surmise from a Native writer's work the realities of his or her life. "Momaday has perhaps become aware," Stevens writes of *The Ancient Child,* "that the Kiowa voice he has claimed is elusive, because it is over-determined by frontier archetypes and a construction of American self-hood that he has uneasily and incompletely assimilated" (613). How does he know? Ironically, Native critics are regularly accused of being naïve essentialists, but here we have someone who places ultimate faith in the supposed transparency of a fictional text to reveal the true thoughts and intentions of its author.

In the end, Stevens argues, "Billy [the Kid] remains ingrained in Moma-day's personal myth. The bitter displacement at the core of the outlaw's story is perhaps as telling of Momaday's labor for ethnic definition as the myth of transformation that the Kiowa bear fails to fulfill" (626). Momaday is, in Stevens's reading, more American frontier than Kiowa. Without a single reference to a work of psychology, Stevens purports to explore the depth of Momaday's consciousness. He treats literary interviews like verbatims from psychoanalysis, portraying Momaday as some-one who can't figure out how to be who he really wants to be.

This article is evidence that things have not changed much since 1980, when, Vine Deloria Jr. says, he was asked by an audience member during a question-and-answer period how she

> would be able to recognize that I was an Indian if she followed me around the streets of Tucson, Arizona, for a week. What could I say in response? That I would be dressed in buckskin, be carrying bow and arrows, have a deer slung over my shoulder, and be carrying some pottery? That picture would have been absurd, of course, but it was precisely the image that I was expected to present which would enable her to correctly identity me as an Indian. ("Foreword: American Fantasy," xiv)

Momaday's musings on his own identity are deeper manifestations of what Deloria presents here. His embrace of the Billy the Kid story confounds many who read *The Ancient Child,* but when we treat it as one more piece of the complex world of ideas and images that Momaday brings to his work, we can see that he writes Native consciousness and agency into a narrative from which they have been excluded.

Readings like Ortiz's or Teuton's, which highlight social realities along with cultural features, make all the more sense when the novel is placed alongside Momaday's nonfiction. Ortiz and Teuton see the possibility of liberation in a text like *House Made of Dawn,* not because of its authen-ticity or the authenticity of its author, but because of the way it provides a platform from which to understand the possibilities of the future for Native communities. Stevens and others from what has become the main-stream of Momaday criticism seem to offer instead a sort of ethnic panop-ticon in which non-Natives stand by and watch Natives wrestle with their identities.

AN ESSAY ON INDIAN HATING

"The Morality of Indian Hating," which Momaday wrote during gradu-ate school, provides perhaps the clearest insight into Momaday's political mind. The essay was not published until he compiled his nonfiction writ-ings in the 1990s. It begins with a story about the Kiowas in the 1830s that would later appear in the "Man Made of Words" presentation at Princeton. Momaday uses that story to talk about the way American Indian history

needs to be understood in its particularities in order to overcome the way
that "the Indian has been for a long time generalized in the mind of the
white man. Denied the acknowledgment of individuality and change, he
has been made to become in theory what he could not become in fact, a
synthesis of himself" (58).

The essay goes on to chronicle various episodes from American Indian
history, from the Pequot War of the seventeenth century to the termination policy and relocation program of the twentieth. He questions the
morality of the intolerance displayed throughout American history and
poses against it the imposition of indignity that comes with colonization.
"The Indian," Momaday writes,

> has been compelled to make his way under an imposed identity of defeat.
> He has been made to live for a long time with the conviction—now indi-
> visibly his and the white man's—that the best possessions of his mind and
> soul are inane. Moralities can be violated and destroyed. Moral degen-
> eration is conceived in guilt and nurtured in prejudice. It is among the
> most hideous of psychological deformities and it perpetuates itself in its
> own infection. The Indian has been afflicted with that for which society
> prescribes neither prevention nor cure. (59)

With these words, Momaday reveals a sense of anger and outrage that rarely
emerges in his later, published writings, especially not in such a long form.

From the Puritans to the present, Momaday argues, the inheritors of
English colonization have lived with two assumptions. "One is the assumption. . . that the Indian is an impediment to the progress of civilization; the other is the related assumption that the rights, both natural and
legal, which dignify the white man are unavailable to the Indian" (63).
These assumptions resulted in an earlier time in intolerance, and in more
recent times in "a morality of pity" (69). That pity, Momaday contends,
was behind the reforms of the 1930s, while a reactive sense of impatience
fueled the movement toward relocation and termination. "The contemporary white American," he writes, "is willing to assume responsibility
for the Indian—he is willing to take on the burdens of oppressed people
everywhere—but he is decidedly unwilling to divest himself of the false
assumptions which impede his good intentions" (71–72).

The false assumption behind relocation, Momaday contends, is the idea
"that the Indian becomes a white man by virtue of living in the presence
of white men" (71–72). Momaday counters that idea not only by pointing

to the statistics of failure that attended the relocation program, but by describing the different sense of identity that he had come to know living in communities in the Southwest, especially among Pueblo people. He finds the "cultural spirit" of the annual Jemez race at dawn to encapsulate the crucial Native response to the idea of Indian absorption into America. Momaday writes, "[T]o watch those runners is to know that they draw with every step some elemental power which resides at the core of the earth" (76). This is, of course, the scene that ends *House Made of Dawn,* one that Momaday suggests is a way to "ward off the immorality of indifference" (76).

Momaday wrote "The Morality of Indian Hating," "The Man Made of Words," and *House Made of Dawn,* of course, in the same ripening era of Indian affairs, even including shared elements among them. Situating "The Man Made of Words" within the era of the activist movement years of the late 1960s and early 1970s is the final move I want to make in building my reading of the speech in Princeton. Reading Momaday in this way makes him not a timeless, romantic figure, but someone speaking from a specific moment. Momaday and the movement years are, thus, of a piece, not merely coincidence. The best example of this comes from those who waged a war against words in taking over the Bureau of Indian Affairs building in Washington, D.C., in 1972, a year and a half after Momaday spoke to the Convocation of American Indian Scholars.

FURY IN THE MOVEMENT YEARS

"Patient fury" is what Bobby Jean Kilberg, then a White House aide, called the destruction that the Trail of Broken Treaties Caravan of two thousand Indian people visited on the Bureau of Indian Affairs building in Washington, D.C., during the election week of 1972 (Smith and Warrior, 167). Having come to town for what was supposed to be a nonviolent set of observances designed to draw attention to the issues of grassroots Indian people and their proposal for the future direction for Indian affairs, the Trail of Broken Treaties instead became an armed confrontation.

American Indians occupied the BIA building when other accommodations fell through and, over the course of a week, the federal installation became a virtual war zone. To defend against federal and district forces that had arrayed against them, the Indian people in the building stacked furniture against doorways and spilled the contents of filing cabinets into corridors. By the end of the confrontation, passersby reported smelling gasoline as they walked near the building. One federal worker's daughter sketched in crayon the source of the smell: a rooftop covered with glass bottles of gasoline at the ready for a spectacular end to the occupation (Smith and Warrior, 157, 160). Warriors inside vied for the right to be the suicide bomber who would strike the match once the building was evacuated, bringing the building to a crumbled wreck of steel, concrete, desks, and the endless paperwork that typified the lives of those stalwarts who held the building, using wrenches, hammers, and crudely fashioned spears against the assault rifles of federal agents in riot gear.

As Paul Smith and I write in our account of the occupation, "[T]he ferocity of the vandalism could not be explained only by the fear of imminent attack. The looting and the trashing was so widespread, so deliberate, that it pointed to a hatred on the part of many Indians for the documents because they were documents; records that must be destroyed because of what they and the building that housed them represented" (162). Indeed. Even today, to ask for BIA records from the years leading up to November 1972 is often fruitless. The bureau has never had the wherewithal to refile the mountain of documents that flooded the corridors.

The deluge of documents and the ferocity of the occupiers speak to larger issues of the facelessness of the bureaucracy that operated during the occupation. The lifeless, yet power-wielding words of hundreds of thousands of memos and reports were the closest the bureaucracy came to the experiences of those whose lives the BIA was supposed to serve. But the nuances of individuality and particularity were hopelessly lost in the chill of the worst sort of literacy. Human experience was translated into millions of words that could conveniently and harmlessly remain locked away in the cold steel of a filing cabinet within the stone walls of a building hundreds and thousands of miles from those to whom those memos and reports mattered.

Kilberg's description of "patient fury" was inspired by a typewriter she found while touring the aftermath once the Trail's participants had been paid off with travel money and they had left town. In the midst of the jangled, sleepless last days of the occupation, someone had "carefully twisted each of the typewriter's forty-four keys beyond repair" (167). Could anything be more symbolic for an occupation in which documents and the words on them had become the source of wrath? How many of the documents that lay strewn in the corridors had been produced using that one typewriter is impossible to know. But its days of being a linguistic weapon against Indian people were surely over.

The occupation was a turning point in the activist movement of those years. Far from the revolutionary euphoria of the student-led occupation of Alcatraz, the people who nearly destroyed the BIA building were on their last stop before the movement's arrival in South Dakota and the gut-wrenching, violent takeover of Wounded Knee. They were desperate to have their voices heard, desperate for any action against a federal bureaucracy they contended did not serve them.

Scholars in Native American literary and cultural studies have not done an adequate job of understanding the connection between moments like the one that produced the BIA takeover and Momaday's literary work. The BIA takeover has been taken to be a moment in radical activism, while Momaday's work has normally been constrained within literary and aesthetic parameters. Yet this is in many ways a false distinction. In *House Made of Dawn,* for instance, Momaday has an office supply company's storage facility sitting atop both the floor of the building where Tosamah, the peyote priest whose sermons take up much of the second part of the novel, lives and the basement where he maintains his church (89). This is a small detail, but a telling one that shows the materiel of bureaucracy weighing down on the everyday realities of one of the major voices in the text.[40]

Tosamah, whose eloquent disputations among the invisible ragtag Natives of relocation Los Angeles call to mind William Apess, is not the only connection to the culture of the office and the written word. Millie, who seeks to help Abel, is a representative of bureaucratic culture and administers questionnaires to him and Benally, his Navajo roommate. These tests remind Abel of similar situations while in prison.

What I am proposing here is that Momaday's ideas on words and language help us understand the lives of Indian people who are surrounded, even imprisoned, by politics and policy and by the words through which policy is propagated. Much of that surrounding force of policy is invisible in terms of public awareness, and one of the important themes that comes across in the intellectual history of American Indian writing and politics, including Momaday's contributions, is the attempt to create spaces in which that force is made visible for public scrutiny or is at least curtailed.[41]

MAKING ARROWS, MAKING WORDS

In reading Momaday in this way, I mean to suggest that regarding his work as conservative vis-à-vis politics is a great disservice, cutting off some of the deepest insights his work offers. In closing his presentation to the

Convocation of American Indian Scholars, Momaday told a story about an arrowmaker that brings all of these themes together. Over a quarter of a century later, in introducing the story in his collected nonfiction, Momaday says, "It remains for me one of the most intensely vital stories in our experience, not only because it is a supernal example of the warrior idea[,] but because it is a story about story, about the efficacy of language and the power of words."[42]

As Momaday tells it, a Kiowa man is sitting in his tipi with his wife. She is sewing while he is about the difficult task of making arrows. As Momaday says, "If an arrow is well made, it will have tooth marks upon it. That is how you know. The Kiowas made fine arrows and straightened them in their teeth. Then they drew them to the bow to see that they were straight" (59–60). As he crafts the arrow shaft, he notices someone standing outside of the door to the tipi. This, then, is a story in which Momaday brings together the idea of the human fashioning of something as important for survival as an arrow (both in hunting and in defense) and the idea of the fashioner of literature through words as sharing a vital, moral positionality.

This story, Momaday writes, "has been the private possession of a very few, a tenuous link in that most ancient chain of language we call the oral tradition; tenuous because the tradition is itself so; for, as many times as the story has been told, it was always but one generation removed from extinction" (60). Oral tradition is important to invoke in this context of the arrowmaker, for, as Momaday contends in another essay, "One who has only an oral tradition thinks of language in this way: my words exist at the level of my voice. If I do not speak with care, my words are wasted. If I do not listen with care, words are lost. If I do not remember carefully, the very purpose of words is frustrated."[43] This belief in words as being wrapped up in the risk of life and death becomes more and more clear as the story unfolds.

Noting the man lurking outside his dwelling, the arrowmaker says to his wife, "Someone is standing outside. Do not be afraid. Let us talk easily, as of ordinary things" (60). Then he takes the arrow he has been making and acts as though he is testing it for its trueness, putting it in his bow and looking in various directions with the arrow fully drawn. Then, he addresses the man outside the tipi, "I know that you are there on the outside, for I can feel your eyes upon me. If you are a Kiowa, you will understand what I am saying, and you will speak your name." When no answer comes, the man points the arrow a few more times, then lets his aim rest on the shadow outside the door. Momaday writes, "He let go of the string. The arrow went straight to the enemy's heart" (60).

Momaday then goes on to his central point, saying the story has been "neither more nor less durable than the human voice, and neither more nor less concerned to express the meaning of the human condition" (60). In this way, he argues, "the story of the arrowmaker is also a link between language and literature. It is a remarkable act of the mind, a realization of words and the world that is altogether simple and direct, yet nonetheless rare and profound" (60). Recall, after all, the man's words to his wife: "Let us talk easily, as of ordinary things." It is as if Momaday is introducing us to a new way of thinking about realism. "Everything," Momaday says, "is ventured in this simple declaration" (61).

This concern for the ordinary as a gateway to the real comes up earlier in the essay when Momaday is speaking of the way "a man looks at a given landscape and takes possession of it in his blood and brain. For this happens, I am certain, in the ordinary motion of life" (53). This is not a magical connection, though certainly some aspect of mysticism seems part of it. It is primarily a connection that Momaday argues should provoke within humans, through the medium of language, the profoundest sense of ethics. "We have sooner or later," Momaday writes, "to come to terms with the world around us" (53). That coming to terms is a matter of choice and decision, a matter, as the arrowmaker story reminds us, that is fraught with life-and-death meaning.

The arrowmaker has become central to the Momaday canon, a necessary stopping place in situating his relationship to language, literature, and the natural world. Yet it is here in this moment, standing in front of a gathering of American Indian scholars, that Momaday seems not only to be carrying forward the aesthetic tradition of Melville, but of politically astute Native writing as well. Not that he wouldn't desire to be in Melville's company; in an excerpt from a letter to Winters, for instance, he writes this allusion to *Moby Dick*: "On the 13th Gaye [then his wife] gave birth to a baby girl, whom we have named Brit Ellen Scott. 'For leagues and leagues it undulated round us, so that we seemed to be sailing through boundless fields of ripe and golden wheat.' Mother and daughter are home now, and fine. The little one is beautiful; she will be a match for her sisters, who are handsomer all the time, if I do say so myself."[44] For all his connections to American modernism and its precursors, Momaday seems at this moment to be also in the company of all those Native nonfiction writers who had gone before him, from Apess to the framers of the Osage Constitution to the Native students who chronicled their educational experiences. Momaday, like Apess before him, seems also in company with his contemporary Clyde Warrior, by then deceased, another proud indigenous intellectual who exhorted Indian scholars to go deeper into themselves and their tribal histories to discover the means by which to move toward the future.

BEYOND BIG DEMANDS

As Momaday says of the arrowmaker, "He ventures to speak because he must: language is the repository of his whole knowledge and experience, and it represents the only chance he has for survival" ("Man Made of Words," 61). Language, then, for Momaday, is much more than words. Language is something out of which humans make their lives, something in which they stand as they fashion their future, and a refuge from the vagaries of the petty politics of the everyday that they inhabit in the modern world.

Rather than banking on the big demands of his era, Momaday goes deeper and deeper into a more direct, simple place. As he says, "[O]f the ominous unknown he asks only the utterance of a name, only the most nominal sign that he is understood, that his words are returned to him on the sheer edge of meaning" (61). This is a place where so many, whether from the academy or the shady world of federal or organizational politics, have been, wondering if their words are registering at all. In such circumstances, cynicism is a tempting choice.

But Momaday offers something else. The arrowmaker gets no answer from the man outside the tipi and he "knows at once what he has not known before: that his enemy is, and that he has gained an advantage over him. This he knows certainly, and the certainty itself is his advantage, and it is crucial" (61). To enter into Momaday's world of language is, contra so much of what has been written of him over the past thirty years, an invitation to what he calls a "procession of words toward meaning. . . . It seems, in fact, to turn upon the very idea that language involves the elements of risk and responsibility; and in this it seeks to confirm itself. In a word, it seems to say, everything is at risk" (61).

It is easy, given the fact that Momaday himself doesn't highlight contemporary politics, to read "The Man Made of Words" as a text bereft of such connections. The activist movement was raging as Momaday, Alfonso Ortiz, Vine Deloria Jr., and other scholars gathered at Princeton. And the message of those scholars was not to go out and throw rocks, to take over buildings, or to form revolutionary cells. Scholars at the convocation argued over how to make sense and make use of the tremendous energy that had been loosed into the Indian world, but they by and large expressed a sense of discomfort with the aspects of the protests that grabbed the most headlines.

What worries me is what happens if we don't see Momaday's message as providing something consonant with the vision being expressed in the corridors of the BIA building and on the streets of Gordon, Nebraska, Chicago, Fort Sill, and lots of other places. The reading of politics in the field of Native literature has been impoverished by a tendency to see activism on one side and a sort of quietistic lack of engagement on the other. As Weaver aptly says of his concept of communitism, "In communities that have too often been fractured and rendered dysfunctional by the effects of more than 500 years of colonialism, to promote communitist values means to participate in the healing of the grief and sense of exile felt by Native communities and the pained individuals in them" (*That the People*, xiii). Is not the arrowmaker a story that is able to empower its Native listeners in exactly this way?

The stark violence of the arrowmaker story should be enough to undercut the idea of Momaday's quietism. To repeat, the man outside the tipi is an "ominous unknown," and "he asks only the utterance of a name, only the nominal sign that he is understood, that his words are returned to him on the sheer edge of meaning. But there is no answer, and the arrowmaker knows at once what he has not known before; that his enemy is, and that he has gained a crucial advantage over him" ("Man Made of Words," 61). Using language, for Momaday, "involves the elements of risk and responsibility; and in this it seems to confirm itself. In a word, it seems to say, everything is a risk" (61).

What I would suggest is that Momaday offers an alternative to protest politics that leads Natives to a deeper sense of themselves as Kiowa, Osage, Pequot, Cherokee, or whatever tribal group they come from. For Momaday, that depth is found in an exploration of what it means to be Kiowa. Though he has acknowledged the extent to which his upbringing at Jemez and among the Navajo gave him an intertribal awareness, at Princeton he most clearly presents himself as part of the Kiowa world, a theme he has intensified over the course of his career (Woodward, *Ancestral Voice,* 38). He takes us to the most elemental level of his own tribal tradition to model a way of confronting the realities of the present. As a man of literature, or as he would have it, the "Man Made of Words," Momaday is more than a protégé of Yvor Winters, more than a former Stegner Fellow, more than an Americanist commanding knowledge of poetics and prosody. He is all that, of course, but more.

The tale of the arrowmaker, in this reading, is not just a profound retelling of an oral traditional story. It does, as Momaday says, tell us about the very idea of story. More than that, though, it is a story that Momaday utters at a specific time that opens, as he says, "a world of definite reality and infinite possibility" (61). Thus, however much Momaday's message transcends the moment at Princeton in which it was uttered, it also stands as an intriguing alternative to the excesses of the movement years. To people caught up in trying to change federal policy, and, hopefully, the lifeless bureaucracy to which it gave rise, Momaday offers us a story of one man facing an invisible foe. That foe, lurking on the outside, seeking to strike fear into those inside the comfort of traditional life, instead falls prey to the well-crafted product of that traditional life.

House Made of Dawn, as I have argued, also features an invisible foe, the unnamed character of federal policy that helps structure the world in which Abel lives. Earlier, in "The Morality of Indian Hating," Momaday presented the centuries-long accretion of ideas about Natives that brought the specifics of contemporary Native life into existence. In the novel, Momaday has Abel back at home at the end, seeking healing through ways that have persisted during the "long outwaiting" of the people of Walatowa. In the student essay, Momaday responds to the American tradition of hating Natives with a call for Indian people to seek out the depth of who they are themselves. Reading "The Man Made of Words" in the movement years suggests that Momaday saw this move as entailing high risk and the potential for decisions that come with grave consequences.

In contrast to the highly public nature of the protests of that era, Momaday leaves his listeners alone to consider his call to morality and the ethics of language. As he writes of the arrowmaker, "And yet the story has it that he is cautious and alone, and we are given to understand that his peril is great and immediate, and that he confronts it in the only way he can. I have no doubt that this is true" (62). While I do not want to belabor the point, let me say one more time that the solitariness that Momaday writes of is no less surrounded by the realities of policy. Rather, Momaday seems to be offering a sharper weapon for overcoming that invisible enemy than what he perceived in the activism of his time. His is a different vision of words and language. Momaday insists on an understanding of language in which words are imbued with moral power reined in only by our fallible, human imaginations and our ability to communicate with those who might bring danger or friendship to our door. In doing so, he insists that language has the power to overcome the faceless enemy, another unnamed character, that threatens our homes and homelands.

Momaday, in short, tells a story. But that story is far from harmless. The storyteller, he says, "tells of his life in language, and of the risk involved. It occurs to us that he is one with the arrowmaker, and that he has survived, by word of mouth, beyond other men. For the storyteller, for the arrowmaker, language does indeed represent the only chance for survival. It is appropriate that he survives in our time and that he has survived over a period of untold generations" (62).

For all that, the meanings of the story are not obvious. Nor are they exhausted through the act of reading or interpretation. As Momaday says in a later, published version, "I have lived with the story of the arrowmaker for many years, and I am sure that I do not yet understand it in all of its consequent meanings. Nor do I expect to understand it so. The stories I keep close to me, day by day, are those that yield more and more of their spirit in time" ("The Arrowmaker," 9). Yet, for all its timelessness, the story yields important meaning in the specific moments of its telling, including at the convocation.

The Arrowmaker's Aim

"The Man Made of Words" offers the sort of complicated critical perspective Satya Mohanty writes of when he says:

> We cannot really claim ourselves morally or politically until we have reconstructed our collective identity, reexamined our dead and our dismembered. This is not simply a project of recovering one's ancestral line, for as we have seen, it often involves fundamental discoveries about what ancestry is, what continuity consists in and which cultural meanings do not sustain themselves through history and are in fact materially embodied and fought for. (227)

In the spring of 1970, Momaday led his listeners at the Convocation of American Indian Scholars into exactly that sort of process, an ineffable move toward a deeper understanding of the moment of history in which Natives found themselves at that time. And an unreconstructed collective identity seems to be what Momaday hopes to evince in his listeners.

In concluding his remarks, Momaday says, "[F]or the arrowmaker, language represented the only chance of survival. It is worth considering that he survives in our own time, and that he has survived over a period of untold generations" (62). This is a prescient statement. For those who gathered at Princeton in 1970, survival must have seemed like something that was closer to being assured than it had been for generations. Budgets were flush and more was happening in terms of programs than ever before. The academy was open in a way it had never been before. People were becoming more interested in how to gather their power to move beyond short-term needs and instead to ascend to even greater heights.

But a few years later the idea of survival resurfaced as the moneys that funded programs and prompted the interest of the public and foundations were on the wane. "It is worth considering," Momaday said. Indeed, it is. And it is worth considering the link between language and experience that Momaday makes in "The Man Made of Words." Momaday includes one of his most enduring phrases in that presentation. Immediately after describing his encounter with the old woman Ko-Sahn, Momaday says:

> Once in his life a man ought to give himself up to a particular landscape in his experience, to look at it from as many angles as he can, to wonder about it, to dwell upon it. He ought to imagine that he touches it with his hands at every season and listens to the sounds that are made upon it. He ought to imagine the creatures that are there and all the faintest motions in the wind. He ought to recollect the glare of moon and all the colors of the dawn and dusk. (52)

If language is the realm in which humans exist and communicate, action is the way in which experience is realized. In this quote, looking, wondering, dwelling, imagining, touching, listening, and recollecting are the ways that we, as humans, mediate our experiences through language.

This is vital in the case of the arrowmaker because, as Momaday says, "language is the repository of his whole knowledge and experience, and it represents the only chance he has for survival" (61). Memory is but one aspect of this, but a crucial one. Memory is "that experience of the mind which is legendary as well as historical, personal as well as cultural" (59). This particular aspect of experience is what gives rise to human imagination, which gives rise to the possibility of story.

Momaday illustrates this by telling of how the Kiowas migrated to the area of what is now southwestern Oklahoma near Rainy Mountain. Due to their history, Momaday argues, "they were a race of centaurs, a lordly society of warriors and buffalo hunters. Along the way they had acquired horses, a knowledge and possession of the open land, and a sense of destiny" (58). By the 1830s, however, their fortunes were changing. The Osages captured one of their most sacred objects, their Tai-Me doll, and not long after an enormous meteor storm crowded the sky, which Momaday says the Kiowas referred to as the time when stars fell.

"Within four years of the falling stars," Momaday writes, "the Kiowas signed their first treaty with the government; within twenty, four major epidemics of smallpox and Asiatic cholera destroyed more than half their number; and within scarcely more than a generation their horses were taken from them and the herds of buffalo were slaughtered and left to waste upon the plains" (57). Demoralized and psychologically wounded, the Kiowas took their remembered experiences and imagined the meaningfulness of those events. And that, according to Momaday, is the process of imagination that gives rise to story and is the deepest root of the literary imagination. The devastated Kiowas "accounted for themselves with reference to that awful memory," he writes. "They appropriated it, recreated it, fashioned it into an image of themselves—imagined it" (57).

This notion of the imagination as an agency that gives shape and meaning to our experiences is Momaday's major contribution to the work of the Convocation of American Indian Scholars. There, in the tangle of perspectives and ideas, Momaday suggests from the midst of the watershed taking up the truths of the arrowmaker. This was not a call to tradition or an admonition to search for a higher sort of wisdom in Native cultural patrimony. Instead, Momaday's invitation was to take up that spot in the unknowingness of the tipi in confronting the shadows outside.

Such a call lingers on the edge of questions that one can answer only through experience and trust in oneself. Have my teeth marks made my arrow true? Can I remain in the ordinariness requisite to keep those shadows at bay long enough to respond to them rightly? Is my aim straight? Can I find the question that will allow me to decide fate not just for myself, but for others inside and outside my world, as well? And, finally, do I have the courage to live with my answers to these questions and act accordingly? The questions derive from the metaphorical aspect of a story, but these are questions that resonate deeply with the times in which they were asked and that continue to resonate today.

In the long run, the Convocation of American Indian Scholars in 1970 may end up being every bit as important to the intellectual history of Native America as *House Made of Dawn*. While its immediate impact never reached the heights for which Costo had hoped, it leaves an indelible imprint on many of those who now encounter it, even in the transcripted form of its proceedings. "The Man Made of Words" is a crucial piece of the whole, demonstrating as it does the power of language and the efficacy of theorizing in the midst of practical problems. Momaday's words provide a nonfiction map from the past to the future, from the traditional to the modern and back again. It is a reminder of who Natives have been, a reflection of who Natives have become, and a rallying cry for who Natives can be.

In the end, Momaday's call for a consideration of these issues of historical and experiential depth was as important, if not more so, than any other challenge presented to the group of scholars who gathered at Princeton in 1970. Amidst a chorus of voices at the convocation—including those who advocated joining the protesters, leading them in another direction, forging the fate of an Indian future through the halls of academia, and unifying everyone under the banner of scholarly leadership—"The Man Made of Words" is a pertinent reminder of the specificity of an intellectual vocation in the midst of historical and political realities. While the Native intellectual may engage in work linked directly to a struggle or set of struggles, Momaday's essay is a reminder that such links are not always obvious, and that some contributions may not be so direct.

CONCLUSION

In reflecting on "The Morality of Indian-Hating" over thirty years later, Momaday contends that "the essential statement of the essay—that the American Indian is, and has been from the moment of contact, engaged in a desperate struggle to persist in his cultural and spiritual being—is at least as true now as it was when I wrote it" ("Morality of Indian Hating," 76). More than just reaffirming his earlier words, Momaday uses the opportunity to take his ideas even further. "My convictions have grown stronger," Momaday writes:

I believe that what most threatens the American Indian is sacrilege, the theft of the sacred. Inexorably the Indian people have been, and are being, deprived of the spiritual nourishment that has sustained them for many thousands of years. This is a subtle holocaust, and it is ongoing. It is imperative that the Indian defines himself, that he finds the strength to do so, that he refuses to let others define him. Children are at greatest risk. We, Native Americans in particular, but all of us, need to restore the sacred to our children. It is a matter of the greatest importance. (76)

As in 1970, Momaday's rhetoric differs from that of most of his contemporaries. Yet here in this statement, he speaks with every bit of the clarity of Ngugi in his description of a colonial "culture bomb" exploding in the midst of indigenous peoples.[45]

This invocation of sacrilege has special meaning for those who agree with Momaday about the link between language and experience. David Moore calls for a profound respect of silences in Native literature, as those silences can be protecting something sacred. "Radical understanding," he writes, "begins with an understanding that 'I cannot understand,' a recognition that the other has a right to not be known. Such a right fits with an epistemology of process and discovery rather than with one of product and commodity" (50).

Janice Gould goes even further in questioning the link between language, literature, and the erotic: "Is there not any place that is sacred, that is safe from violation? Perhaps there are places within the psyche that can and must remain beautifully inarticulate and mute. I would like to think there is a vast reserve of silence that can never be colonized, that can never be taught to speak. I would like to imagine that there is a place of power that never becomes knowledge, a place of knowledge that never becomes power" (43).

Momaday, both recently and earlier in his career, writes himself into the tradition of Native nonfiction. Far from being eclipsed (except perhaps in the minds of critics), that tradition continues to grow. As with William Apess, the framers of the Osage Constitution, the producers of generations of educational narratives, and many others, Momaday provides a way, through narrating experiences in nonfiction, to join in the process of imagination and morality. Nonfiction has been a means of engagement, a way of gaining perspective and taking a stand. Momaday, as much as anyone before or since, offers in his nonfiction a way toward a deeper ethical and political space.

This, then, is Momaday in the movement years and beyond, not apolitical or disengaged, but grappling with a different order of challenge than that of his more practically minded contemporaries. And, of course, *practicality* is perhaps not the right term. After all, the issues Momaday reaches toward remain. Though he would not use the same language, Momaday's arrowmaker has something to do with Frantz Fanon's "new man," someone searching for a position from which to understand the precariousness of where indigenous people stand, while also embodying the strength and power that comes from abiding traditions and the courage that derives from abiding and the abiding experience that accrues along the way.

Conclusion

Intellectual Trade Routes

*T*hough I have always preferred critical language that is less, rather than more, figural, I have found myself repeatedly fixing on the metaphor of intellectual trade routes as I have considered how to conclude this work. Perhaps the sheer variety of the texts covered here and the vast geography from which their writers have come prompted this image, but my travel itinerary over the time I wrote these chapters and the concomitant opportunities I've had to share these ideas in far-flung places has probably done at least as much to make me think of the particular ways that ideas become mobile and settle elsewhere.

Edward Said, who passed away while I was working on the last stages of this book, famously took up the question of what happens when ideas, specifically theories, travel "from person to person, from situation to situation, from one period to another. Cultural life and intellectual life are usually nourished and often sustained by this circulation of ideas" (*The World,* 226). While it is hard to argue against the concept of ideas traveling—one can argue, for instance, that ideas travel when one person speaks to another or even as they undergo the neurological processes that give them life in one person's mind—Said takes great pains to point out that no idea travels without being transformed by the process.

Ideas that travel not just across a synapse or a room, but across great geographical or cultural divides, he says, can have the good effect of providing alternatives to moribund theoretical positions or dogma. Criticism,

Said says, benefits from all of this, since "what is critical consciousness at bottom if not an unstoppable predilection for alternatives?" (247).

The routes that ideas follow in their travels are oftentimes the same ones that trade goods follow from their points of origin to markets. Through extended visits by voyagers and even the idle chatter of merchants and caravaners, ideas have moved from time immemorial along the same paths as foodstuffs, medicines, textiles, tools, and toys. Books, too, have played an enormous role in this exchange, combining as they do their role as goods and as vessels for ideas. The process of transporting ideas has often been as informal as formal, and the equation of knowledge and power has been evident throughout history in the favorable relationships between some nations and the inequitable, exploitative ones between others.

Ideas do not, however, need to make their way literally across geographical or cultural space to travel. At times, ideas have traveled through the medium of a single person's mind across time and space. That is, a fallow idea from long ago or new knowledge that comes from the juxtaposition of two or more ideas can grow in a highly localized situation—a serendipitous moment in an archive or the sudden realization of a connection between things that had seemed disparate. The metaphor of intellectual trade routes encompasses both of these possibilities and everything in between.

The movement in the history of ideas that occurred in the encounter between Europeans and the indigenous people of the Americas has most often been considered a one-way process, with Western ideas and the Western classical tradition making their way to the Indian world from metropolitan centers to colonial indigenous margins along with technology (e.g., metal making), pathogens (e.g., syphilis), and aggressive religious ideologies (e.g., missionary Christianity). Some attention, most of it popular but some scholarly, has been paid to ideas and goods that made their way from the Americas to Europe (potatoes, chocolate, female participation in democratic politics), but the routes of most interest have been those from Europe to the Americas.

Trade routes, however, have existed in the Americas since the first pathways linking people emerged in a time that no one can remember. Those pathways became trails and then networks of trails that crisscrossed the single landmass that is the Americas. The many hundreds of cultures and civilizations that dot the American landscape are connected by those crisscrossing trails, and the supposed European discovery of the continent took place along those trails. Different indigenous groups have made more or less extensive use of these routes, but certainly all of them have had some knowledge of the world beyond their homelands. Even among a highly insulated group of people who exhibit next to no interest in such a world, it is hard to imagine that a generation could pass without at least a few people developing a strong curiosity about the world over the next hill, through the next stand of trees, a little further downriver, or over a looming range of mountains.

Under the sign of modernity, some of these old routes have been forgotten through disuse, while others have been appropriated so people can better get to shopping malls and theme parks. In other cases, older trails have become roads, highways, or interstates. Perhaps my favorite example comes from California, a state whose mythologies make it a *terra nullius,* in which placid, passive indigenes sparsely populated the area's least attractive locales when, in fact, what is now California was well traveled by the scores of indigenous groups that lived there, and virtually every present-day walkway and major roadway has taken the place of an earlier system of footpaths as intricate and well traveled as any in the world.

The tradition of Native nonfiction has developed along the modern version of such trade routes and is written on palimpsests of earlier forms of intellectualism. William Apess embraced a foreign religious tradition—though Scott Stevens is right to say that by his time that tradition was far from new and had arguably become Pequot—and represented his life and thoughts using Western writing and the modern technology of the book. At the same, he was shaped by his experiences in the Native world of New England, finding those he called his brethren along olden paths that the Iroquois and Algonquians had used to communicate with each other and which the Pequots used to trade the quahog shells that would become wampum beads. Apess used other paths to reconnect with his father in the hidden corners of their ancestral homeland and developed a political and intellectual praxis by finding his way to the mix of old and new ideas that would result in the Mashpee revolt. He spent his last days on the rising tide of New York, a center of trade and commerce, but at least part of what led him to the boarding house by the piers where he died may have been a knowledge of the Native whalers who had traveled the world from the fisheries their people had been using for generations.

The Osages, it is fair to say, have traditionally been one of those groups more interested in developing knowledge of their own traditions than in incorporating new ideas into their world, but clearly by the time of their constitution, their leaders knew the way to the knowledge centers of their old enemies, the Cherokees. Their embrace of democracy was as much a means of maintaining their identity as a way to erase it. But more than providing a way to hold on to their ancient integrity as a people, their constitution was also an attempt to negotiate the exigencies of modernity in a way akin to how the Osages had done so in trading and dealing with the French and Spanish.

The educational narratives of chapter 3 provide an illuminating contrast between the attitudes of white educators, who saw themselves as completely remaking Indian students, and the students themselves, like Luther Standing Bear and others, who saw themselves as going to school to gain new knowledge so they could work more effectively in the service of older forms of knowledge and existence. Momaday's work demonstrates, among other things, the extent to which traversing these older intellectual trade routes as part of a response to modernity remains a possibility in our own time. He is perhaps the exemplar of what it means to find the richest veins in his own tradition and those he encounters elsewhere, rather than attaching himself to the intellectual equivalents of baubles and trinkets.

The figure of intellectual trade routes stands in contrast to what I called in my first book, following John Joseph Mathews, "Blackjacks discourse." The Blackjacks is the name Mathews gave the little stone house he built on his allotment land after he returned to the Osage following his travels through Europe and Africa during and after World War I. As he writes about that house in his book, *Talking to the Moon*, Mathews's Blackjacks discourse, as I figured it, entailed creating an intellectual space and regulating the process by which visitors enter that space. The value of such discourse, I argued, was that it allowed an envisioning of the intellectual process that helped me sort through the cacophony of voices competing for critical attention. More important, such a practice was key to what I termed "intellectual sovereignty," through which I attempted to link what intellectuals do with what is happening among those seeking to change the realities of people in Native American communities. Blackjacks discourse was my way of declaring a boundary around my intellectual practice and seeking a modicum of individual determination over the way new ideas came into my intellectual and critical space.

Intellectual trade routes are, of course, something qualitatively different, but I want to suggest that these are complementary ideas. Mathews's isolated little house, after all, was linked eventually to the roads that took him away from the Osage and brought him back. And by highlighting the importance of the ways that ideas travel great distances, I am not forgetting how crucial stability and rootedness can be to the lives of ideas. I recall from studying Western philosophy that Kant never traveled more than 150 miles from Konigsberg, Germany. Traditional Osages traveled much further than that twice a year on their buffalo hunts, but plenty of ideas that grew up in the indigenous world of the Americas, including the Osage corner of it, did so in highly specified places.

Journeying on the intellectual trade routes of the Americas, then, is all the more valuable when done with knowledge of the more controlled environment of the Blackjacks. Clyde Warrior has shown up a number of times in this work, something I did not plan. I would venture that his intellectual hold on my imagination comes from the way he combined highly specified knowledge of his own Ponca tradition, a vast library of knowledge of the traditions of other Indian people, and endless curiosity about the world around him. He embodied the best ideals of the powwow world and its intertribal ethic. Far from Pan-Indianism, the powwow world exhibits strong awareness of and respect for tribal differences. The trail that powwow people follow, in fact, is perhaps the closest modern version that remains of an older world of North American indigenous trade routes.

In thinking of myself as having traveled on intellectual trade routes in developing these four chapters, I hope to evince something of this intense love and knowledge for some place very specific interacting with a love and appreciation for what can be gained from new knowledge from new places. Plenty of indigenous intellectuals have brought new knowledge into their work, but too often that process has been burdened by the assumption that knowledge from the colonial center counts more than knowledge from the indigenous world. My trade routes here are part of networks that, in their oldest forms, were linked to the indigenous world of the Americas long before they became part of modern, global networks.

The idea of Blackjacks discourse lent itself to a picture of kitchen table conversations happening over steaks and spaghetti in the safety of a space of withdrawal, away from what Mathews called the "roaring river of civilization" (*Talking to the Moon*, 3). Intellectual trade routes conjure noisier, more active images. In these pages I have imagined myself covering the same physical and intellectual terrain as Apess, inheriting the legacy of the forward-thinking framers of the Osage Constitution in the homeland they fought to protect for me and their other progeny, mapping the shared geographies of Native students across eras and centuries, and affirming with Momaday the moral and ethical space of the imagination. Sometimes I have thought of myself as encountering these figures in their spaces; at other times I have felt as though we were traveling together or meeting at a spot that was home for neither of us.

This is a different agenda from my earlier advocacy of withdrawing into an intellectual space that can be seen as sovereign, but intellectual trade routes have not in my mind supplanted intellectual sovereignty. The geography I mapped in my earlier work remains a necessary point of departure, but more, it is also a point of reference and return. And though intellectual sovereignty has been taken wrongly to be a "poorly defined . . . separatist intellectual sentiment," a call for Native intellectuals to "operate autonomously . . . in a manner fully independent . . . and without reference to the Euramerican tradition," an insular, navel-gazing approach in which Natives intellectuals focus only on other Native intellectuals, and strictly separatist and antitheoretical, I always intended the intellectual practice I advocated in *Tribal Secrets* to be highly specific and robust in content, highly aware of the intellectual world beyond Native America, and against naïve separatism.[1]

That is why I was careful in that work to go out of my way to trace the specificity of the critical approaches of Vine Deloria Jr. and John Joseph Mathews, delineating an approach to politics that critiques cultural pluralism and cultural radicalism using concepts from treaties, federal policy, and material realities; discussing the importance of non-Native thinkers to the development of mature thought in Native studies; and explicitly rejecting separatist ideology ("we must . . . withdraw without becoming separatists, being willing to reach out for the contradictions within ourselves and open ourselves to the joy and pain of others" [*Tribal Secrets*, 124]). The best evidence of this, of course, was my choice of Mathews and Deloria as subjects, two cosmopolitan thinkers who always looked far and wide for intellectual inspiration.

The attention to and respect for the specific situations of indigenous communities and their struggles for justice that were constitutive in formulating intellectual sovereignty remain in my conception of trade routes. I have learned in my travels to politically charged places around the world (including Northern Ireland, Palestine, Israel, Pine Ridge, and Guatemala) not to be too quick to express my opinion on local affairs, but that doesn't mean I have ever purposefully blinded myself to the political realities of the places I have visited.

While politics is central to the way I have conceived of my critical work (which, of course, has more often than not been the case in the development of modern criticism), my championing here of intellectual trade routes has at least as much to do with the genuine love and passion I have for the modern development of intellectualism among indigenous people and the figures who have been instrumental to that development. The fact is, I love reading and charting the ways indigenous intellectuals have risen to the challenge of responding to the hardships that they and their communities face.

Those responses have sometimes been misguided, but I almost always find something worth considering in my encounters with the work of Native writers and scholars. More, I find fulfillment in understanding myself as connected to that work, however flawed. That, in the end, is what keeps me on these trade routes—my sense that I have something to learn about my own intellectual challenges by paying attention to the tracks and traces of my fellow travelers, past, present, and future. The nonfiction tradition of Native writing in North America has provided a wide but less-traveled path and, for the most part, the tourists in their air-conditioned buses have yet to arrive.

Maybe we'll see each other along some of these old roads, including the ones that take me to those places, intellectual and otherwise, that I call home. If so, let's compare notes. Then again, I am like most travelers in preferring to stay one step ahead of the crowds.

Appendix

The 1881 Constitution of the Osage Nation

*T*he Constitution of the Osage Nation, prepared by the authorized committee and adopted by the National Council.

The Great and Little Osages having united and become one body politic, under the style and title of the Osage Nation; therefore,

We, the people of the Osage Nation, in National Council assembled, in order to establish justice, insure tranquility, promote the common welfare, and to secure to ourselves and our posterity the blessing of freedom—acknowledging with humility and gratitude the goodness of the Sovereign Ruler of the universe in permitting us so to do, and imploring his aid and guidance in its accomplishment—do ordain and establish this Constitution for the government of the Osage Nation.

ARTICLE I.

Section 1. The boundary of the Osage Nation shall be that described in the treaty of 1876 between the United States and the Great and Little Osages, except that portion purchased by the Kaws.

Sec. 2. The lands of the Osage Nation shall remain common property, until the National Council shall request an allotment of the same, but the improvements made thereon and in possession of the citizens of this Nation are the exclusive and indefeasible property of the citizens respectively who made or may rightfully be in possession of them. *Provided,* That the citizen of this Nation possessing exclusive and indefeasible[1] right to their improvements, as expressed in this article, shall possess no right or power to dispose of their improvements in any manner whatever, to the United States, individual States, or to individual citizens thereof; and that, whenever any citizen shall remove with his effects out of the limits of this Nation, and become a citizen of any other government, all his rights and privileges as a citizen of this Nation shall cease; *Provided, nevertheless,* That the National Council shall have power to re-admit by law, to all the rights of citizenship any such persons who may at any time desire to return to the Nation, on memorializing the National Council for such readmission.

Moreover, the National Council shall have power to adopt such laws and regulations as it may deem expedient and proper to prevent citizens from monopolizing improvements with the view of speculation.

ARTICLE II.

Section 1. The power of this government shall be divided into three distinct departments, the Legislative, the Executive, and the Judicial.

Sec. 2. No person or persons belonging to one of these departments shall exercise any of the powers properly belonging to either of the others, except in the cases hereinafter expressly directed or permitted.

ARTICLE III.

Section 1. The legislative power shall be vested in a National Council, and the style of their acts shall be:—Be it enacted by the National Council.

Sec. 2. The National Council shall make provision, by law, for laying off the Osage Nation into five districts, and, if subsequently it should be deemed expedient, one or two may be added thereto.

Sec. 3. The National Council shall consist of three members from each district, to be chosen by the qualified electors in their respective district, for two years, the elections to be held in the respective districts every two years, at such times and places as may be directed by law.

The National Council shall, after the present year, be held annually, to be convened on the first Monday in November, at such place as may be designated by the National Council, or, in case of emergency, by the Principal Chief.

Sec. 4. Before the districts shall be laid off, any election which may take place, shall be by general vote of the electors throughout the Nation, for all officers to be elected.

The first election for all officers of the government[2]—Chiefs, Executive Council, members of the National Council, Judges, and Sheriffs—shall be held at Pawhuska, before the rising of this council; and the term of service of all officers elected previous to the first Monday in November, 1882, shall be extended to embrace, in addition to the regular constitutional term, the time intervening from their election to the first Monday in November, 1882.

Sec. 5. No person shall be eligible to a seat in the National Council, but an Osage male citizen, who shall have attained to the age of twenty-five years.

Sec. 6. The members of the National Council shall in all cases, except those of felony or breach of the peace, be privileged from arrest during their attendance at the National Council, in going to, and returning.

Sec. 7. In all elections by the people the electors shall vote *viva voce*. All male citizens, who shall have attained to the age of eighteen years, shall be equally entitled to vote at all public elections.

Sec. 8. The National Council shall judge of the qualifications and returns of its own members, determine the rules of its proceedings, punish a member for disorderly behavior, and with the concurrence of two-thirds,[3] expel a member; but not a second time for the same offence.

Sec. 9. The National Council, when assembled, shall choose[4] its own officers; a majority shall constitute a quorum to do business, but a small number may adjourn from day to day and compel the attendance of absent members, in such manner, and under such penalty as the council may prescribe.

Sec. 10. The members of the National Council shall each receive a compensation for their services, which shall be one hundred dollars per annum: *Provided,* That the same may be increased or diminished by law; but no alteration shall take effect during the period of services of the members of the National Council by whom such alteration may have been made.

Sec. 11. The National Council shall regulate by law, by whom, and in what manner, writs of elections shall be issued to fill the vacancies which may happen in the Council thereof.

Sec. 12. Each member of the National Council, before he takes his seat, shall take the following oath or affirmation:

"I, A.B., do solemnly swear (or affirm, as the case may be) that I have not obtained my election by bribery, treat, or any undue and unlawful means, used by myself, or others, by my desire or approbation for that purpose; that I consider myself constitutionally qualified as a member of _____, and that on all questions and measures which may come before me, I will so give my vote, and so conduct myself, as, in my judgment, shall appear most conducive to the interest and prosperity of this Nation, and that I will bear true faith and allegiance to the same, and to the utmost of my ability and power, observe, conform to, support, and defend the constitution thereof."

Sec. 13. No person who may be convicted of felony shall be eligible to any office or appointment of honor, profit,[5] or trust, within this Nation.

Sec. 14. The National Council shall have power to make all laws and regulations which they shall deem necessary and proper for the good of the Nation, which shall not be contrary to this constitution.

Sec. 15. It shall be the duty of the National Council to pass such laws as may be necessary and proper to decide differences by arbitration, to be appointed by the parties who may choose that summary mode of adjustment.

Sec. 16. No power of suspending the laws of this Nation shall be exercised, unless by the National Council or its authority.

Sec. 17. No retrospective law, nor any law impairing the obligations of contracts, shall be passed.

Sec. 18. The National Council shall have power to make laws for laying and collecting taxes for the purpose of raising a revenue.

Sec. 19. All acknowledged treaties shall be the supreme law of the land, and the National Council shall have the sole power of deciding on the constructions of all treaty stipulations.

Sec. 20. The Council shall have the sole power of impeaching. All impeachments shall be tried by the National Council, when sitting[6] for that purpose; the members shall be upon oath or affirmation; and no person shall be convicted without the concurrence of two-thirds of the members present.

Sec. 21. The Principal Chief, Assistant Principal Chief, and all civil officers shall be liable to impeachment for misdemeanor in office; but judgment in such cases shall not extend further than removal from office, and disqualification to hold any office of honor, trust, or profit under the government of this Nation. The party, whether convicted or acquitted, shall, nevertheless, be liable to indictment, trial, judgment, and punishment according to law.

Article IV.

Section 1. The supreme executive power of this Nation shall be vested in a Principal Chief, who shall be styled "The Principal Chief of the Osage Nation." The Principal Chief shall hold his office for the term of two years, and shall be elected by the qualified electors on the same day, and at the place where they shall respectively vote for members to the National Council. The returns of the elections for Principal Chief shall be sealed up and directed to the President of the National Council, who shall open and publish them in the presence of the Council assembled. The person having the highest number of votes shall be Principal Chief, but if two or more shall be equal and highest in votes, one of them shall be chosen by vote of the National Council; the manner of determining contested elections shall be directed by law.

Sec. 2. No person, except a natural born citizen, shall be eligible to the office of Principal Chief; neither shall any person be eligible to that office who shall not have attained to the age of thirty-five years.

Sec. 3. There shall also be chosen, at the same time, by the qualified electors, in the same manner, for two years, an Assistant Principal Chief, who shall have attained to the age of thirty-five years.

Sec. 4. In case of the removal of the Principal Chief from office, or of his death, or resignation, or inability to discharge the powers and duties of the said office, the same shall devolve on the Assistant Principal Chief.

Sec. 5. The National Council may, by law, provide for the case of removal, death, resignation, or disability of both the Principal and Assistant Principal Chief, declaring what officer shall then act as Principal Chief until the disability be removed or a Principal Chief shall be elected.

Sec. 6. The Principal Chief and Assistant Principal Chief shall, at stated times, receive for their services a compensation which shall neither be increased nor diminished during the period for which they shall have been elected, and they shall not receive within that period any other emolument from the Osage Nation or any other government.[7]

Sec. 7. Before the Principal Chief enters on the execution of his office, he shall take the following oath or affirmation: "I do solemnly swear or affirm that I will faithfully execute the duties of Principal Chief of the Osage Nation, and will, to the best of my ability, preserve, protect, and defend the Constitution of the Osage Nation."[8]

Sec. 8. He may, on extraordinary occasions, convene the National Council at the seat of government.

Sec. 9. He shall, from time to time, give to the Council information of the state of the government, and recommend to their consideration such measures as he may deem expedient.

Sec. 10. He shall take care that the laws be faithfully executed.

Sec. 11. It shall be his duty to visit the different districts at least once in two years, to inform himself of the general condition of the country.

Sec. 12. The Assistant Principal Chief shall, by virtue of his office, aid and advise the Principal Chief in the administration of the government at all times during his continuance in office.

Sec. 13. Vacancies that may occur in offices, the appointment of which is vested in the National Council shall be filled by the Principal Chief during the recess of the National Council, by granting commissions, which shall expire at the end of the next session thereof.

Sec. 14. Every bill, which shall pass the National Council, shall, before it becomes a law, be presented to the Principal Chief; if he approves, he shall sign it, but if not, he shall return it with his objections to the Council, who shall enter the objections at large on their journals, and proceed to reconsider it.

If, after such reconsideration, two-thirds of the Council shall agree to pass the bill, it shall[9] become a law, if any bill shall not be returned by the Principal Chief within five days (Sunday excepted) after the same has been presented to him, it shall become law, in like manner as if he had signed it. Unless the National Council, by their adjournment, prevent its return, in which case it shall be a law, unless sent back within three days after their next meeting.

Sec. 15. Members of the National Council and all officers, executive and judicial, shall be bound by oath, to support the Constitution of their Nation; and to perform the duties of their respective offices with fidelity.

Sec. 16. The Principal Chief shall, during the session of the National Council, attend at the seat of government.

Sec. 17. The Principal Chief shall recommend three persons, to be appointed by the National Council, whom the Principal Chief shall have full power at his discretion to assemble; he, together with the Assistant Principal Chief and the Counsellors, or a majority of them, may, from time to time, hold and keep a Council for ordering and directing the affairs of the Nation according to law.

Sec. 18. The members of the Executive Council shall be chosen for the term of two years.

Sec. 19. The Treasurer of the Osage Nation shall be chosen by the National Council for the term of two years.

Sec. 20. The Treasurer shall, before entering on the duties of his office, give bond to the Nation with Sureties to the satisfaction of the National Council, for the faithful discharge of his trust.

Sec. 21. No money shall be drawn from the treasury, but by warrant from the Principal Chief, and in consequence of appropriations made by law.

Sec. 22. It shall be the duty of the Treasurer to receive all public moneys, and to make a regular statement and account of the receipts and expenditures of all public moneys at the annual session of the National Council.

Sec. 23. The "Fiscal Year" of the Osage Nation shall begin on the 1st day of October, and close on the 30th day of September of each year; and all books and accounts of the Treasurer, shall be kept, and duties of his office performed with regard to the beginning and ending of the fiscal year.[10] The National Treasurer shall receive for his services ten (10) per cent[11] of all moneys that may pass through his hands as provided by law.

ARTICLE V.

Section 1. The judicial powers shall be vested in a supreme court, and such circuits and inferior courts as the National Council may from time to time ordain and establish.

Sec. 2. The judges of the supreme and circuit courts shall hold their commission for the term of two years, but any of them may be removed from office on the address of two-thirds of the National Council to the Principal Chief, for that purpose.

Sec. 3. The judges of the supreme court and circuit[12] courts, shall at stated times receive a compensation which shall not be diminished[13] during their continuance in office, but they shall receive no fees or perquisites of office, nor hold any other office of profit or trust under the government of this Nation or any other power.

Sec. 4. No person shall be appointed a judge of any of the courts, until he shall have attained the age of thirty years.

Sec. 5. The judges of the Supreme and Circuit courts shall be elected by the National Council.

Sec. 6. The judges of the Supreme court[14] and of the Circuit courts shall have complete criminal jurisdiction in such cases and in such manner as may be pointed out by law.

Sec. 7. No judge shall sit on trial of any cause when the parties are connected (with him) by affinity or consanguinity except by consent of the parties. In case all the judges of the supreme court shall be interested in the issue of any court or related to all or either of the parties, the National Council may provide by law for the selection of a suitable number of persons of good character and knowledge for the determination thereof, and who shall be specially commissioned for the adjudication of such case by the Principal Chief.

Sec. 8. All writs and other process shall run "in the name of the Osage Nation" and bear test and be signed by the respective clerks.

Sec. 9. Indictments shall conclude against the peace and dignity of the Osage Nation.

Sec. 10. The supreme court shall, after the present year, hold its session three times a year, at the seat of government, to be convened on the first Monday in October, February, and August, of each year.

Sec. 11. In all criminal prosecutions the accused shall have the right of being heard; of demanding the nature of the accusation; of meeting the witnesses face to face; of having compulsory process for obtaining witnesses in his or their favor, and in prosecutions by indictment or information a speedy public trial; nor shall the accused be compelled to give evidence against himself.

Sec. 12. All persons shall be bailable by sufficient securities, unless for capital offences when the proof is evident or presumption great.

Article VI.

Section 1. No person who denies the being of a God or a future state of reward and punishment, shall hold any office in the civil department in this Nation.

Sec. 2. When the National Council shall determine the expediency of appointing delegates, or other public agents for the purpose of transacting business with the Government of the United States, the Principal Chief shall recommend, and by the advice and consent of the National Council appoint and commission such delegates or public agents accordingly on all matters of interest touching the rights of the citizens of this Nation which may require the attention of the United States Government.

Sec. 3. All commissions shall be in the name and by the authority of the Osage Nation, and signed by the Principal Chief. The Principal Chief shall make use of his private seal until a national one shall be provided.

Sec. 4. A sheriff shall be elected in each district by the qualified electors thereof, who shall hold his office two years unless sooner removed. Should a vacancy occur subsequent to[15] election, it shall be filled by the Principal Chief as in other cases, and the person so appointed shall continue in office until the next regular election.

Sec. 5. The appointment of all officers not otherwise directed by this constitution shall be voted for[16] in the National Council.

Sec. 6. The National Council may propose such amendments to this Constitution as two-thirds of the Council may deem expedient, and the Principal Chief shall issue a proclamation directing all officers of the several districts to promulgate the same as extensively as possible within their respective districts at least six months previous to the next general election, and if, at the first session of council after such general election, two-thirds of the council shall by ayes and noes ratify such proposed amendments, they shall be valid to all extent and purposes as part of this Constitution, *Provided,* that such proposed amendments shall be read on three several days in Council, as well as when the same are proposed as when they are ratified.

Done in convention at Pawhuska, Osage Nation, this thirty-first day of December, A.D. 1881.

James Bigheart, *President of the National Convention*[17]
Ne-kah-ke-pon-ah
Wah-ti-an-kah
Saucy Chief
Tah-wah-che-he
William Penn
Clamore
Two-giver

Tall-chief
Sa-pah-ke-ah
Black Dog
Thomas Big-chief
Ne-kah-wah-she-ton-kah
Joseph Pawnee-no-pah-she
White Hair
Cyprian Tayrian

Paul Akin, *Interpreter*
E. M. Matthews, *Secretary*

Notes

Introduction

1. Momaday, "The Man Made of Words," 49–52.

2. Green, "Rosebuds of the Plateau: Frank Matsura and the Fainting Couch Aesthetic."

3. Occom, *A Sermon Preached at the Execution of Moses Paul*; Hochbruck and Dudensing-Reichel, "'Honoratissimi Benefactores': Native American Students and Two Seventeenth-Century Texts in the University Tradition"; Wyss, *Writing Indians*. Occom was an important writer of hymns. Among his published hymnody is *A Choice Collection of Hymns and Spiritual Songs Intented* [sic] *for the Edification of Sincere Christians of all Denominations*. Though now showing signs of age, the most complete bibliography of early and contemporary Native literature is *American Indian Literatures* by A. LaVonne Brown Ruoff.

To avoid repetition and broaden the scope of my bibliography, I have focused in this introduction on texts that I do not discuss in the chapters that follow.

4. See Littlefield and Parins, *American Indian and Alaska Native Newspapers and Periodicals*. Boudinot's writings are collected in Perdue, *Cherokee Editor*.

5. For a concise telling of the story of Native journalism, see Trahant, *Pictures of Our Nobler Selves*.

6. The works of Eastman and Bonnin are discussed in chapter 3 of this work.

7. See, for instance, Standing Bear, *My People the Sioux*.

8. For early Native fiction, see Peyer, *The Singing Spirit*.

9. After Ridge's novel, next in line appears to be S. Alice Callahan's *Wynema*, and after that is Simon Pokagon's *O-gi-Maw-Kwi Mit-I-gwa-ki (Queen of the Woods)*. Novels of the 1920s and 1930s include Mourning Dove's (Humi Ishu-Ma, Christine Quintasket) *Cogewea, the Half-Blood*; John Milton Oskison's *Black Jack*

Davy, Brothers Three, and *Wild Harvest;* John Joseph Mathews's *Sundown;* and D'Arcy McNickle's *The Surrounded.*

10. For a partial list of Native novels since *House Made of Dawn,* see Owens, *Other Destinies,* 283–85.

11. See, for instance, Larson, *American Indian Fiction;* Wiget, *Native American Literature;* Allen, *The Sacred Hoop;* Owens, *Other Destinies;* Sarris, *Keeping Slug Woman Alive;* Donovan, *Feminist Readings of Native American Literature;* Hoy, *How Should I Read These?;* and Parker, *The Invention of Native American Literature.*

12. For another perspective on the history of repression in Guatemala, see Weaver, "Scaling Rios Montt," 201–25.

13. Cardinal, *The Unjust Society;* Welch, *Killing Custer;* Vizenor, *Earthdivers;* and Maracle, *Crazywater.*

14. Maracle, *I Am Woman;* and Alfred, *Peace, Power, Righteousness.*

15. Ortiz, *Speaking for the Generations;* and Armstrong, *Looking at the Words of Our People.*

16. For a discussion of the rise of criticism from print culture and the public sphere in the early eighteenth century, see Eagleton, *The Function of Criticism;* and Habermas, *Structural Transformation of the Public Sphere.*

17. For a recent discussion of the status of experience in criticism, see Ireland, "The Appeal to Experience and Its Consequences."

18. More widely cited is a shortened version of this essay, "Experience," in Butler and Scott, *Feminists Theorize the Political,* 22–40. Subsequent textual references refer to the original essay. See also Kruks, *Retrieving Experience.*

19. Sean Teuton uses similar language to describe Native expressions of identity as theories; see "On These Grounds: The Red Power Novel and the Retaking of American Indian Identity."

20. See Mignolo, *The Darker Side of the Renaissance,* esp. 82ff., 109, and 121ff.

1. Eulogy on William Apess

1. Apess, *On Our Own Ground,* 310. Apess spelled his name with both one and two *s*'s. O'Connell, who edited and wrote an introduction for *On Our Own Ground,* argues convincingly that Apess clearly chose by the end of his life to use two *s*'s to spell his name rather than using "Apes," as he had in his first two publications (xiv). The name continues to exist among contemporary Pequots and, whatever the spelling, is usually pronounced with one syllable.

2. All of these works are reprinted in *On Our Own Ground.*

3. All biographical information on Apess here is taken from Barry O'Connell's introduction to *On Our Own Ground.* Following O'Connell's example, I have used *Apes* for the parents since this spelling is the only one that shows up in historical documents in which they appear (xxvii). O'Connell has traced what

can be known of Apess's parents. His father, William Apes, shows up in census documents as a free white man, but the name *Apes* is clearly of Pequot origin and O'Connell is most certainly correct in pointing to faulty racial classification in those times as the reason for the confusion. Though Apess never names her, his mother was most probably the woman listed in the 1820 census, Candace, as the wife of William Apes. Similar to the confusion regarding her husband, in the census and in other documents she is described variously as a "Negro" who was freed from slavery in 1805, a "free white woman," and a Pequot (O'Connell, xxvii). It is very likely, then, that Apess's ancestry was a mix of Pequot, white, and black.

4. Among the collections and anthologies are Brooks, "Six Hymns by Samson Occom"; Murray, *To Do Good to My Indian Brethren*; Perdue, *Cherokee Editor*; Peyer, *The Elders Wrote*; and Vizenor, *Touchwood*. Book-length projects include Konkle, *Writing Indian Nations*; Peyer, *The Tutor'd Mind*; Wyss, *Writing Indians*; and Weaver, *That the People Might Live*. Konkle's book came out while I was making one of the last rounds of revisions on this work. I have incorporated some references to her book here, though I did not have access to it during most of the process of research and writing.

Cusick's major work, *Sketches of Ancient History of the Six Nations,* has not been recently reprinted.

5. See Walker, "Saving the Life That Is Your Own," "Zora Neale Hurston," and "Looking for Zora."

6. Ron Welburn has speculated that Apess left New England for a career in whaling. He imagines Apess signing up to sail on the *Pequod* with Captain Ahab in search of Moby Dick (*Roanoke and Wampum,* 105).

7. Inquisition on the View of the Body of William Apes, New York County, New York, April 10, 1839, New York County Coroner, Department of Records and Information Services, 31 Chambers Street, Municipal Archives of the City of New York.

8. O'Connell speculates that Apess perhaps wrote *A Son of the Forest* in New York City, based on his 1829 copyright deposit of the book there (*On Our Own Ground,* xlii). Given that the evidence of Apess's 1939 death in New York City had not surfaced when he wrote his introduction, O'Connell's supposition was especially prescient (though, of course, still not proved). Though it does not reference Apess, a thorough literary history of New England can be found in Buell, *New England Literary Culture*.

9. Rayna Green of the Smithsonian Institution's Museum of American History, upon hearing a public presentation of this evidence, told me that, based on her interactions with forensic anthropologists, Apess's symptoms suggest an acute case of pancreatitis. Though I have been unable to do the work necessary to establish this possibility, conversations with various medical doctors, including

faculty colleagues, suggest pancreatitis exacerbated by heavy alcohol use as a likely cause of Apess's death.

10. In her admirably researched and documented study, Konkle, in fact, bases her argument for Mary's death on the fact that her husband married Elizabeth prior to his death. She admits that no record of Mary's death has been uncovered, saying instead, "Elizabeth apparently married Apess in 1836 . . . which indicates that Mary died and he married Elizabeth" (*Writing Indian Nations,* 154). This highly questionable reasoning comes immediately before Konkle's transcription of Elizabeth's testimony during her husband's inquest, which also presents that testimony with no indication that other readings of the handwritten document are possible (154–55). Her transcription, it seems obvious to me, having examined a copy of the document, ought to at least indicate that there are other ways of deciphering the handwriting.

11. Among many accounts of what Jennings calls "the Second Puritan Conquest of New England," see Jennings, *Invasion,* 298ff.; and Calloway, "Introduction: Surviving the Dark Ages."

12. Included in this population loss is a significant amount of absorption into other tribal groups, especially the Mohegans (see McBride, 105ff.).

13. Among the many works that detail the history of Native Americans in New England, see Fawcett, *The Lasting of the Mohegans*; Peters, *The Wampanoags of Mashpee*; O'Brien, *Dispossession by Degrees*; Hauptmann and Wherry, *The Pequots*; and Calloway, *After King Philip's War.* Peters has also written a children's book, *Clambake: A Wampanoag Tradition.* An interesting collection of writings by contemporary New England Native writers is found in Carlson, *Rooted Like the Ash Trees.*

14. These whalers, of course, are models for the Native whalers who show up most famously in Herman Melville's *Moby Dick.*

15. See also Calloway, *The American Revolution.*

16. Weaver points out that Apess presents the story of his backsliding as happening only when away from the company of other Indians. "He never encounters problems in the community of Natives," Weaver writes, "where he seems to be an integrated whole" (*That the People,* 57).

17. For an insightful discussion of the rhetorical strategies of Winnemucca and Eastman, see Powell, "Rhetorics of Survivance." Copway's writings include *The Traditional History and Characteristic Sketches of the Ojibway.* For a general discussion of the phenomenon of Natives and non-Natives dressing up in supposedly authentic Native dress, see P. Deloria, *Playing Indian.*

18. For a discussion of the criticism that Apess's work has sparked in recent years, see Weaver, *That the People,* 53ff.

19. Recent accounts of Native Christians in the process of becoming ordained lend credence to this claim. Part of Vine Deloria Jr.'s famous assault on Christianity

in his early writings is based on long-standing complaints about the unwillingness of American churches to allow the development of Native leadership through ordination; see *Custer Died for Your Sins,* 110ff. Even more recently, a Methodist pastor has recounted her struggles with ordination as a Navajo woman; see Sombrero, "Black Robes."

20. Asbury and Coke were responsible for leading American Methodism in its formative years. Their focus was more on the moral content of Christianity that John and Thomas Wesley had developed in England. For more on Methodism, see Hempton, *The Religion of Hope;* Richey, *Early American Methodism;* and Schneider, *The Way of the Cross.*

21. See Hatch, *The Democratization of American Christianity;* and Richey, *Early American Methodism.*

22. Walker, *Appeal to the Colored Citizens of the World;* Stewart, *Productions of Mrs. Maria W. Stewart.* See also Hinks, *To Awaken My Afflicted Brethren;* Romero, *Home Fronts;* and Porter, *Early Negro Writing, 1760–1837.*

23. Peters's published transcription of the names includes 98 people (*The Wampanoags,* 33). Nielsen reports that 102 people signed the petition (409).

24. See note 10 on this subject, above.

25. See Bender, *New York Intellect.*

26. See Smith and Warrior, *Like a Hurricane,* 36ff. Though Smith and I collaborated on every word of the book, I took the lead in researching and drafting the chapter featuring Clyde Warrior.

27. Sandra Gustafson makes interesting parallels between Apess and Emerson in her "Nations of Israelites."

2. Democratic Vistas of the Osage Constitutional Crisis

1. The Osage Constitution circulates in various forms. The earliest printed edition I have found is *The Constitution and Laws of the Osage Nation Passed at Pawhuska, Osage Nation, In the Years 1881 and 1882.* See also Fitzpatrick, *Treaties and Laws of the Osage Nation,* 51–62. The full text of the Osage Constitution of 1881 is in the appendix at the end of this book.

2. See T. Wilson, *The Underground Reservation,* 24ff. The literature on Cherokee removal and its aftermath is immense. See, among many, McLaughlin, *After the Trail of Tears;* and Wilkins, *Cherokee Tragedy.* The Cherokee Constitution of 1839 is available at http://www.cherokeeobserver.org/Issues/1839constitution .html. The Cherokee version of the preamble reads as follows: "The Eastern and Western Cherokees having again re-united and become one body politic, under the style and title of the Cherokee Nation: Therefore, We, the people of the Cherokee Nation, in National Convention assembled, in order to establish justice, insure tranquility, promote the common welfare, and secure to ourselves and our

posterity the blessings of freedom acknowledging, with humility and gratitude, the goodness of the Sovereign Ruler of the Universe in permitting us so to do, and imploring His aid and guidance in its accomplishment—do ordain and establish this Constitution for the government of the Cherokee Nation."

Though it misses many of the nuances of the Cherokee case, Priscilla Wald's reading of this document is nonetheless insightful; see *Constituting Americans,* 26ff.

3. I am grateful to Jace Weaver for his legal expertise in helping me understand the basic principles of how a judge in American jurisprudence comes to a decision in equity, focusing on remedying injustice in the face of laws through which such equity cannot occur.

4. I participated in each of these votes as a nonshareholder (I became a shareholder after the death of my father, Allen David Warrior, in 1997), and I remember the details of these events vividly. In reconstructing them, I have consulted information sheets and other materials published by the Osage Commission following its creation after the 1992 district court decision. These various documents were gathered together, along with a press release, a copy of the Tenth Circuit's reversal, the 1994 Osage Constitution, and the 1906 Osage Allotment Act in a press packet that supporters of the Osage National Council assembled in June 1997 (hereafter referred to in the text as "Press Packet"). Vice president Whitehorn's statement is from the June 13, 1997, press release in the packet. I should add that, as a supporter of the National Council, I assisted in duplicating and disseminating the packet.

5. The congress was sponsored by the Guatemalan Department of Culture and Sports and was held July 1997 in Guatemala City. I was one of nine U.S. delegates, including Simon Ortiz, Jace Weaver, and Denise Sweet, who attended as guests of the United States Information Agency of the U.S. State Department. The congress brought together writers from throughout the Americas.

6. Osage historiography is extensive. Among the most important written accounts are Mathews, *The Osages*; Burns, *A History of the Osage People*; T. Wilson, *The Underground Reservation*; Din and Nasatir, *The Imperial Osages*; and Rollings, *The Osage*. Though now somewhat out of date, an excellent resource for scholarship on the Osages is T. Wilson, *Bibliography of the Osage*.

7. Pierce demonstrates convincingly that treaty making was, for the fledgling United States, a matter of manipulating situations by any means necessary. The Osage Treaty of 1808, for instance, was signed by only one of the two most important Osage leaders, Pawhuska, while Claremore, the undisputed war chief, refused to be party to it (11). Pierce reveals the individual cash inducements the United States used to entice supposed chiefs to sign and legitimate similar Cherokee documents (12). For an illuminating discussion of the treaty-making process, see Deloria and DeMallie, *Documents of American Indian Diplomacy,* esp. 177–80.

8. See R. White, *"It's Your Misfortune,"* 216–20. As White argues, overhunting was but one factor in the decline of the buffalo herd. Disease and drought also played a role.

9. See Miner and Unrau, *The End of Indian Kansas.*

10. For much of the information on the Osages in Kansas and in the Osage Nation in Indian Territory and the state of Oklahoma, I am drawing on the *Annual Report of the Commissioner of Indian Affairs,* 1850–1922. I will refer to these reports as *Annual Report* followed by the year.

11. Agents reported 4,561 Osages (with births double the rate of deaths) in the 1850 report to the Commissioner of Indian Affairs and 4,941 Osages in the 1852 report (1850, 35, 37; 1852, 105). W. J. J. Morrow, author of the 1852 report, believed that his figure was high due to the practice of repeat enrollments in some bands to increase their share of annuities, but Father John Schoenmakers, principal of the Osage school starting in 1847, reported the Osage population around the time of his arrival among the tribe to be 5,000. I have used Schoenmakers's estimate as a baseline for my discussion here.

12. The Osages never received the actual title to the land. The United States eventually arranged with the Cherokees to have the title held in trust by the United States. Annual agent reports include a number of references to various leaders insisting that the agent inquire about the status of the document proving Osage ownership of the land. The 1906 Act extinguished that trust title when the land was allotted.

13. This is consistent with the work of Duane Champagne, who has done the most extensive analysis of tribal constitutional democracies. Champagne persuasively contends that such governments come from tribal groups that already had "differential" social systems in which "political action . . . is based primarily on political interests and contingencies," rather than on "prerogatives . . . of religion, culture, kinship, economy, and social solidarity. Such differentiation, based on the ability of Native people to act politically in the political realm, helped pave the way for adopting new forms of government." See Champagne, *Social Order and Political Change.*

14. Prucha, 671. This phrase is often attributed to Theodore Roosevelt, but Prucha points out that Roosevelt adopted it from Gates.

15. See *Fletcher v. United States,* 1323ff.

16. In this, the court failed to note that the Congress was, at the time of the 1906 Act, following the mandates of the Supreme Court in *Lone Wolf v. Hitchcock* (1903), which completely undermined the concept of tribal sovereignty for the next three decades. See Prucha, 776.

17. Appiah makes this suggestion in the midst of discussing the relationship between postmodern and postcolonialism. Postcolonialism, especially, has generated controversy among North American indigenous writers, with some calling

for a rejection of it on the grounds that it represents continuing subjection to the conditions of colonization. While I agree with much of what is contained in that sentiment, I do not think it reflects a broad understanding of what is happening in postcolonial discourse (see Loomba, *Colonialism/Postcolonialism*). As several commentators have argued, the *post* in *postcolonial* and *postmodern* represents not so much a sense of "after" as it does "above and beyond" (Appiah, 143).

3. The Work of Indian Pupils

1. Deloria, "Knowing and Understanding," 139. Deloria's essays on education are among the most influential writings of the most recent part of his career. They appeared originally in *Winds of Change,* a magazine published by the American Indian Science and Engineering Society (AISES). The essays published in *Winds of Change* (which are listed in the bibliography) were also collected and published by AISES in a single volume, *Indian Education in America: Eight Essays.* Along with being reprinted in *Spirit and Reason,* these essays are also revised and reprinted in *Power and Place: Indian Education in America,* edited by Vine Deloria Jr. and Daniel R. Wildcat. *Power and Place* is, in essence, Wildcat's amplification of Deloria's ideas in the original *Winds of Change* essays. References here are to the essays as published in *Spirit and Reason.*

2. All issues of the *Helper* that I have read from 1888 to 1890 include this statement.

3. Noley, 117–18; Mihesuah, *Cultivating the Rosebuds,* 22, and "'Graves of the Polluted Debauches,'" 503–21.

4. See Eastman, *Pratt: Red Man's Moses.* Eastman does not comment on the irony of giving Pratt the pride of place as a mosaic figure for Natives. It makes me wonder how Jewish people would feel if Moses weren't a Jew.

5. Lindsey points out that the St. Augustine prisoners were not, in fact, the first Natives to attend Hampton. They were preceded by Ute student Richard Johnson. Johnson was one of three Ute students who previously attended Lincoln University, another African American school, in the 1870s. Howard University in Washington, D.C., also had Native alumni (Lindsey, 19–21). See also Anderson, *The Education of Blacks in the South,* 33–78.

6. Washington, *Up from Slavery,* 80. Washington indicates that in 1879 he was in charge of the first group of male Native students at Hampton, but more likely he was in charge of the first group the year after Pratt left to establish Carlisle.

7. For an interesting analysis of Standing Bear and the other Sioux authors in this chapter, see Heflin, *"I Remain Alive": The Sioux Literary Renaissance.*

8. For details on Eastman's life, see R. Wilson, *Ohiyesa: Charles Eastman, Santee Sioux;* and Powell, "Rhetorics of Survivance." Eastman's autobiographical writing includes *Indian Boyhood* and *From the Deep Woods to Civilization.*

9. For a discussion of Native literacy, see Blaeser, "Learning 'The Language the Presidents Speak,'" 230–35.

10. Another resource for the voices of Native students and other Native writers is Daniel F. Littlefield Jr. and James Parins, *A Biobibliography of Native American Writers, 1772–1924.* Littlefield and Parins, who detail the careers of hundreds of Native writers, including many students, give lie to the idea that Native people produced little in the way of written records until recently.

11. Paul DeMain, editor and publisher of *News from Indian Country,* is a descendant of Dennison Wheelock and was generous in passing along information about him. The Oneida Nation Cultural Heritage Department (P.O. Box 365, Oneida, Wisconsin, 54155) has clippings and other material about him in its collection. Wheelock has been of increasing interest among scholars who study boarding schools, so no doubt more and more will be known of him in time to come. An unfortunate aspect of much research of this type, I should say, has been for researchers to assume, bizarrely, that figures who emerge in boarding-school research have no living family members, much less tribal historical societies and cultural heritage departments that carry memories and other important information about them. It should go without saying that a primary legacy of these former students is the families who followed in their footsteps, especially when those families include significant numbers of people who have committed themselves in their work to the future of their Native communities.

12. While writing about the synchronicity that these bridging narratives create, I found a remarkable example. Joy Harjo, in her short story "How to Get to Venus," presents a boarding-school narrative in which a young woman from an abusive home situation attends an arts-based residential school that is clearly based on the Insitute of American Indian Arts in Santa Fe, New Mexico, where Harjo attended high school. The young woman talks about trips she takes to the moon as an escape from her home life. At school, she befriends a troubled young woman from a similar background and, in a moment of crisis, comforts her. "All night I held her," Harjo writes, "while she cried for her mother, for home. All night, as we flew through the stars to the planet Venus" (176). The story is a beautiful evocation of the boarding-school experience.

The moment of synchronicity comes from an 1890 edition of Carlisle's *Indian Helper,* which included a story by Nellie Robertson, "one of our imaginative Sioux girls," about visiting the moon. "Of the many strange lands and queer places I have visited in my life," she writes, "the strangest and the one [on which] I have experienced [the most] pleasure was my trip to the moon in 1900." She describes humanoid creatures in unisex dress who are "very kind and polite." In perhaps the most telling observation, Robertson writes, "Up in the moon they have no school-houses nor books of any kind from which to read or study. They are a blissful people." She goes on to describe a people who live apart from all except what they need for their own subsistence. "I hope sometime in the future," she writes, "to take another trip and see more things of interest."

13. One notable exception is Forbes, "An American Indian University."

14. See Crum, "Henry Roe Cloud"; and Tetzloff, "Cloud, Henry Roe."

15. When "Philadelphia Flowers" was first published, Roberta Hill's legal name was Roberta Hill Whiteman.

16. *Thunder in My Soul,* 88. Monture-Angus has also written movingly of her educational experience in a 1998 essay, "On Being Homeless: One Aboriginal Woman's 'Conquest' of Canadian Universities, 1989–1998."

4. Momaday in the Movement Years

1. Thornton, "The Demography of Colonialism," 19. The 1900 number of 375,000 is without controversy among demographers, according to Thornton. I use Thornton's own estimate of seven million for the 1492 population, which is a moderate one. As he reports, early demographic estimates of one to one and a half million are widely seen as extreme underestimates, while later estimates of ten to twelve million seem equally extreme as overestimates. Seven million is on the upper end of current scholarly work, which places between two and seven million indigenes above the Rio Grande and in Greenland in 1492. See also Thornton, *American Indian Holocaust and Survival.*

2. See Tallchief, *Maria Tallchief: America's Prima Ballerina*; and Livingston, *American Indian Ballerinas.*

3. See Wheeler, *Jim Thorpe: World's Greatest Athlete.*

4. See P. Deloria, "'I Am of the Body,'" 329.

5. See Oxendine, *American Indian Sports Heritage,* 87–89.

6. See Archuleta, "'The Indian Is an Artist,'" 91–95; and P. Deloria, "'I Am of the Body,'" 329.

7. See Churchill, Hill, and Hill, "Examining Stereotyping," 39–40.

8. See Singer, *Wiping the War Paint,* 20–21.

9. See Black, "Humorous Betrayals: American Indians and Film." For a discussion of what it has meant for American Indians to be relegated to being extras in Hollywood representations of American Indians, see Smith, "The Big Movie," in *Exile on Main Street,* cyberbook, http://redplanet.home.mindspring.com/exile/exile.htm.

10. Graham Greene's credits include *Dances with Wolves* (1990), *Thunderheart* (1991), and *Skins* (2002). Tantoo Cardinal was also in *Dances,* as well as *Grand Avenue* (1998) and *Smoke Signals* (1998). Bedard was the voice of the title character in the animated feature *Pocahontas* (1995) and has also been in *Smoke Signals* and *Naturally Native* (1998). Studi starred in *Geronimo* (1993) and has also appeared in Michael Mann's *Heat* (1995).

11. See Singer, *Wiping the War Paint,* for information on the work of these individual filmmakers.

12. For a discussion of American Indian participation in the war, see Bernstein, *American Indians and World War II.* Bernstein includes a brief discussion of the Code Talkers (46, 48–49). My grandfather, Robert Edward Warrior, was an Osage soldier in World War II. He was killed as a member of the medical corps in the aftermath of the D-Day invasion in 1944; see my "Souvenirs of the Indian Wars."

13. See Sando, *Pueblo Nations,* 100–101, 261; see also Deloria, *God Is Red,* 7–11. Sando's book is a revision of his *The Pueblo Indians.*

14. Johnny Cash marked his death in a famous song, "The Ballad of Ira Hayes," by Pat LaFarge. The song was on LaFarge's albums in 1961 and 1962, and Cash recorded the song in March 1964. LaFarge was the son of Oliver LaFarge, author of *Laughing Boy.*

15. See Koehler, "Jim Thorpe: Legend and Legacy"; and Thorpe, "Jim Thorpe."

16. Mills provides an account of the race in the transcript of one of his many speeches; see Mills, "Twenty Seconds of Pain."

17. See Unrau, *Mixed-Bloods and Tribal Dissolution.*

18. For a searchable electronic database of Academy Award nominees and winners, see http://www.oscars.org/awardsdatabase/index.html.

19. Robertson and The Band appear with Bob Dylan on *Before the Flood (Live with The Band, 1974)* and *The Basement Tapes* (1975). Robertson's recent work includes *Music for the Native Americans* (1994) and *Contact from the Underworld of Red Boy* (1998). The Band's final concert as a quintet is the subject of a famous Martin Scorcese documentary, *The Last Waltz* (1978).

20. For a discussion of Mathews's novel, see the second chapter of my book *Tribal Secrets* (45–86).

21. Letter from Momaday to Winters, Amherst, March 17, 1967, Yvor Winters and Janet Lewis Papers (collection number M352), box 1, folder 9 (personal correspondence, Marcus-Momaday), Special Collections and University Archives, Green Library, Stanford University.

22. For discussion of the United Scholarship Service (USS) program, see Deloria, *Custer Died for Your Sins,* 270.

23. See Momaday, "An Edition of the Complete Poems of Frederick Goddard Tuckerman," and *The Complete Poems of Frederick Goddard Tuckerman.*

24. Momaday discusses his work as a painter in "Only an Appearance" and includes a large amount of his visual art in *In the Presence of the Sun.* None of Momaday's plays are published, though one of his recently published pieces is written in the form of a play (see "The Bear-God Dialogues" in *In The Bear's House*). The most well-known of Momaday's plays is "The Indolent Boys," about three Kiowa boarding-school students who freeze to death while running away (see *http://www.buffalotrust.org/indolent.htm*). His children's book is *Circle of*

Wonder: A Native American Christmas Story and his nonfiction is collected in *The Man Made of Words: Essays, Stories, Passages.*

25. See Lincoln, "From Tai-Me to Rainy Mountain." In his recent work on Kiowa storytelling, Gus Palmer Jr. makes a more nuanced and insightful point regarding Momaday's work. Palmer argues that Kiowa storytelling, while not having a formal training structure, does follow a clear pattern of grandparents having the privileged position of passing along Kiowa oral stories—in the Kiowa language—to their grandchildren. While demonstrating abundant and abiding respect for Momaday's contributions to contemporary literature, Palmer argues against "people [who] naturally assume he is a storyteller, which he is, though not in the Kiowa sense, not insofar as the term applies to the oral Kiowa world." Interestingly, then, the reports Lincoln unearthed may, in fact, have a strong basis in a traditional Kiowa sensibility, even if the animus of the report writers that one can presume from Lincoln's description seems misplaced. See Palmer, *Telling Stories the Kiowa Way,* 58.

26. For an insightful discussion of one alternative to criticism that chooses to focus either on the cultural aspects of *House Made of Dawn* or the novel's modernist forms, see Landrum, "The Shattered Modernism." Landrum argues that Momaday indulged in modernist form in order to break out of those formal strictures, and, in doing so, he creates aesthetic space for the cultural material he uses. As Landrum argues, "[T]he relentless individuation of the other in . . . *House Made of Dawn* and the strategies for countering modernist hegemony suggest that the crucial issues (and perhaps a reason Momaday has had so much influence on Native American authors) involve how to articulate cultural differences within textual forms hostile to it" (781).

27. This quote and the one that follows appear in *The Names* on the page following the genealogical chart and preceding the prologue.

28. Momaday to Winters, Goleta, California, January 4, 1968, Winters and Lewis papers.

29. Though I direct this comment at contemporary criticism in general, I refer specifically to Bhabha, *The Location of Culture*; and Haraway, *Simians, Cyborgs, and Women.*

30. See Smith and Warrior, *Like a Hurricane.*

31. For instance, this is the position Troy Johnson takes in *The Occupation of Alcatraz Island.*

32. For an insider discussion of the development of SRIYC on the cusp of the National Indian Youth Council (NIYC), see Minton, "The Place of the Indian Youth Council."

33. See *Uncommon Controversy: Fishing Rights of the Muckleshoot, Puyallup, and Nisqually Indians,* esp. 108.

34. Alfonso Ortiz was one of the most important Native scholars of the twen-

tieth century and helped define excellence for generations to follow. Princeton would later deny him tenure in its anthropology department, one of several such dismissals from elite U.S. universities that litter the history of the development of Native American scholarship.

35. Nabokov, "The Indian Oral Tradition" (interview with N. Scott Momaday).

36. See, for instance, Schubnell, *N. Scott Momaday.* Landrum provides a thorough review of the broad outlines of cultural approaches to *House Made of Dawn* in "The Shattered Modernism."

37. For a recent reading of *House Made of Dawn* that includes extensive references to the criticism that has grown up around the novel, see Teuton, "'Where Are You Going?'"

38. Since Ortiz is not the first to see the novel as a story of learning, but his reading takes account of what others have missed. Bernard Selinger notes that the bildungsroman has been a major form for Native novels ("*House Made of Dawn*: A Positively Ambivalent Bildungsroman"). As he says, "One wonders why this essentially European bourgeois form with its middle-class hero has been so appealing to our best Native authors" (39).

In tracing out the ways that *House Made of Dawn* follows and does not follow the form of the bildungsroman, Selinger argues that Abel seeks "to achieve some sort of self-transcendence and accommodation to society" (49). Tosamah, the peyote priest in the novel, and Benally, Abel's more well-adapted roommate and confidant, are ambivalent models for Abel to follow in his quest. This ambivalence is also present in the case of Abel's grandfather, who for Selinger becomes a "heavy-handed . . . model *par excellence*" for Abel (54). Yet Selinger, who finds the ending lacking, doesn't consider the possibility that Abel, in fact, chooses a nonambivalent path over one that he has learned is filled with ambivalence.

39. See Ortiz's introduction to his *Woven Stone,* 31–32.

40. I am indebted to Landrum's article for leading me to this connection (775). However, he misses the boat not long after in arguing for an equation of traditional spirituality with peyotism in the "Christian contamination of local knowledge" (776). Peyotism would be more accurately read as a movement that seeks to alter Christianity through the application of local knowledge. This equation of Tosamah's peyote ministry with a move toward primitivism on Momaday's part ignores the emergence of peyote religion as a response to colonialism and modernity.

41. According to Vine Deloria Jr. in 1991, policy studies is among the most underdeveloped areas in Native American studies. As he writes, "No in-depth study of federal policy exists, and most of us would be hard pressed to name half of the people who have served as Indian Commissioner or Assistant Secretary of the Interior for Indian Affairs" ("Federal Policy," 19). See also Deloria, *American Indian Policy.*

42. "The Arrowmaker," in *Man Made of Words,* 9. In this volume, various components of the Princeton presentation are presented separately.

43. "On Indian-White Relations: A Point of View," in *Man Made of Words,* 55.

44. Momaday to Winters, November 20, 1967, Winters and Lewis papers. This letter indicates no place of writing, but is almost certainly from Santa Barbara or nearby Goleta.

45. One example of an indigenous nation seeking to overcome just this sort of epistemological barrier in addressing the sacrilegious degradation of its lands is described in Good Striker, "TEK Wars: First Nations' Struggles for Environmental Planning," in Weaver, *Defending Mother Earth.* The other essays in Weaver's volume also address the connections between local struggles and scholarly knowledge. Another source for contemporary environmental struggles of local indigenous groups and the political strategies they have used is Winona LaDuke, *All Our Relations.*

Conclusion

1. See Owens, *Mixedblood Messages,* 52; Krupat, *The Turn to the Native,* 18; Lyons, "Rhetorical Sovereignty," 457; and Pulitano, *Toward a Native American Critical Theory.*

Appendix

Except for instances noted in the text, this text reproduces the Osage Constitution of 1881 as printed in *The Constitution and Laws of the Osage Nation Passed at Pawhuska, Osage Nation, in the Years 1881 and 1882.*

1. Reads *indeasible* in the 1883 text.

2. The 1883 text includes a period at this point.

3. Reads *two-third* in the 1883 text.

4. Text here reads *chose* instead of *choose.*

5. The 1883 text does not include a comma, as in other examples of this phrase.

6. Reads *setting.*

7. The text includes a closing quotation mark at the end of this line, which is clearly a typesetting mistake as the following section is missing that same mark.

8. See note 7.

9. The word *shall* does not occur in the 1883 text, but syntax indicates it is missing. Also, a single space in the text may indicate a missing word in the typeset.

10. The 1883 text includes a comma instead of a period at the end of this sentence.

11. The 1883 text includes a period at this point.

12. This section and sections three and six following read *circuits courts.*

13. Reads *deminished* in 1883 text.

14. Reads *Supreme courts* in the 1883 text.

15. Reads *te* in the 1883 text.

16. Reads *for voted* in the 1883 text.

17. The 1883 text includes periods after all names except *Bigheart*'s and *Pawnee-no-pah-she*'s.

Bibliography

Ahmed, Aijaz. *In Theory: Classes, Nations, Literatures.* London: Verso, 1992.

Aldama, Frederick Luis. *Postethnic Narrative Criticism: Magicorealism in Oscar "Zeta" Acosta, Ana Castillo, Julie Dash, Hanik Kureishi, and Salman Rushdie.* Austin: University of Texas Press, 2003.

Alfred, Taiaiake. *Peace, Power, Righteousness: An Indigenous Manifesto.* Toronto: Oxford University Press, 1999.

Allen, Paula Gunn. *The Sacred Hoop: Recovering the Feminine in American Indian Traditions.* Boston: Beacon, 1986.

Alvord, Lori Alviso, and Elizabeth Cohen Van Pelt. *The Scalpel and the Silver Bear: The First Navajo Woman Surgeon Combines Western Medicine and Traditional Healing.* New York: Bantam, 1999.

Anderson, James D. *The Education of Blacks in the South, 1860–1935.* Chapel Hill: University of North Carolina Press, 1988.

Annual Report of the Commissioner of Indian Affairs, 1850–1922. Washington, D.C.: Government Printing Office.

Apess, William. *On Our Own Ground: The Complete Writings of William Apess, A Pequot.* Edited by Barry O'Connell. Amherst: University of Massachusetts Press, 1992.

Appiah, Kwame Anthony. *In My Father's House: Africa in the Philosophy of Culture.* New York: Oxford, 1992.

Archuleta, Margaret. "'The Indian Is an Artist': Art Education," In Archuleta, Child, and Lomawaima, *Away from Home,* 84–97.

Archuleta, Margaret L., Brenda J. Child, and K. Tsianina Lomawaima, eds. *Away from Home: American Indian Boarding School Experiences, 1879–2000.* Phoenix: Heard Museum, 2000.

215

Arieff, Allison. "A Different Sort of P(R)eservation: Some Thoughts on the National Museum of the American Indian." *Museum Anthropology* 19, no. 2 (Fall 1995): 78–90.

Armstrong, Jeanette, ed. *Looking at the Words of Our People: First Nations Analysis of Literature.* Penticton, British Columbia: Theytus, 1993.

Barsh, Russel Lawrence. "Contemporary Marxist Theory and Native American Reality." *American Indian Quarterly* 12 (Summer 1988): 187–211.

Bataille, Gretchen M., and Charles L. P. Silet, eds. *The Pretend Indians: Images of Native Americans in the Movies.* Ames: University of Iowa Press, 1980.

Batstone, David, Eduardo Mendieta, Lois Ann Lorentzen, and Dwight N. Hopkins, eds. *Liberation Theologies, Postmodernity, and the Americas.* London: Routledge, 1997.

Bender, Thomas. *New York Intellect: A History of Intellectual Life in New York City from 1750 to the Beginning of Our Time.* Baltimore: The Johns Hopkins University Press, 1987.

Bernstein, Alison. *American Indians and World War II: Toward a New Era in Indian Affairs.* Norman: University of Oklahoma Press, 1991.

Bhabha, Homi. *The Location of Culture.* New York: Routledge, 1994.

Bird, Gloria. "Towards a Decolonization of the Mind and Text 1: Leslie Marmon Silko's *Ceremony. Wicazo Sa Review* 9, no. 2 (Fall 1993): 1–9.

Black, Liza. "Humorous Betrayals: American Indians and Film." Unpublished ms.

Blaeser, Kimberly M. "Learning 'The Language the Presidents Speak': Images and Issues of Literacy in American Indian Literature." *World Literature Today* 66, no. 2 (Spring 1992): 230–35.

Bronson, Ruth Muskrat. *Indians Are People, Too.* New York: Friendship House, 1944.

Brooks, Joanna. "Six Hymns by Samson Occom." *Early American Literature* 38, no. 1 (2003): 67–87.

Buell, Lawrence. *New England Literary Culture: From Revolution to Renaissance.* Cambridge: University of Cambridge Press, 1986.

Burns, Louis. *A History of the Osage People.* Fallbrook, Calif.: Ciga Press, 1989.

———. *Osage Indian Bands and Clans.* Fallbrook, Calif.: Ciga Press, 1984.

———. *Osage Indian Customs and Myths.* Fallbrook, Calif.: Ciga Press, 1984.

———. *Osage Mission Baptisms, Marriages, and Interments, 1820–1886.* Fallbrook, Calif.: Ciga Press, 1986.

———. *Symbolic and Decorative Arts of the Osage People.* Fallbrook, Calif.: Ciga Press, 1984.

Burrows, Edwin G., and Mike Wallace. *Gotham: A History of New York City to 1898.* New York: Oxford University Press, 1999.

Callahan, S. Alice. *Wynema: A Child of the Forest.* 1891. Reprint, edited and with an introduction by A. LaVonne Brown Ruoff. Lincoln: University of Nebraska Press, 1997.

Calloway, Colin G., ed. *After King Philip's War: Presence and Persistence in Indian New England*. Hanover, N.H.: University Press of New England, 1997.

———. *The American Revolution in Indian Country: Crisis and Diversity in Native American Communities*. Cambridge: Cambridge University Press, 1995.

Cardinal, Harold. *The Unjust Society*. 1969. Reprint, Seattle: University of Washington Press, 1999.

Carney, Cary Michael. *Native American Higher Education in the United States*. New Brunswick, N. J.: Transaction Publishers, 1999.

Champagne, Duane. *Social Order and Political Change: Constitutional Governments among the Cherokee, the Choctaw, the Chickasaw, and the Creek*. Stanford, Calif.: Stanford University Press, 1992.

Cherokee Constitution of 1839. *http://www.cherokeeobserver.org/Issues/1839 constitution.html*.

Child, Brenda J. *Boarding School Seasons: American Indian Families, 1900–1940*. Lincoln: University of Nebraska Press, 1998.

Churchill, Ward, Mary Anne Hill, and Norbert S. Hill Jr. "Examining Stereotyping: An Analytic Survey of Twentieth-Century American Indian Entertainers." In *The Pretend Indians: Images of Native Americans in the Movies*, edited by Gretchen M. Bataille and Charles L. P. Silet, 35–48. Ames: University of Iowa Press, 1980.

The Constitution and Laws of the Osage Nation Passed at Pawhuska, Osage Nation, In the Years 1881 and 1882. Washington, D.C.: R. O. Polkinhorn, Printer, 1883.

Copway, George. *The Traditional History and Characteristic Sketches of the Ojibway Nation*. London: Gelpin, 1850. Republished as *Indian Life and Indian History, by an Indian Author: Embracing the Traditions of the North American Indian Tribes Regarding Themselves, Particularly the Most Important of All the Tribes, the Ojibways*. 1858. Reprint, New York: AMS, 1977.

Cronin, William. *Changes in the Land: Indians, Colonists, and the Ecology of New England*. New York: Hill and Wang, 1983.

Crum, Steven J. "Henry Roe Cloud, A Winnebago Indian Reformer: His Quest for American Indian Higher Education." *Kansas History* 11, no. 3 (Summer 1988): 171–84.

Cruse, Harold. *The Crisis of the Negro Intellectual: From Its Origins to the Present*. New York: Morrow, 1977.

Cusick, David. *Sketches of Ancient History of the Six Nations*. 3rd ed. Lockport, New York: Turner & McCollum, Printers, Democrat Office, 1848.

Dannenberg, Anne Marie. "'Where, Then, Shall We Place the Hero of the Wilderness?' William Apess's *Eulogy on King Philip* and Doctrines of Racial Destiny." In Jaskoski, *Early Native American Writing*, 66–82.

Deloria, Barbara, Kristen Foehner, and Sam Scinta, eds. *Spirit and Reason: The Vine Deloria Jr. Reader*. Golden, Colo.: Fulcrum Publishing, 1999.

Deloria, Ella C. *Speaking of Indians*. New York: Friendship House, 1944.

Deloria, Philip. "'I Am of the Body': Thoughts on My Grandfather, Culture, and Sports." *South Atlantic Quarterly* 95, no. 2 (Spring 1996): 321–38.

———. *Playing Indian*. New Haven: Yale University Press, 1998.

Deloria, Vine Jr., ed. *American Indian Policy in the Twentieth Century*. Norman: University of Oklahoma Press, 1985.

———. "The Burden of Indian Education." Reprinted in Deloria, Foehner, and Scinta, *Spirit and Reason*, 159–86.

———. *Custer Died for Your Sins: An Indian Manifesto*. New York: Macmillan, 1969.

———. "Federal Policy and the Indian Question." *American Indian Quarterly* 15 (Winter 1991): 19–21.

———. "Foreword: American Fantasy." In Bataille and Silet, *The Pretend Indians: Images of Native Americans in the Movies*, ix–xvi.

———. *God Is Red*. New York: Grosset and Dunlap, 1973.

———. "Higher Education and Self-Determination." *Winds of Change* 6, no. 1 (Winter 1991): 18–25. Reprinted in Deloria, Foehner, and Scinta, *Spirit and Reason*, 144–53.

———. "Implications of the 1968 Civil Rights Act in Tribal Autonomy." In *Indian Voices: The First Convocation of American Indian Scholars*, 85–104.

———. *Indian Education in America: Eight Essays*. Boulder, Colo.: AISES Publishing, 1991.

———. "Knowing and Understanding: Transitional Education in the Modern World." *Winds of Change* 5, no. 3 (Summer 1990): 10–15. Reprinted in Deloria, Foehner, and Scinta, *Spirit and Reason*, 137–43.

———. "The Perpetual Education Report." *Winds of Change* 6, no. 2 (Spring 1991): 12–18.

———. "Property and Self-Government as Educational Initiatives." *Winds of Change* 5, no. 4 (Autumn 1990): 26–31.

———. "Traditional Education in the Modern World." *Winds of Change* 5, no. 1 (Winter 1990): 12–18.

———. "Traditional Technology." *Winds of Change* 5, no. 2 (Spring 1990): 12–17.

Deloria, Vine, Jr., and Raymond J. DeMallie. *Documents of American Indian Diplomacy: Treaties, Agreements, and Conventions, 1775–1979*, vol. 1. Norman: University of Oklahoma Press, 1999.

Deloria, Vine, Jr., and Daniel R. Wildcat. *Power and Place: Indian Education in America*. Golden, Colo.: Fulcrum Publishing, 2001.

Din, Gilbert C., and A. P. Nasatir. *The Imperial Osages: Spanish-Indian Diplomacy in the Mississippi Valley*. Norman: University of Oklahoma Press, 1983.

Donovan, Kathleen. *Feminist Readings of Native American Literature*. Tucson: University of Arizona Press, 1998.

Drinnon, Richard. *Facing West: The Metaphysics of Indian Hating and Empire Building.* 1980. Reprint, New York: Schocken Books, 1990.

Du Bois, W. E. Burghardt. "The Field and the Function of the American Negro College." In Paschal, *W. E. B. Du Bois: A Reader,* 51–69.

———. *The Souls of Black Folk; Essays and Sketches.* 1903. Reprint, Greenwich, Conn.: Fawcett, 1961.

Duran, Eduardo, and Bonnie Duran. *Native American Postcolonial Psychology.* Albany: State University of New York Press, 1995.

Eagleton, Terry. *The Function of Criticism: From the Spectator to Post-Structuralism.* London: Verso, 1984.

Eastman, Charles Alexander. *From the Deep Woods to Civilization.* Boston: Little, Brown, 1916.

———. *Indian Boyhood.* New York: McClure, Phillips & Co., 1902.

Eastman, Elaine Goodale. *Pratt: Red Man's Moses.* Norman: University of Oklahoma Press, 1935.

Emerson, Ralph Waldo. "The American Scholar." In Whicher, *Selections from Ralph Waldo Emerson; An Organic Anthology,* 63–80.

Erdrich, Heid, and Laura Tohe, eds. *Sister Nations: Native American Women Writers on Community.* Minneapolis: Minnesota Historical Society Press, 2002.

Erdrich, Louise. *Jacklight.* New York: Holt, Rinehart, and Winston, 1984.

———. *Love Medicine.* 1984. New and expanded edition, New York: HarperCollins, 1993.

Fanon, Frantz. *The Wretched of the Earth.* Translated by Constance Farrington. New York: Grove, 1963.

Fawcett, Melissa Jayne. *The Lasting of the Mohegans, Part I: The Story of the Wolf People.* Uncasville, Conn.: The Mohegan Tribe, 1995.

Fitzpatrick, W. S., compiler. *Treaties and Laws of the Osage Nation as Passed to November 26, 1890.* Cedar Vale, Kans.: Commercial Press, 1890. Reprinted as *The Constitutions and Laws of the American Indian Tribes* 4: 51–62. Wilmington, Del.: Scholarly Resources, 1973.

Fletcher v. United States. 116 F.3d 1315 (10th Cir. 1997).

Forbes, Jack D. "An American Indian University: A Proposal for Survival." *Journal of American Indian Education* 5, no. 2 (January 1966): 1–7.

Garrod, Andrew, and Colleen Larimore, eds. *First Person, First Peoples: Native American College Graduates Tell Their Life Stories.* Ithaca: Cornell University Press, 1997.

Good Striker, Duane. "TEK Wars: First Nations' Struggles for Environmental Planning." In Weaver, *Defending Mother Earth,* 144–52.

Gould, Janice. "Disobedience (in Language) in Texts by Lesbian Native Americans." *ARIEL: A Review of International English Literature* 25, no. 1 (January 1994): 32–43.

Green, Rayna. "Rosebuds of the Plateau: Frank Matsura and the Fainting Couch Aesthetic." In Lippard, *Partial Recall,* 46–53.

Green, Rayna, and John Troutman. "By the Waters of the Minnehaha: Music and Dance, Pageants and Princesses." In Archuleta, Child, and Lomawaima, *Away from Home,* 60–83.

Gustafson, Sandra. "Nations of Israelites: Prophecy and Cultural Autonomy in the Writings of William Apess." *Religion and Literature* 26, no. 1 (Spring 1994): 31–53.

Habermas, Jürgen. *Structural Transformation of the Public Sphere: An Inquiry into a Category of Bourgeois Society.* Translated by Thomas Burger. Cambridge, Mass.: MIT Press, 1991.

Haraway, Donna J. *Simians, Cyborgs, and Women: The Reinvention of Nature.* New York: Routledge, 1991.

Harjo, Joy. "How to Get to Venus." In Erdrich and Tohe, *Sister Nations,* 162–76.

———. *A Map to the Next World.* New York: W. W. Norton, 2000.

———. *The Woman Who Fell from the Sky.* New York: W. W. Norton, 1994.

Harjo, Joy, and Gloria Bird. "Introduction," In *Reinventing the Enemy's Language,* 19–31.

Harjo, Joy, and Gloria Bird, eds. *Reinventing the Enemy's Language: Contemporary Native Women's Writing of North America.* New York: W. W. Norton, 1997.

Hatch, Nathan. *The Democratization of American Christianity.* New Haven: Yale University Press, 1989.

Hauptman, Laurence. "The Pequot War and Its Legacies." In Hauptman and Wherry, *The Pequots in Southern New England,* 69–80.

Hauptman, Laurence M., and James D. Wherry, eds. *The Pequots in Southern New England: The Fall and Rise of an American Indian Nation.* Norman: University of Oklahoma Press, 1990.

Haynes, Carolyn. "'A Mark for the All to Hiss . . . at': The Formation of Methodist and Pequot Identity in the Conversion Narrative of William Apess." *Early American Literature* 31 (1996): 25–44.

Heflin, Ruth J. *"I Remain Alive": The Sioux Literary Renaissance.* Syracuse: Syracuse University Press, 2000.

Hempton, David. *The Religion of Hope: Methodism and Popular Religion c. 1750–1900.* New York: Routledge, 1996.

Herndon, Ruth Wallis, and Ella Wilcox Sekatau. "The Right to a Name: The Narragansett People and Rhode Island Officials in the Revolutionary Era." In Calloway, *After King Philip's War,* 114–43.

Hinks, Peter P. *To Awaken My Afflicted Brethren: David Walker and the Problem of Antebellum Slave Resistance.* University Park: Pennsylvania State University Press, 1997.

Hochbruck, Wolfgang, and Beatrix Dudensing-Reichel. "'Honoratissimi Benefactores': Native American Students and Two Seventeenth-Century Texts in the University Tradition." In Jaskoski, *Early Native American Writing*, 1–14.

hooks, bell. "Essentialism and Experience." *American Literary History* 25, no. 1 (1991): 172–83.

Houchins, Sue, ed. *Spiritual Narratives.* New York: Oxford University Press, 1988.

Hoxie, Frederick E., ed. *Encyclopedia of North American Indians.* Boston: Houghton Mifflin, 1996.

Hoy, Helen. *How Should I Read These? Native Women Writers in Canada.* Toronto: University of Toronto Press, 2001.

Huff, Delores. *To Live Heroically: Institutional Racism and American Indian Education.* Albany: State University of New York Press, 1997.

Hurtado de Mendoza, William. "A Learning Song." In Noriega, *Pichka Harwikuna: Five Quechua Poets,* 44–47.

Indian Voices: The First Convocation of American Indian Scholars. San Francisco: Indian Historian Press, 1970.

"Inquisition on the View of the Body of William Apes." New York County, New York, April 10, 1839. New York County Coroner, Department of Records and Information Services, 31 Chambers Street, Municipal Archives of the City of New York.

Ireland, Craig. "The Appeal to Experience and Its Consequences: Variations on a Persistent Thompsonian Theme." *Cultural Critique* 52 (Fall 2002): 86–107.

Jahner, Elaine. "Introduction: American Indian Writers and the Tyranny of Expectations." *Book Forum* 5, no. 3 (1981): 343–48.

Jaskoski, Helen, ed. *Early Native American Writing: New Critical Essays.* Cambridge: Cambridge University Press, 1996.

Jennings, Francis. *The Invasion of America: Indians, Colonialism, and the Cant of Conquest.* 1975. Reprint, New York: W. W. Norton, 1976.

Johnson, Troy. *The Occupation of Alcatraz Island: Indian Self-Determination and the Rise of Indian Activism.* Urbana: University of Illinois Press, 1996.

Jump, Kenneth Jacob. *The Legend of John Stink, or Roaring Thunder "Child of Nature."* Pawhuska, Oklahoma: Self-published, 1977.

———. *Osage Indian Anthology: Indian—Religious—General.* Pawhuska: Florence Jump Quinata, Arita G. Jump, 1983.

———. *Osage Indian Poems and Short Stories.* Pawhuska, Oklahoma: Self-published, 1979.

Koehler, Michael D. "Jim Thorpe: Legend and Legacy." *Indian Education* 15, no. 3 (May 1976): 3–6.

Konkle, Maureen. *Writing Indian Nations: Native Intellectuals and the Politics of Historiography.* Chapel Hill: University of North Carolina Press, 2004.

Kruks, Sonia. *Retrieving Experience: Subjectivity and Recognition in Feminist Politics.* Ithaca, N.Y.: Cornell University Press, 2001.

Krupat, Arnold. *The Turn to the Native: Studies in Criticism and Culture.* Lincoln: University of Nebraska Press, 1996.

LaDuke, Winona. *All Our Relations: Native Struggles for Land and Life.* Boston: South End Press, 1999.

LaFlesche, Francis. *The Middle Five: Indian Schoolboys of the Omaha Tribe.* Madison: University of Wisconsin Press, 1963. Originally published as *The Middle Five: Indian Boys at School.* Boston: Small, Maynard, and Co., 1900.

Landrum, Larry. "The Shattered Modernism of Momaday's *House Made of Dawn.*" *Modern Fiction Studies* 42, no. 2 (1996): 763–86.

Larson, Charles. *American Indian Fiction.* Albuquerque: University of New Mexico Press, 1978.

Lewis, David Levering. *W. E. B. Du Bois: Biography of a Race, 1868–1919.* New York: Henry Holt, 1993.

Lincoln, Kenneth. "From Tai-Me to Rainy Mountain: The Makings of American Indian Literature." *American Indian Quarterly* 10, no. 2 (Spring 1986): 101–17.

Lindsey, Donal F. *Indians at Hampton Institute, 1877–1923.* Urbana: University of Illinois Press, 1995.

Lippard, Lucy, ed. *Partial Recall.* New York: New Press, 1992.

Littlefield, Daniel F. Jr. *Seminole Burning: A Story of Racial Vengeance.* Jackson: University of Mississippi Press, 1996.

Littlefield, Daniel F., and James W. Parins. *American Indian and Alaska Native Newspapers and Periodicals,* vol. 1 (1826–1924). Westport, Conn.: Greenwood Press, 1984.

———. *A Biobibliography of Native American Writers, 1772–1924.* Metuchen, N.J.: Scarecrow Press, 1981.

Livingston, Lili Cockerille. *American Indian Ballerinas.* Norman: University of Oklahoma Press, 1997.

Lomawaima, K. Tsianina. *They Called It Prairie Light: The Story of the Chilocco Indian School.* Lincoln: University of Nebraska Press, 1994.

Loomba, Ania. *Colonialism/Postcolonialism.* New York: Routledge, 1998.

Lyons, Scott Richard. "Rhetorical Sovereignty: What Do American Indians Want from Writing?" *CCC* 51, no. 3 (February 2000): 447–68.

Mann, Henrietta. *Cheyenne-Arapaho Education, 1871–1982.* Boulder: University Press of Colorado, 1997.

Maracle, Brian. *Crazywater: Native Voices on Addiction and Recovery.* Toronto: Viking, 1993.

Maracle, Lee. *I Am Woman: A Native Perspective on Sociology and Feminism.* 1988. Reprint, Vancouver, British Columbia: Press Gang, 1996.

Martin, Tony. "Of the NAACP and Integrationists, and Garvey and Separatists, or, The Integrationist Onslaught." In *Race First: The Ideological and Organi-*

zational Struggles of Marcus Garvey and the Universal Negro Improvement Association, 273–343. Westport, Conn.: Greenwood Press, 1976.

Mathews, John Joseph. *Life and Death of an Oilman: The Career of E. W. Marland.* Norman: University of Oklahoma Press, 1951.

———. *The Osages: Children of the Middle Waters.* Norman: University of Oklahoma Press, 1961.

———. *Sundown.* New York: Longman, Green, 1934.

———. *Talking to the Moon.* Chicago: University of Chicago Press, 1945.

———. *Wah'Kon-Tah: The Osage and the White Man's Road.* Norman: University of Oklahoma Press, 1932.

McAuliffe, Dennis Jr. *The Deaths of Sybil Bolton: An American History.* New York: Times Books, 1994.

McBride, Kevin A. "The Historical Archaeology of the Mashuntucket Pequots, 1637–1900." In Hauptman and Wherry, *The Pequots in Southern New England,* 96–116.

McLaughlin, William G. *After the Trail of Tears: The Cherokees' Struggle for Sovereignty, 1839–1880.* Chapel Hill: University of North Carolina Press, 1993.

McMaster, Gerald, ed. *Reservation X: The Power of Place in Aboriginal Contemporary Art.* Seattle: University of Washington Press, 1998.

McNickle, D'Arcy. *The Surrounded.* New York: Dodd, Mead, 1936.

Mignolo, Walter. *The Darker Side of the Renaissance: Literacy, Territoriality, and Colonization.* Ann Arbor: University of Michigan Press, 1995.

Mihesuah, Devon A. *Cultivating the Rosebuds: The Education of Women at the Cherokee Female Seminary, 1851–1909.* Urbana: University of Illinois Press, 1993.

———. "Out of the 'Graves of the Polluted Debauches': The Boys of the Cherokee Male Seminary." *American Indian Quarterly* 15 (Fall 1991): 503–21.

Mills, Billy. "Twenty Seconds of Pain." *Journal of American Indian Education* 13, no. 3 (May 1974): 1–8.

Miner, Craig, and William E. Unrau. *The End of Indian Kansas: A Study of Cultural Revolution, 1854–1871.* Lawrence: University of Kansas Press, 1978.

Minton, Charles. "The Place of the Indian Youth Council in Higher Education." *Journal of American Indian Education* 1, no. 1 (June 1961): 29–32.

Mohanty, Satya. *Literary Theory and the Claims of History.* Ithaca: Cornell University Press, 1997.

Momaday, N. Scott. *The Ancient Child.* New York: Doubleday, 1989.

———. *Angle of Geese and Other Poems.* Boston: Godine, 1974.

———. *Circle of Wonder: A Native American Christmas Story.* Albuquerque: University of New Mexico Press, 1999.

———. *The Complete Poems of Frederick Goddard Tuckerman.* Oxford: Oxford University Press, 1965.

——"A Divine Blindness: The Place of Words in a State of Grace." In *The Man Made of Words,* 80–88.

——. "An Edition of the Complete Poems of Frederick Goddard Tuckerman." Ph.D. diss., Stanford University, 1963.

——. "A First American Views His Land." In *The Man Made of Words,* 30–41.

——. *The Gourd Dancer.* New York: Harper and Row, 1976.

——. *House Made of Dawn.* New York: Harper and Row, 1968.

——. "The Indolent Boys." Unpublished play.

——. *In the Bear's House.* New York: St. Martin's, 1999.

——. *In the Presence of the Sun: Stories and Poems, 1961–1991.* New York: St. Martin's Press, 1992.

——. *The Journey of Tai-me.* Santa Barbara: Privately printed, 1967.

——. "The Man Made of Words." In *Indian Voices: The First Convocation of American Indian Scholars,* 49–84.

——. *The Man Made of Words: Essays, Stories, Passages.* New York: St. Martin's Press, 1997.

——. "The Morality of Indian Hating." In *The Man Made of Words,* 57–75.

——. *The Names: A Memoir.* New York: Harper and Row, 1976.

——. "The Native Voice in American Literature." In *The Man Made of Words,* 13–20.

——. "Only an Appearance." *Forum* 1 (November 1989): 1–8.

——. *The Way to Rainy Mountain.* Albuquerque: University of New Mexico Press, 1969.

Montejo, Victor. *Testimony: The Death of a Guatemalan Village.* Willimantic, Conn.: Curbstone, 1987.

Monture-Angus, Patricia. "On Being Homeless: One Aboriginal Woman's 'Conquest' of Canadian Universities, 1989–1998." Unpublished essay, 1998.

——. *Thunder in My Soul: A Mohawk Woman Speaks.* Halifax, Nova Scotia: Fernwood, 1995.

Moore, David L. "Rough Knowledge and Radical Understanding: Sacred Silence in American Indian Literatures." *American Indian Quarterly* 21, no. 4 (Fall 1997): 633–62.

Mourning Dove [Humi Ishu-Ma, Christine Quintasket]. *Cogewea, the Half-Blood: A Depiction of the Great Montana Cattle Range.* With notes and biographical sketch by Lucullus McWhorter. Boston: Four Seasons, 1927.

Murray, Laura J., ed. *To Do Good to My Indian Brethren: The Writings of Joseph Johnson, 1751–1776.* Amherst: University of Massachusetts Press, 1998.

Nabokov, Peter. "The Indian Oral Tradition." Interview with N. Scott Momaday. Pacifica Radio Archives, North Hollywood, Calif., 1969.

Nielsen, Donald M. "The Mashpee Indian Revolt of 1833." *New England Quarterly* 58 (1985): 400–20.

Noley, Homer. *First White Frost: Native Americans and United Methodism.* Nashville: Abingdon Press, 1991.

Noriega, Jorge. "American Indian Education in the United States." In *The State of Native America: Genocide, Colonization, and Resistance,* edited by M. Annette Jaimes. Boston: South End Press, 1992.

Noriega, Bernuy, Julio, ed. *Pichka Harawikuna: Five Quechua Poets.* Translated by Maureen Ahern. Pittsburgh, Penn.: Latin American Literary Review Press, 1998.

Northrup, Jim. *Walking the Rez Road.* Stillwater, Minn.: Voyager, 1993.

O'Brien, Jean. *Dispossession by Degrees: Indian Land and Identity in Natick, Massachusetts, 1650–1790.* New York: Cambridge University Press, 1997.

———. "'Divorced' from the Land: Resistance and Survival of Indian Women in Eighteenth Century New England." In Calloway, *After King Philip's War,* 144–61.

Occom, Samson. *A Choice Collection of Hymns and Spiritual Songs Intented for the Edification of Sincere Christians of all Denominations.* London: Green, 1774.

———. *A Sermon Preached at the Execution of Moses Paul, an Indian Who Was Executed at New Haven, on the 2d of September 1772.* Bennington: William Watson, 1772.

O'Connell, Barry. "'Once More Let Us Reconsider': William Apess in the Writing of New England Native American History." In Calloway, *After King Philip's War,* 162–77.

Ortiz, Alfonso. "American Indian Philosophy and Its Relation to the Modern World." In *Indian Voices,* 18–19.

Ortiz, Simon. *Speaking for the Generations: Native Writers on Writing.* Tucson: University of Arizona Press, 1998.

———. "Towards a National Indian Literature: Cultural Authenticity in Nationalism." *MELUS* 8, no. 2 (Summer 1981): 7–12.

———. *Woven Stone.* Tucson: University of Arizona Press, 1992.

Osage National Council. Press Packet. June 13, 1997.

Oskison, John Milton. *Black Jack Davy.* New York: D. Appleton, 1926.

———. *Brothers Three.* New York: Macmillan, 1935.

———. *Tecumseh and His Times.* New York: Dunlap, 1938.

———. *Wild Harvest.* New York: D. Appleton, 1925.

Owens, Louis. *Mixedblood Messages: Literature, Film, Family, Place.* Norman: University of Oklahoma Press, 1998.

———. *Other Destinies: Understanding the American Indian Novel.* Norman: University of Oklahoma Press, 1992.

Oxendine, Joseph. *American Indian Sports Heritage.* 1988. Reprint, Lincoln: University of Nebraska Press, 1995.

Palmer, Gus. *Telling Stories the Kiowa Way.* Tucson: University of Arizona Press, 2003.

Parker, Arthur. *The Indian How Book*. New York: Doran, 1927.

Parker, Robert Dale. *The Invention of Native American Literature*. Ithaca, New York: Cornell University Press, 2003.

Paschal, Andrew, ed. *W. E. B. Du Bois: A Reader*. New York: Collier Books, 1971.

Paschen, Elise. *Infidelities: Poems*. Brownsville, Ore.: Story Line Press, 1996.

Perdue, Theda, ed. *Cherokee Editor: The Writings of Elias Boudinot*. Athens: University of Georgia Press, 1996.

Peters, Russell M. *Clambake: A Wampanoag Tradition*. Minneapolis: Lerner Publications, 1992.

———. *The Wampanoags of Mashpee: An Indian Perspective on American History*. Somerville, Mass.: Media Action, 1987.

Peyer, Bernd C. *The Elders Wrote: An Anthology of Early Prose by North American Indians, 1768–1931*. Berlin: Dietrich Reimer Verlag, 1982.

———. *The Singing Spirit: Early Short Stories by North American Indians*. Tucson: University of Arizona Press, 1989.

———, ed. *The Tutor'd Mind: Indian Missionary-Writers in Antebellum America*. Amherst: University of Massachusetts Press, 1997.

Pierce, Drew. "A Legal History of the Osage Tribe: From European Contact to *Fletcher v. United States*." Unpublished manuscript.

Pokagon, Simon. *O-gi-Maw-Kwi Mit-I-gwa-ki (Queen of the Woods)*. Hartford, Mich.: C. H. Engle, 1899.

Porter, Dorothy, ed. *Early Negro Writing, 1760–1837*. Baltimore: Black Classic Press, 1995.

Powell, Malea. "Rhetorics of Survivance: How American Indians *Use* Writing." *CCC* 53, no. 3 (February 2002), 396–434.

Prucha, Francis Paul. *The Great Father: The United States Government and the American Indians*. Lincoln: University of Nebraska Press, 1984.

Red Corn, Charles. *A Pipe for February*. Norman: University of Oklahoma Press, 2002.

"Representative Indians." Reprinted in the *Red Man,* June 1900, 3.

Revard, Carter. *Cowboys and Indians: Christmas Shopping*. Norman, Okla.: Point Riders Press, 1992.

———. *An Eagle Nation*. Tucson: University of Arizona Press, 1993.

———. *Family Matters, Tribal Affairs*. Tucson: University of Arizona Press, 1998.

———. *Ponca War Dancers*. Norman, Okla.: Point Riders Press, 1980.

———. *Winning the Dust Bowl*. Tucson: University of Arizona Press, 2001.

Richey, Russell E. *Early American Methodism*. Bloomington: University of Indiana Press, 1991.

Ridge, John Rollin. *The Life and Adventures of Joaquín Murieta, the Celebrated California Bandit*. 1854. Reprint, Norman: University of Oklahoma Press, 1977.

Robertson, Nellie. "A Trip to the Moon." *Indian Helper,* June 20, 1890.

Rollings, Willard H. *The Osage: An Ethnohistorical Study of Hegemony on the Prairie-Plains.* Columbia: University of Missouri Press, 1992.

Romero, Lora. *Home Fronts: Domesticity and Its Critics in the Antebellum United States.* Durham, N.C.: Duke University Press, 1997.

Ruffo, Armand Garnet. "Why Native Literature?" *American Indian Quarterly* 21, no. 4 (Fall 1997): 663–73.

Ruoff, A. LaVonne Brown. *American Indian Literatures: An Introduction, Bibliographic Review, and Selected Bibliography.* New York: MLA, 1990.

———. "Three Nineteenth-Century American Indian Autobiographers." In Ruoff and Ward, *Redefining American Literary History,* 251–69.

Ruoff, A. LaVonne Brown, and Jerry W. Ward Jr., eds. *Redefining American Literary History.* New York: Modern Language Association of America, 1990.

Said, Edward W. *Culture and Imperialism.* New York: Knopf, 1993.

———. *The World, the Text, and the Critic.* Cambridge, Mass.: Harvard University Press, 1983.

Sainsbury, John A. "Indian Labor in Early Rhode Island." *New England Quarterly* 48, no. 3 (September 1975), 378–93.

Sando, Joe S. *The Pueblo Indians.* San Francisco: Indian Historian Press, 1976.

———. *Pueblo Nations: Eight Centuries of Pueblo Indian History.* Santa Fe: Clear Light, 1992.

Sarris, Greg. *Keeping Slug Woman Alive: A Holistic Approach to Native American Texts.* Berkeley and Los Angeles: University of California Press, 1993.

Schneider, Gregory A. *The Way of the Cross Leads Home: The Domestication of American Methodism.* Bloomington: University of Indiana Press, 1993.

Schubnell, Matthias. *N. Scott Momaday: The Literary and Cultural Background.* Norman: University of Oklahoma Press, 1986.

Scott, Joan W. "The Evidence of Experience." *Critical Inquiry* 17 (Summer 1991): 773–97.

———. "Experience." In *Feminists Theorize the Political,* edited by Judith Butler and Joan W. Scott, 22–40. New York: Routledge, 1992.

Selinger, Bernard. "*House Made of Dawn*: A Positively Ambivalent Bildungsroman." *Modern Fiction Studies* 45, no. 1 (1999), 38–68.

Serequeberhan, Tsenay. *The Hermeneutics of African Philosophy: Horizon and Discourse.* New York: Routledge, 1994.

Silko, Leslie Marmon. *Storyteller.* New York: Arcade Publishing, 1981.

Singer, Beverly. *Wiping the War Paint off the Lens: Native American Film and Video.* Minneapolis: University of Minnesota Press, 2001.

Smith, Linda Tuhiwai. *Decolonizing Methodologies: Research and Indigenous Peoples.* New York: Zed Books, 1999.

Smith, Paul Chaat. "The Big Movie." In *Exile on Main Street,* cyberbook, http://redplanet.home.mindspring.com/exile/exile.htm.

——. "The Meaning of Life." In McMaster, *Reservation X,* 31–40.

Smith, Paul Chaat, and Robert Allen Warrior. *Like a Hurricane: The Indian Movement from Alcatraz to Wounded Knee.* New York: New Press, 1996.

Sombrero, Tweedy. "Black Robes: Native Americans and the Ordination Process." In Weaver, *Native American Religious Identity,* 173–77.

Standing Bear, Luther. *Land of the Spotted Eagle.* 1933. Reprint, Lincoln: University of Nebraska Press, 1978.

——. *My People the Sioux.* 1928. Reprint, Lincoln: University of Nebraska Press, 1975.

Starna, William A. "The Pequots in the Early Seventeenth Century." In Hauptman and Wherry, *The Pequots in Southern New England,* 33–47.

Stevens, Jason W. "Bear, Outlaw, and Storyteller: American Frontier Mythology and the Ethnic Subjectivity of N. Scott Momaday." *American Literature* 73, no. 3 (2001): 599–631.

Stevens, Scott Manning. "William Apess's Historical Self." *Northwest Review* 35, no. 3 (1997), 67–84.

Stewart, Maria. *Productions of Mrs. Maria W. Stewart.* 1835. Reprinted in Houchins, *Spiritual Narratives.*

Strickland, Rennard. *Fire and the Spirits: Cherokee Law from Clan to Court.* Norman: University of Oklahoma Press, 1982.

——. *The Indians in Oklahoma.* Norman: University of Oklahoma Press, 1981.

——. *Tonto's Revenge.* Albuquerque: University of New Mexico Press, 1997.

Stone-Mediatore, Shari. "Chandra Mohanty and the Revaluing of 'Experience.'" *Hypatia* 13, no. 2 (1998), 116–33.

Swisher, Karen Gayton. "Why Indian People Should Be the Ones to Write about Indian Education." *American Indian Quarterly* 20, no. 1 (Winter 1996): 83–90.

Szasz, Margaret Connell. *Education and the American Indian: The Road to Self-Determination Since 1928.* Albuquerque: University of New Mexico Press, 1977.

Tallchief, Maria. *Maria Tallchief: America's Prima Ballerina.* With Larry Kaplan. New York: Henry Holt, 1997.

Tetzloff, Jason. "Cloud, Henry Roe." In Hoxie, *Encyclopedia of North American Indians,* 125–27.

Teuton, Sean. "'Where Are You Going?': The Social Motion of Place in N. Scott Momaday's *House Made of Dawn.*" In "On These Grounds: The Red Power Novel and the Retaking of American Indian Identity," unpublished ms., 174–226.

Thiong'o, Ngugi wa. *Decolonising the Mind: The Politics of Language in African Literature.* Oxford, England: James Currey, 1986.

Thornton, Russell. *American Indian Holocaust and Survival: A Population History Since 1492.* Norman: University of Oklahoma Press, 1987.

——. "The Demography of Colonialism and 'Old' and 'New' Native Americans." In *Studying Native America: Problems and Prospects,* 17–39.

———, ed. *Studying Native America: Problems and Prospects.* Madison: University of Wisconsin Press, 1998.

Thorpe, Grace. "Jim Thorpe." In Hoxie, *Encyclopedia of North American Indians,* 627–29.

Tinker, George, E. *Missionary Conquest: The Gospel and Native American Cultural Genocide.* Minneapolis: Fortress Press, 1993.

Tonemah, Stuart A. "Philosophical Perspectives of Gifted and Talented American Indian Education." *Journal of American Indian Education* 31, no. 1 (October 1991): 3–9.

Trahant, Mark N. *Pictures of Our Nobler Selves: A History of Native American Contributions to News Media.* Nashville, Tenn.: The Freedom Forum, 1995.

Two Bears, Davine Ruth Begaye. "I Walk in Beauty." In Garrod and Larimore, *First Person, First Peoples,* 43–63.

Uncommon Controversy: Fishing Rights of the Muckleshoot, Puyallup, and Nisqually Indians. Seattle: University of Washington Press, 1970.

Unrau, William E. *Mixed-Bloods and Tribal Dissolution: Charles Curtis and the Quest for Indian Identity.* Lawrence: University of Kansas, 1989.

Utley, Robert, ed. *Battlefield and Classroom: Four Decades with the American Indian, 1867–1904.* New Haven: Yale Univesity Press, 1964.

Vickers, Daniel. "The First Whalemen of Nantucket." In Calloway, *After King Philip's War,* 90–113.

Vizenor, Gerald. *Earthdivers: Tribal Narratives on Mixed Descent.* Minneapolis: University of Minnesota Press, 1981.

———. *Interior Landscapes: Autobiographical Myths and Metaphors.* Minneapolis: University of Minnesota Press, 1990.

———. *Manifest Manners: Postindian Warriors of Survivance.* Hanover, N.H.: Wesleyan University Press, 1994.

———, ed. *Touchwood: A Collection of Ojibway Prose.* 1987. Reprint, Minneapolis: New Rivers Press, 1994.

Wald, Priscilla. *Constituting Americans: Cultural Anxiety and Narrative Form.* Durham, N.C.: Duke University Press, 1995.

Walker, Alice. *In Search of Our Mothers' Gardens: Womanist Prose.* San Diego: Harcourt Brace Jovanovich, 1983.

Walker, David. *Appeal to the Colored Citizens of the World, But in Particular, and Very Expressly, to Those of the United States of America.* 1829. Revised edition, Sean Wilentz, ed. New York: Hill & Wang, 1965.

Warrior, Robert Allen. "Souvenirs of the Indian Wars," *C & C* 51, March 4, 1991, 55–56. Reprinted as "Reflections from the War Zone" in *Collateral Damage; The New World Order at Home and Abroad,* edited by Cynthia Peters, 299–304. Boston: South End Press, 1992.

———. *Tribal Secrets: Recovering American Indian Intellectual Traditions*. Minneapolis: University of Minnesota Press, 1995.

———. "William Apess: A Pequot and a Methodist under the Sign of Modernity." In Batstone, Mendieta, Lorentzen, and Hopkins, *Liberation Theologies, Postmodernity, and the Americas*, 188–202.

Washington, Booker T. *Up from Slavery* (1901), in *Three Negro Classics*. New York: Avon, 1965.

Watt. Ian. *The Rise of the Novel: Studies in Defoe, Richardson, and Fielding*. Berkeley and Los Angeles: University of California Press, 1957.

Weaver, Jace, ed. *Defending Mother Earth: Native American Perspectives on Environmental Justice*. Maryknoll, N.Y.: Orbis, 1996.

———, ed. *Native American Religious Identity: Unforgotten Gods*. Maryknoll, New York: Orbis Books, 1998.

———. *Other Words: American Indian Literature, Law, Culture*. Norman: University of Oklahoma Press, 2001.

———. "Scaling Rios Montt: Indigenous Peoples, International Human Rights, and the *Pinochet* case." In Weaver, *Other Words*, 201–25.

———. *That the People Might Live: Native American Literatures and Native American Community*. New York: Oxford, 1997.

———. *Turtle Goes to War: Of Military Commissions, the Constitution, and American Indian Memory*. New Haven, Conn.: Trylon and Perisphere Press, 2002.

Welburn, Ron. *Roanoke and Wampum: Topics in Native American Heritage and Literatures*. New York: Peter Lang, 2000.

Welch, James. *Fools Crow*. New York: Viking Press, 1986.

Welch, James, with Paul Stekler. *Killing Custer: The Battle of the Little Bighorn and the Fate of the Plains Indians*. New York: W. W. Norton, 1994.

Wheeler, Robert W. *Jim Thorpe: World's Greatest Athlete*. Norman: University of Oklahoma Press, 1975.

Wheelock, Dennison. Untitled essay, originally published in *Indian Helper,* November 18, 1887.

Whicher, Stephen E., ed., *Selections from Ralph Waldo Emerson; An Organic Anthology*. Boston: Houghton Mifflin, 1957.

White, Richard. *"It's Your Misfortune and None of My Own": A History of the American West*. Norman: University of Oklahoma Press, 1991.

Whiteman, Roberta Hill. *Philadelphia Flowers*. Duluth, Minn.: Holy Cow! Press, 1996.

Whitman, Walt. "Democratic Vistas." In *Leaves of Grass and Selected Prose,* edited by Ellman Crasnow, 504–58. London: J. M. Dent, 1994.

Wiget, Andrew. *Native American Literature*. Boston: Twayne, 1985.

Wilkins, Thurman. *Cherokee Tragedy: The Ridge Family and the Decimation of a People*. 2d revised edition. Norman: University of Oklahoma Press, 1986.

Wilson, Raymond. *Ohiyesa: Charles Eastman, Santee Sioux.* Urbana: University of Illinois Press, 1983.

Wilson, Terry P. *Bibliography of the Osage.* Native American Bibliography Series no. 6. Metuchen, N.J.: Scarecrow Press, 1985.

———. *The Underground Reservation: Osage Oil.* Lincoln: University of Nebraska Press, 1985.

Winters, Yvor, and Janet Lewis Papers. Collection number M352. Special Collections and University Archives, Green Library, Stanford University.

Womack, Craig. *Red on Red: Native American Literary Separatism.* Minneapolis: University of Minnesota Press, 1999.

Woodward, Charles. *Ancestral Voice: Conversations with N. Scott Momaday.* Lincoln: University of Nebraska Press, 1989.

Wyss, Hilary E. *Writing Indians: Literacy, Christianity, and Native Community in Early America.* Amherst: University of Massachusetts Press, 2000.

Zitkala-Sa [Gertrude Bonnin]. *American Indian Stories.* Washington, D.C.: Haworth Publishing, 1921.

Index

*R*obert Warrior is author of *Tribal Secrets: Recovering American Indian Intellectual Traditions* (Minnesota, 1995) and, with Paul Chaat Smith, *Like a Hurricane: The Indian Movement from Alcatraz to Wounded Knee.* His award-winning writing has been published in the *Village Voice, Utne Reader, The Progressive, News from Indian Country,* and *American Quarterly.*